Young Guns

D0800490

Young Guns

Inside the Violent World of
Britain's Street Gangs

STEVE HACKMAN

Milo Books Ltd

Published in November 2010 by Milo Books

ISBN 978 1 903854 92 1

Edited by Rebecca Macklin
Typeset by e-type

Printed in Great Britain by
Cox & Wyman Ltd, Reading, Berkshire

MILO BOOKS LTD
The Old Weighbridge
Station Road
Wrea Green
Lancs PR4 2PH
United Kingdom
www.milobooks.com

Contents

Introduction

ON 22 AUGUST 2007, an eleven-year-old boy named Rhys Jones was shot in the neck as he walked home from football training on the Croxteth Park estate in Liverpool. He died the innocent victim of a feud he neither knew nor cared about. It was a tragedy that thrust an age-old issue back into the public consciousness: gangs.

Gangs take various forms, and academics argue over definitions. Some are territorial; others are focussed on acquisitive crime. For most purposes, a gang is simply a criminal collective working towards a common goal. They are not a modern phenomenon in Britain. Newspaper articles from the mid-1800s spoke of rising rates of mob violence and the corrosive impact of youth crime in our bigger cities: Birmingham, Glasgow, Liverpool, London, Manchester and Edinburgh. Criminal subcultures are neither new, nor are they necessarily more violent than they have been in the past. They are a constant, immovable threat.

Today, however, Britain is enduring a gang crisis. One in ten young people, between the ages of ten and nineteen, class themselves as belonging to a gang. Gang members are responsible for just under a third of criminal offences and represent around fifteen per cent of known offenders. Although the situation in the UK is nowhere near as severe as it has become in the United States, it is widely accepted that gang membership has seen a substantial, and continuing, rise.

So what is my connection to gangland Britain? What makes me suited to writing a book about such a difficult area? My knowledge of this little-explored area stems from a year of immersion in the British prison system. I have worked, eaten and slept within the company of convicted gang members. I have spent time with every sector of criminal society, from low-level drug runners to national crime bosses. I have studied gangs from within their midst in one of the toughest jails in the UK.

In August 2008, I was sentenced to two-and-a-half years in prison for selling ecstasy whilst at university. It was a crime of immense naivety: I was attempting to supplement my student loan by dabbling in things I knew little about. The second I stepped through the prison gates, I realised that I was in for a rough time. HMP Leeds, commonly known as Armley Gaol, is one of the longest-running operational jails in the country. It is a large, stone building covered from top to bottom in barbed wire. It is icy cold during the winter and swelteringly hot during the summer. The walls of the cells are caked in racist graffiti and a thick, brown phlegm. Rapists, paedophiles, torturers and murderers are indistinguishable from the general population.

Prison inmates are fiercely territorial. The first question a new arrival is asked is 'Where are you from?' closely followed by 'What estate?' Many of the offenders have their postcodes tattooed on their arms and some have maps of their home-towns etched across the back of their necks. They segregate themselves in terms of the town or city that they were living in up until their arrest, slotting into one of a number of different 'firms' – geographically determined gangs. Acceptance into a firm is the key to survival: prison is a hostile environment and membership of a gang can mean the difference between an easy sentence and an unbearably hard one.

I was intrigued by the territorialism of the other inmates on the wing. There were inter-county rivalries: South Yorkshire and West Yorkshire were in a state of constant competition to prove whose area was the 'hardest'. Then there were individual cities that hated each other, and there were even different parts of the same city that were at each other's throats. I began to wonder if the same area-based conflict existed outside of the prison. I started asking questions, quizzing the other prisoners on the exact nature of their rivalries and why they had started. The majority of the inmates that I encountered had been in a gang at some point in their lives. So I conducted interviews, carried out research and attempted to gain an insight into the daily workings of a modern British street gang, all within the prison system.

Young Guns tells, often in the words of gang members themselves, the reality of life for many of what are a new breed of young gang member: youths who, in the first decade of the twenty-first century, have dragged the problem in the UK to new depths. Almost all of those I interviewed spoke on the strictest conditions of anonymity, which is why I have changed the names of interviewees throughout. Most are still involved in 'the game', despite protestations that they have given it up. What this book is not is an attempt at a comprehensive history of the problem, nor is it an exploration of the various solutions that have been tried or mooted. Rather it is a series of personal accounts, and telling snapshots, direct from the streets.

While gang culture has been documented in places like Croxteth and Norris Green, there are regions where it has received almost no media attention. So I have written this book as a guide to the various firms that exist throughout the UK – some in places where you would expect to find them, others in more obscure locations. Partway through my sentence, I was transferred to HMP Wolds, bringing me into contact with prisoners from another diverse range of towns and cities. Gangs are rife within the worst estates of every town in Britain – and even in the most surprising places.

The true extent of the problem is far greater than the authorities currently admit. From feral groups of territorial youths to major drug-dealing cartels, gangland violence is a threat to the fabric of our society. For those at the more affluent end of the social scale, the UK is a gang-free paradise, where fear is an abstract concept. For those within the bottom one per cent, it is a different story altogether.

Sheffield

TO THE NATIONAL newspapers, he was 'The General'. To fellow inmates in HMP Wolds, Nigel Ramsey was 'Rocky'. He was a popular prisoner with a lot of friends; he had a kindly demeanour and, when I arrived, did his best to make me feel welcome on the wing. You can imagine my shock when I heard that he had ordered a gangland execution. I knew that Rocky was involved in gangs in his native Sheffield but I had assumed that he stuck to drug dealing and robberies. I had no idea that he was responsible for the shooting of a seventeen-year-old boy. He had called an accomplice on a mobile phone and arranged for a rival gang member to be shot in the back in broad daylight. It was the talk of the jail.

Rocky was the leader of the S3 gang, named after the post-code for Burngreave and Pitsmoor. They are a largely black and mixed race firm who sell crack and commit armed robberies. Their main rivals, S4, live a matter of minutes away. 'It's some dumb shit really,' another inmate from Sheffield told me. 'Some of Pitsmoor is in S3 and some of it's in S4, so it isn't even two rival areas, it's parts of the same area.' The conflict is thought to have stemmed from a row over drug money. It has since escalated and claimed the lives of several members on both sides.

Sixteen-year-old Jonathan 'Venomous' Matondo was the

first casualty of the feud. He was shot in the head at a recreation area in Pitsmoor. Matondo was a known member of the S3 gang. He had arrived in Sheffield from the Democratic Republic of Congo at the age of six, relocating to what his family thought would be a safer environment. Although it was a distinct improvement on the Congo, Pitsmoor was still not an easy place to live. Thirteen-year-olds delivered drugs on pedal bikes and teenage boys carried guns for protection.

Matondo got caught up in the gun and gang culture of the area: he was part of a group of teenagers that would listen to violent rap songs and attempt to emulate what they heard. 'It's the S3 army, I'm invincible, got soldiers behind me,' he rapped in one home-recorded song. 'Pussy you can't merk [kill] me, come test me and I'm gonna go barmy.' In his music he would portray himself as an untouchable, Godfather-like figure. In reality, he was a teenage boy caught up in a dangerous subculture of guns and bravado.

Siobhan Sterling was talking to Matondo on his phone at the time of his death. He was walking through a recreation area on Nottingham Cliff, Burngreave, when he heard a gunshot whistle past his head.

'Yo did you hear that?' he asked his friend Kyle 'Kasman' Crosby. 'Yo, that nearly licked you Kasman.'

Kasman had no intention of staying put to find out who was shooting.

'Come on Venomous, run!'

'I'm not running for no-one,' Matondo retorted.

There was another bang and the phone went silent. He had been shot in the head, sending him sprawling onto the playground floor. His refusal to back down from confrontation had left him fatally wounded. Youthful tenacity had cost a young boy his life.

Matondo's parents were distraught. Knowing nothing of his gang affiliation, they cherished him as a devout churchgoer and loving son. They pleaded for his death to bring an end to gang violence in the city, though their pleas were ignored and the feud intensified. The S3 were enraged that one of their members had been taken: they wanted revenge.

From that moment on, the two gangs carried weapons wherever they went. None of them wanted to be the next Jonathan Matondo. Whenever they met their rivals, guns would be drawn and shots fired. Things had gone way beyond the level of a petty postcode rivalry.

The next to lose his life died at the hands of a fellow S3 gang member. Whereas many of these area-based gangs claim to be a single unified outfit, they often end up killing more of their own members than their rivals do. Brett Blake and Barrington 'Wasman' Wallis grew up together. Brett was an S3 veteran, whereas Wasman was a relative newcomer. For some reason, they fell out. Voices were raised and tempers were frayed.

'It was over something petty,' I was told. 'Just one of those arguments that comes out of nowhere.'

Wasman had a temper and didn't appreciate being spoken to in raised tones. A self-proclaimed hard man, he didn't take kindly to people challenging his authority. He pulled out a knife and slashed Blake across the face, the blade cutting deep enough to scar but not cause a life-threatening injury. Blake was furious. He was a senior gang member yet he had been sliced up by a new jack.

Blake and Wasman's feud split the gang. Some members sided with the former, others with the latter. In criminal circles, a slashing is more a sign of disrespect than a genuine attempt upon the victim's life. If Wasman had wanted to kill Blake, he would have found a way to do it. The fact that he chose to cut him meant that he wanted to leave a lasting mark; it was Wasman's way of saying, 'Mess with me and this is what you'll get.'

Danny Hockenhull, a longstanding gang member and friend of Matondo, was part of the group who chose to ally with Wasman. This would prove to be problematic, as Hockenhull moved in the same circles as Blake and would regularly see him. In May 2008, Hockenhull punched Blake in the eye at a popular city nightspot. Blake was furious. He later caught Hockenhull at a carwash and sliced him down the face with a knife. In return, Hockenhull smashed Blake's car windscreen and threatened to kill him.

On June 7, 2008, he followed up his threat. Danny Hockenhull and fellow S3 member Curtis Goring stabbed Brett Blake to death at the Uniq nightclub in Sheffield city centre. CCTV footage displayed at the trial showed Hockenhull severing Blake's jugular vein in the middle of the dance floor and Goring stabbing him in the stomach before making his way out of the club. Blake was taken to hospital, where he died from his injuries an hour and a half later.

Goring and Hockenhull were sentenced to a minimum of twenty-one years in prison. They showed no remorse during the court case, despite Blake's sobbing mother sitting metres away from where they stood in the dock. These were young men for whom violence was a part of everyday life.

On the day of Blake's funeral, tensions ran high. Not content with mourning his death, some of Blake's friends took it upon themselves to seek revenge. Learning that Isiah Nelson had been quizzed over the killing, Junior 'Bam Bam' Liversidge and Brett's brother Leyton ambushed him, stole his VW Golf and burnt it. They felt that even if he had played only a small role in the murder, he should suffer. As it was, he had played no part at all – but he did take part in a near-fatal stabbing later that day.

Isiah Nelson and Esmond Thompson tracked Junior Liversidge down to the car park of the Wincobank Hotel and stabbed him repeatedly all over his body. He received puncture wounds to his right arm, chest, left armpit and back, resulting in the collapse of both of his lungs and a loss of blood supply to his liver and bowel. Medical examiners remarked that it was rare for anyone to sustain such injuries and live. Liversidge was very lucky to pull through. He had been stabbed at least four times and several of his vital organs were seriously damaged.

The theft of a car had resulted in an attempt upon his life. Only a few hours since his good friend had been placed in a casket, he had narrowly avoided the same fate. On the spur of the moment, Liversidge broke the gang's strict code of silence and identified Nelson and Thompson as his attackers. He would have to live with the consequences.

On the day that his assailants were due to stand trial, Liversidge was nowhere to be seen. Scared for his life, he had fled; in the underworld, 'grasses' can expect to be stigmatised even by their closest friends and family. Not wanting to go out the same way as Blake had done, he thought it best to keep his mouth firmly shut – although at this point it was already too late. The police raided address after address and traced Liversidge's relatives and friends in a bid to find his whereabouts. They eventually found him leaving a house in Burngreave. He evaded capture and ran for his life.

When he was finally apprehended, Liversidge retracted his statement and claimed that he had lied about the identity of his attackers. He said that he had wanted someone to get convicted to help him with his claim for compensation. He added that he had not seen the faces of the men who had stabbed him and had no idea who they were. Whilst he was on the run, his aunt found a piece of paper entitled 'Reasons I Lied' and handed it in to the police. He denied all knowledge of it, as it was clearly evidence that his excuse was premeditated. Yet it had his fingerprints all over it.

In March 2009, Junior Liversidge was jailed for eleven weeks for contempt of court. Police records stated that he was 'fearful' of giving evidence and that he had been 'expressing concerns about attending court through fear of being branded a grass'. The sentencing judge told him, 'The only explanation for what you were doing is that you have some sort of code of silence within the little group of which you are part.' He was unsympathetic to the grave danger that Liversidge had placed himself in by even considering naming his attackers.

Isiah Nelson and Esmond Thompson were found guilty of attempted murder and sentenced to twenty-two years' imprisonment. Both men had a lengthy catalogue of previous offences, including a joint armed robbery in which £6,000 was stolen from Brightside Post Office.

DESPITE SEVERAL KEY players being behind bars, the dispute between the two factions continued to rage. Teenager Tarek Chaiboub was said to have had a foot in both camps; he was a neutral player, unwilling to side with either of the splinter groups. However, he was also insecure and desperate to prove himself. Although not directly involved with either faction, he was thought to have had prior knowledge that one of the gang was going to get stabbed. Rather than stepping in to prevent it from happening, the word on the street was that he had stood back and let it go ahead.

In a rap song uploaded by Tarek onto the Internet, he states:

Just 'cause I'm the skinny sort and my skin is kind of light… [they] always give it the biggest talk like they really wanna see me fight… niggers really think I can't back beef but no I ain't talking beef you can eat, more like the beef 'pon street.

It is clear that he had hang-ups about both his race and his build. Perhaps this is what had attracted him to the gang life; maybe it was an attempt to overcome his insecurities. Whatever the reason, it cost him his life.

On 6 July 2008, Chaiboub was stabbed in the stomach, legs, hands and back by two men. His liver was perforated and he need urgent treatment but he survived. Five days later, he was shot whilst leaving Frenchie's barbers in Burngreave. He quickly drew a gun of his own but was killed before he had a chance to fire it. It was daylight: a gunfight on the streets of Sheffield raged in the middle of the day.

'Rocky' Ramsey had ordered Tarek Chaiboub's execution from a mobile phone hidden in his prison cell. It was revenge for his role in the stabbing of Rocky's friend, though all Chaiboub had done was fail to intervene. Ramsey was already serving an indefinite sentence, for wounding with intent, at the time. He was later convicted of murder and given a minimum term of thirty-five years.

Although he was in jail at the time of the murder, Ramsey was deemed to have been just as much a part of the killing as the two assassins: his younger brother Denzil Ramsey and next-door neighbour Levan Menzies. He was transferred to a category A prison, where he is due to remain until he is in his fifties.

Less than a week after Ramsey was convicted, there were reports that another S3 member had been subjected to repeated attacks inside Doncaster prison. He was hit with a chair leg, threatened with a razor blade and scalded with boiling water. Ishmael Thompson was only eighteen and a low-ranking member of the gang. He was a 'joey', an odd job man, used to mind guns for older members of the firm. He could hardly be classed as an active gang member.

Thompson committed the cardinal sin of grassing. He had been minding guns for an S3 member when the police burst into his house in Rotherham. Panicking, Thompson told the police that the guns had been left in his car and that he was waiting for their owner, an S3 member, to pick them up. He named the person, a mistake that he would later regret. The police raided the house of the man named and found class A drugs, ammunition and a heroin press.

Tests on the two weapons revealed that one of them had been used during an armed robbery in Low Bradfield, Sheffield, in which a prominent businessman had been shot at close range and his girlfriend's Porsche stolen from the driveway. The house had been ransacked and riddled with bullets from the gun that Thompson was minding.

The judge remarked that the possibility that the guns had been left in Thompson's car was highly implausible, given their street value. He suggested that Thompson had known exactly what he was doing and that he had been charged with minding them for those higher up in the gang hierarchy. Thompson had fifteen previous convictions on his record, including a robbery and a vicious assault with a baseball bat. He was hardly a naïve innocent. For two counts of firearm possession and one of possessing ammunition he was sentenced to five years' imprisonment.

Given that Tarek was shot dead for his supposed treachery, the fate that awaited Thompson upon his release was not one to be envied. He lived in Rotherham, not Pitsmoor or

Burngreave, and could have steered clear of gang life. He had entered a world in which he did not fully understand the rules, and may have made himself a target for life.

THE FEUD BETWEEN the S3 and S4 crews was the first prolonged gang conflict in the city to make the headlines since the days of legendary hard man Sam Garvin in the 1920s. The police were quick to point out how 'rare' gang violence was and how it was relatively unheard of in the city, but this was a futile attempt to downplay the gang activities as a series of isolated incidents.

In fact it would be wrong to assume that the S3 versus S4 rivalry was the first of Sheffield's modern gang feuds. Instead, it was merely the first to receive large-scale attention. This was partly due to the sudden surge in media focus upon postcode rivalries in the wake of Rhys Jones's murder in Liverpool, and partly, perhaps, to do with race. Whereas groups of violent black adolescents are often seen as 'gangs', their white counterparts are less quick to be labelled. They fail to fit the stereotype set by the infamous Bloods and Crips of America and tend to pass below the radar. White-on-white gang violence appears to be frequently under-reported.

There are white street gangs scattered all over Sheffield. There are the S8 'Boyz' from Batemoor, Greenhill, Lowedges, Meadowhead, Jordanthorpe and Woodseats; the S6 Crew from Fox Hill; the Shirecliffe Boys; the Birley Boys; the Parson Cross Crew and no doubt others. They are often portrayed as 'troublemakers' rather than crooks and their behaviour described as 'antisocial' rather than criminal. The reality couldn't be further from the truth.

The Parson Cross Crew are amongst the most prolific of the white gangs. They caught the public's attention after several of their members posed with guns, knives and a spiked mace on Internet social networking sites. A community campaigner was so fed up of gang violence on the estate where they lived that she set about scouring the Web for as many incriminating images as she could find. This resulted in the arrest of twenty-three-year-old Joe Brent-Mitchell and eighteen-year-old Jamie Howden, who were charged with firearms possession and received a total of seven-and-a-half years in prison.

The youth with the spiked mace was identified as sixteen-year-old Reece Mendez. This was not the first time he had been in trouble with the police and he was no stranger to weapons. In April 2009, he was convicted of fatally stabbing eighteen-year-old Dale Robertson at a teenage girl's birthday party in Parson Cross; his victim was attacked by a group of almost forty youths following an argument about the owner-ship of an Xbox game. Another youth, who appeared on the photos wielding a knife, was convicted of violent disorder in the build-up to the same incident. There were initially rumours that the killing was part of an ongoing feud between the Parson Cross Crew and the S6 Crew from neighbouring Foxhill, but although members of both gangs were allegedly present at the party, there was no evidence to support these claims.

A seventeen-year-old Parson Cross Crew member, who was cleared of violent disorder, was later imprisoned for slashing a youth with a knife at another party. Rather than learning from the mistakes of his friends, he had carried out a strikingly similar crime to that which led to Dale's death, although luckily his victim survived. Jail did little to deter him. He regularly updated a social networking page whilst he was locked up and used it to gloat about his gang affiliation. This was presumably done on a mobile phone that he had smuggled into the prison.

His page showed graffiti tags, bearing the initials 'PXC' (Parson's Cross Crew) and 'S5 Soldiers', and a rap that said, 'I got loose screws... since nursery I rolled on youths.' His profile picture displayed him brandishing a knife alongside Reece Mendez, who was holding an extendable cosh. He was brazenly showing off the weapon he had used in the slashing.

S5 Soldiers is a reference to the postcode that encompasses some of Sheffield's most deprived areas. It consists of Parson Cross, Firth Park, Shiregreen, Shirecliffe, Southey Green, Longley and Fir Vale, all of which have levels of crime and poverty that are well above the national average. It is also home to three separate gangs: the predominantly white Parson Cross Crew and Shirecliffe Boys, and the racially mixed S5 gang, mostly from the Firth Park area. Although the Parson Cross Crew are the best known of these gangs, S5 gained notoriety during a standoff with the Teck 9 crew at Farrars funfair in 2005. It cost one of their members his life.

Teck 9 was a predominantly Asian gang, whose name was a misspelling of the TEC-9 semi-automatic pistol. They pledged allegiance to no specific area or postcode but were tied together through bonds of race and religion. Despite their name they rarely fought with guns, preferring knives, machetes and baseball bats. On March 4, 2005, large numbers of Teck 9 and S5 attended a travelling fair in Hillsborough. The two gangs argued and drew blades. Armed with a kitchen knife, eighteen-year-old Jovan Bethune squared up ready for combat but was assaulted before he had the chance to use his weapon; he was stabbed eight times in the eye, chest and arm by Teck 9 member Shakeel Mohammed, from Pitsmoor.

Bethune was rushed to hospital but died within half an hour. The knife that Mohammed had stabbed him with was nine inches long and had cut straight through one of his bones.

Bethune had paid the ultimate price for his membership in a postcode gang – his life.

I tracked down a member of the Teck 9 crew. Like most of the gang members I spoke to for this book, he was prepared to provide only sparing information, but he was able to fill me in on what happened afterwards.

'Teck 9 is not a gang no more after all that,' he said. Presumably, they had either closed down due to the attention that the killing had generated, or out of genuine regret at what had happened. 'The name lives on though,' he added. 'Nowadays we're just a group of friends that hang out together.' He was reluctant to say too much about what had gone on that day, but implied that there was a lot more to the fight than had been reported in the media. 'Half of what they said in their articles was bullshit. They don't know the real reasons for what happened.'

Another source close to the gang confirmed this. 'Trust me,' he said, 'there's things that the papers didn't report. The people who were there know the full story, but I don't think the general public will ever fully know.'

Even though they were no longer officially a gang, Teck 9 and their affiliates were sticking to their code of silence. The truth was hidden behind an impenetrable wall of fear: talking to the press was a form of 'dry snitching', or informing via gossip. Whatever the reasons for the gang's actions, they had left a young man lifeless and another with a lengthy jail sentence.

During my attempt to get to the bottom of what had happened at the fair that day, I found that the same name continued to crop up – not in relation to the specific incident, but with regard to the Sheffield gangland in general. 'You want to look into the UTC,' I was told. 'They ain't no kids stabbing each other up over postcodes: they are the real bad men.' I heard the same story from a few different criminals. 'They ruled the city, trust me,' another source said. 'They've got the main guys locked up for something they didn't do now though; couldn't get them for anything they actually did.'

The UTC was separated from the other gangs within the city by one key factor: they were born out of the desire to make money, rather than a rivalry with a neighbouring area. The police have described them as a 'criminal enterprise' rather than a postcode gang and they were, in their prime, very powerful. UTC is a shortened form of Upperthorpe Crew, Upperthorpe being the main area in which the gang operated. It is a part of the city in which two men held great sway: Ashley and David Cohen.

Upperthorpe is a deprived area to the northwest of the city. It is a place where the name 'Cohen' is synonymous with intimidation. Whereas gangs like Teck 9 and S5 had no strict leadership, the UTC ran as a dictatorship with the Cohens firmly in charge. David was the leader, whilst Ashley acted as his second-in-command. They ruled through fear: anyone who stood in their way could expect brutal reprisal.

Even before David and Ashley came into their prime, their family were immersed in violence. Their half-brother, Lester Divers, was a well known associate of the Blades Business Crew, Sheffield United's football hooligan firm; indeed some regarded him as the 'top boy'. He was also well connected in the city's underworld and drove a £20,000 Lexus. On New Year's Day, 2003, he was shot in the head from point blank range as he started up his car outside his home in Walkley. He died almost instantly.

In the wake of Divers' murder, police were given extra powers in order to prevent a revenge attack. Divers had a number of associates in Pitsmoor and Burngreave and officers felt it necessary to stop and search anybody acting suspiciously in these areas. Their power to search pedestrians was increased and three armed vehicles, an extra patrol car and a riot van were deployed. All of the officers on duty were equipped with bulletproof vests.

After months of intense speculation about the circumstances surrounding Divers' death, Kevin Smith, of Barnsley, and Michael Ullah, of Wincobank, were charged with his murder. It was alleged that the killing had taken place as the result of a feud between two factions. On one side were the heroin-addicted Ullah and his two associates, who believed that Divers was planning to kidnap them to learn the location of their boss and drug supplier. On the other side, were Divers and his firm, who were thought to have specialised in robbing drug dealers. Fearing for his safety, Ullah had got his retaliation in first by firing a sawn-off shotgun through the window of Divers' car. He then jumped into a getaway car, driven by Smith, and the two men sped away.

Kevin Smith pleaded not guilty but was convicted and jailed for eighteen years for his part in the killing. Michael Ullah was given sixteen years. A third man who was accused of master-minding the murder, walked free after being acquitted. The jury's decision was met with angry shouts from Divers' friends and relatives.

Around 2,500 people attended Divers' wake; he commanded a huge amount of respect even after his death. Indeed his passing was mourned across the country, with members of West Ham United's Inter-City Firm among the many football mobs to send condolence cards to his family.

Several of Divers' relatives commented that it was particu-larly upsetting that a bullet had killed him, as he had an extreme hatred of guns. This was somewhat inconsistent with his reputation as a gangland taxman, but may well have been true. David Cohen, however, seemed fascinated by guns. At fifteen, he had been charged with possession of a firearm and ammunition and given a supervision order. It was the start of a fixation that would carry on into his adult life.

In September 2003, seventy-two-year-old Lester Cohen, father of David and Ashley, and his partner, Patricia Sharpe, were evicted from their council house in Netherthorpe. Their family were accused of having terrorised the estate for the previous eight years. Their fourteen-year-old son was said to be the leader of a gang of unruly teenagers who threatened the locals and made their lives a misery. Witnesses claimed that they had threatened to burn down the property of a local shop-keeper after she attempted to ban them from her shop. Sharpe was said to have sat back and encouraged her son, even issuing threats of her own. But all of this paled into insignificance when compared to the accusations levelled against her two older sons, David and Ashley. Whereas Patricia and the four-teen-year-old were nuisance neighbours, the older Cohen brothers took things a step further. They proved that they were more than willing to carry out the family's threats.

David and Ashley were accused of attacking a woman who came to the house to complain about the family's behaviour. They were alleged to have sprayed her with petrol and threat-ened her with a handgun. She said that David had handed the gun to Ashley and told him to shoot her with it and that she had driven away in fear for her life with Ashley in hot pursuit, ramming her car from behind. The Cohens were not the type of people that took criticism lightly.

When they weren't scaring the neighbours or intimidating the local community, the Cohens were thought to be involved in extortion and protection rackets. They were said to have pressurized club owners and door staff in an attempt to take over the city's door trade. Their right-hand men were known as the UTC: a collective of local villains feeding off their reputation and enacting their criminal plans.

In March 2007, Imran Khan, of Pitsmoor, made the mistake of getting into a fight with the Cohens' younger brother Mathew in a city centre nightclub. He then went to David Cohen's house in Philadelphia Gardens, Upperthorpe, with a weapon. He later denied firing shots at the house and claimed that the gun was an imitation weapon; although police later found a bullet lodged in a window frame, they could not say who had fired it. In any event, going there was a bad move: anybody with sense knew to leave the Cohens well alone.

Khan was now a wanted man, with the UTC on his tail. Luckily for him, he was in the safest place possible: locked away in a holding cell. He was taken in for questioning over a motoring offence and was being quizzed by the local police just as the gang were deploying to look for him. Try as they might, the UTC could not get their hands on him.

However, there is an unsavoury convention amongst some hard-core criminals that if a wanted man is difficult to locate, then it is fair game to go after one of his family instead. Imran's father, Younis, was an open target. He lived in Pitsmoor, an area that the gang were familiar with, and drove a black cab, an easily identifiable vehicle that would ensure that they got the right man. He was an innocent man and his killers were fully aware of this fact.

On 14 March 2007, six shots were fired into Younis's taxi as he drove along Scott Road in Pitsmoor. One of the bullets struck him in the chest, causing him to crash the car. He was rushed to the nearest hospital but was pronounced dead on arrival. The car used by the gunmen was found burnt out on the Langsett estate in Upperthorpe.

David and Ashley Cohen were convicted of organising Younis Khan's murder and sentenced to life in prison. Ashley was also accused of having perverted the course of justice, after it was proven that he helped to destroy the getaway car. The victim's family were too scared of the Cohens to appear in court and were kept informed of proceedings over the telephone. His widow, Pervez, said that even if the pair received ten life sentences it would be too short. The gang had taken away her husband over a dispute in which he had no involvement. To her, nothing could atone for what they had done.

Pervez's grief was made worse by the actions of some of the Cohens' relatives, who seemed more outraged that the brothers had been convicted than they were about the death of an innocent man. David's father-in-law declared that the streets of Sheffield would see a 'bloodbath' now that the two were behind bars. He said that David had been a 'peacekeeper' on the streets of Upperthorpe and Patricia Sharpe demanded to know why Imran Khan was not being charged with attempted murder.

Imran was charged with firearm possession on the basis that he had initiated the feud by allegedly shooting at David Cohen's house. The case against him was dropped despite the fact that he had admitted possessing a gun. His solicitor argued that the police had led him to believe he would avoid prosecution if he was to provide evidence against the Cohens. The point was stressed that, without Imran having admitted to going to David's house with the gun, it was unlikely that the brothers would have been brought to justice.

The Cohens continue to maintain their innocence and they are not alone: their family have been vocal in their requests for a retrial and appear to genuinely believe that the brothers are innocent. Patricia Sharpe has even offered to put her house up for sale to pay their legal bills. She stated that she would rather live in a tent than have her boys spend the next thirty years in prison.

On 24 June 2008, a café previously owned by Ashley Cohen was set ablaze in what his relatives claimed to be a revenge attack. A few days earlier, a family friend was followed and robbed. According to Patricia Sharpe, these were almost certainly the actions of somebody who opposed her family's protests about the 'truth' behind the murder.

Sheffield has been blighted by gang-related killings over the past few years and its gangs are relying increasingly heavily upon guns. From its juvenile street gangs to more organised firms like the UTC, it is a city in the midst of a wave of violence. Sheffield Police are quick to point out that the amount of gun crime within the city is well below that of Manchester or London, but the fact remains that it is an undoubtedly escalating problem. There are a number of gangs that have not yet entered the public consciousness: the S2 Mandem, the Darnall Mob, the S9 Boyz from Darnall and Attercliffe and the S13 Boyz from Handsworth. The disaffected youth of Sheffield are becoming increasingly territorial and, as a result, lives are being lost. It is a problem, as elsewhere, for which there is no quick fix.

Halifax

I F I LEARNT anything during my time in prison, it was that gun crime has infiltrated almost every corner of society: no longer is it confined to inner-city estates. I met armed robbers from Harrogate and Redcar, gun-wielding drug dealers from York and Wakefield, and armed gang members from a small town just outside of Halifax.

Elland is a historic market town with a population of 14,500. It is one of the poorer areas in the region, but is nothing out of the ordinary: it is an archetypal, small West Yorkshire town. It has no large council estates and the majority of the residents live in modest terraced housing – hardly the type of place where you might expect an armed gang to stalk the streets.

HX5 is the postcode for Elland and Blackley. It is a postcode that I first encountered when I saw it tattooed across the back of a convicted drug dealer. The next time it was brought to my attention was in the context of a rivalry with HX2, the postcode for the Pellon area of Halifax.

'HX2 come to Elland and they get dealt with,' a small, stocky inmate with a particularly manic stare boasted to me. 'Our firm run Halifax.'

So who were HX5 and what did they have against HX2?

'It's just rival areas, innit?' he said. 'All the places around Halifax have their own firm and they all hate each other.

There's a few in Elland: HX5, the Elland Mad Dogs, the Elland Bongheads. Then you've got the gangs in Halifax. There's HX2, the Mixenden Crew, the Furnace Crew from Illingworth, the Lee Mount Loonies and then there's the Brighouse Crew nearby as well.'

HX5 are testament to the spread of gangland culture from major cities to small towns and villages. Did they really 'run' Halifax? I suspected not; most of the top firms that I had encountered were unconcerned with whose postcode was the 'hardest'. They were out for money and they would work with anyone from any area to acquire it.

Whilst they were probably nowhere near to the top of the ladder, HX5 were the type of gang that posed the biggest threat to innocent civilians: they had a lot to prove and they were determined to make a name for themselves. 'Come to Elland and you will see guns, knives, knuckle-dusters and nunchucks,' I was told. 'If you're from HX2, you'll be lucky to come out alive.'

It was hard to imagine gun crime in a place like Elland. I wondered if I was being told the truth or if he was merely exaggerating.

'How much can you get a gun for?' I asked.

'For a used one you'd be looking at around a hundred and fifty pounds.'

This was in line with what I'd been told by an inmate who was serving a sentence for supplying firearms.

'If you want a new one, it can be anything from six hundred pounds to fifteen hundred pounds for a nine-millimetre, depending on who you get it off.'

I asked how willing were they to use these weapons, if need be. Not very, it seemed.

'The lads normally only use them as a last resort, or if

they're doing a graft,' he said. A graft is street slang for an illegal means of earning money. 'If it's just area beef we use all types of things: samurai swords, knives, machetes, knuckle dusters, nunchucks, bats, hockey sticks…we like to get up close and personal.'

He went on to boast of numerous encounters in which he had beaten, bludgeoned, slashed and stabbed his enemies. HX2 were clearly the gang's main rivals. From what I could gather, the feud had reached fever pitch after a man from Elland was attacked by several HX2 members at a Halifax nightclub. That night, twenty HX2 members travelled to Elland to finish what they had started. They were greeted by a much larger number of HX5, who proceeded to beat them to a pulp.

'It was great!' said Liam, the stocky HX5 member. 'There was this one guy the lads threw off a bridge; my mate went down afterwards and smashed him in the face with a brick. He went off in an ambulance – his head was a mess.'

A few days later, HX2 came back for a rematch and were rammed off the road. Four men from Elland were taken in for questioning, but were eventually released without charge.

HX5's reign of terror, however, was not restricted to inter-gang turf wars. During his youth, Liam had committed at least two street robberies every day. At just fourteen years old, he went out armed with a metal bar and mugged unsuspecting civilians in Halifax town centre. He would take their money, jewellery and mobile phones and any resistance was met with violence.

'It was only ever men that got robbed,' he claimed, by way of mitigation. 'If people get done over as part of a robbery, it's nothing personal: it's just part of the business.'

Liam and his friends claim to have earned up to £1,500 a

night this way and seemed to get a rush from preying on the weak. 'It's the type of thing that's fun when you're that age. I wouldn't do it nowadays: the only crime I'd consider doing now is selling drugs. I don't believe in taking things from law-abiding people any more.'

Drugs were another of the gang's fortes. Another HX5 member I met had received his first custodial sentence at fifteen for selling crack, heroin, speed and ketamine in Halifax town centre. According to him, there were not enough addicts in Elland, so he had to travel to Halifax to sell his wares.

'There's a few of the lads involved in selling coke and a couple robbing dealers as well,' he told me. 'The thing is that's their business though. It's nothing to do with them being in a gang: everybody acts as individuals but if it comes down to it then we back each other up.'

Although Liam would toy with cocaine every now and again, drink was his main vice. He would become violent when drunk and it seemed that alcohol was the catalyst for most of his offences. He had lived a hard life. Several of his friends were dead, including one who had been killed with a samurai sword. Newspaper clippings of his fallen comrades lined the walls of his cell. He had been stabbed in the lip, bludgeoned with an empty beer bottle and badly beaten on numerous occasions. The gang life was no easy ride.

'If you think things are bad in Elland, you want to see what they get up to in Brighouse,' Liam told me. 'They are notorious for using shooters. Some of their boys came down here last year firing shots off outside of the pub.'

Brighouse is another town near Halifax and Elland, and an equally unlikely setting for gun-wielding gangs to roam the streets. But Liam was telling the truth. I typed 'Elland' and 'shooting' into Google and, sure enough, there was an article about a sawn-off shotgun being fired at the front of the Royal Oak pub. Shortly after the shooting, the vehicle used by the gunmen was found parked outside the Black Swan pub in Brighouse. A shotgun, machete and meat cleaver were found inside. The incident was thought to be the result of a conflict between rival factions from Elland and Brighouse.

In January 2009, a man from Brighouse and another from nearby Rastrick received seven-year jail terms after pleading guilty to possession of a firearm with intent to cause fear of violence. A third man was later sentenced to six years. He was a well-known criminal with a suspected mental disorder.

'There's a lot of stuff like that happens but it only gets reported if it's in a public place,' Liam said. 'It's not just Elland and Brighouse though, there's guns everywhere nowadays, just they only get in the papers when people get shot with them.'

When they weren't pursuing their rivalry with Elland, gangs from Brighouse would frequently fight with those from the neighbouring village of Rastrick. Rastrick is home to the Field Lane estate, a deprived council estate where gang violence is more common than one might suspect. Large groups of youths regularly fight with each other, sometimes unarmed, sometimes using knives. Violence on the estate was highlighted in September 2007, when a sixty-year-old terminally ill man had his throat slashed in his own flat.

Rastrick itself was the site of a shooting in March 2006 and there have been several serious knife attacks. On New Year's Eve 2007, a group of forty youths from Brighouse and Rastrick descended upon an estate in Southowram, a small village roughly equidistant from Halifax and Brighouse, intent on causing havoc. All in their teens, they had consumed large amounts of alcohol and a mass brawl ensued. A teenage boy was stabbed in the arm and had a large chunk of flesh bitten out of his ear, resulting in forty stitches. When the police arrived, they were pelted with missiles.

When questioned about the night's events, the residents of Southowram claimed that they were not in the least bit surprised, as gangs had been fighting in the village for years. Many said that they felt under siege and that their quality of life had been destroyed: what was once a peaceful village had been reduced to anarchy by a few individuals determined to cause trouble.

Although Halifax and the surrounding areas are not in the same league as cities like Sheffield in terms of gang activity, serious violent crime is beginning to take hold in small towns and villages. A problem that was previously restricted to large cities such as London, Birmingham and Manchester is now taking root in places like Elland and Rastrick – a disturbing thought at a time when the country as a whole faces an extended period of economic hardship in the wake of the global recession.

Glasgow

WHEREAS YOUTH GANGS are only just beginning to make the news in Halifax, there is a city where they have been a way of life for generations. Dubbed 'gang city' by the media, it is a place where young people are members of gangs that their fathers and grandfathers fought in decades before them. Glasgow is thought to have at least 170 gangs, an equal number to London despite being only a sixth of the size. It is, in many ways, the gang capital of Britain.

Youth gangs have existed in Glasgow for over 200 years. In the 1800s, 'penny mobs' terrorized the city. They were often fined rather than imprisoned and members would chip in a penny each to ensure the freedom of their comrades. Eventually several of these gangs united and larger mobs formed, some of which still exist.

The Real Calton Tongs started off as the Calton Tongs, an early twentieth century gang made up of penny mobs. They are one of Scotland's longest running street gangs and are perhaps best known for their graffiti slogan 'Tongs Ya Bass', which was sprayed on walls all over the streets of Glasgow throughout the 1960s and '70s. 'Bass' is a bastardisation of a Gaelic phrase meaning 'battle and die': it perfectly sums up the outlook of many of the Tongs members.

To understand why the Tongs – originally a name applied to

criminal brotherhoods of Chinese origin – came into being, it is important to gain an insight into life in Calton, one of the UK's most deprived areas. It is a place where life expectancy is more akin to that of Iraq or Palestine than to Western Europe: estimated at a mere 53.9 years, compared to the nationwide average of seventy-eight. Children growing up in Calton are ten times more likely to have unemployed parents than those born in the wealthier western suburbs of the city and adults are three times more likely to develop heart disease. Drug use is at near-epidemic proportions.

At the start of their existence, the Tongs' main rivals were the Brigtonderry gang, hailing from the Protestant area of Bridgeton. They were mainly Irish immigrants, rationalizing that, if the English could add the prefix of London to the Northern Irish city of Derry, they could add the suffix of 'Derry' to Bridgeton. The Tongs were Catholic and resented the existence of a Protestant gang so close to their territory. They would stab, slash or beat any of the Brigtonderry that dared to cross over into Calton. They did, however, have a policy of only attacking other gang members – civilians were allowed to come and go as they pleased.

In the late 1970s, the gang branched out into more lucrative forms of crime. They would smash through the windows of jewellery shops using hammers and crowbars, helping themselves to the contents. This gave rise to the Calton Hammer Gang (CHG), a subdivision of the Tongs. Most of the CHG hailed from the area around Well Street, a notorious part of Calton known locally as 'Nightmare Alley'. They were, in effect, the financial wing of the Tongs. Whereas the rest of the gang concentrated on defending their territory, the CHG were strictly profit-orientated and carried out a prolific spate of commercial burglaries across the city.

The CHG are a rarity on the streets of Glasgow, in that they seem motivated by money. Whereas gangs in other towns and cities are often focused on drug turf, most of Glasgow's street gangs fight purely for recreational reasons. During my time at HMP Wolds, I met a prisoner from Barnsley who had spent a year living in the Gorbals, one of Glasgow's gang hotspots. 'It's worse than anywhere round here,' he said. 'They love to fight there: they'll slash you up and leave your wallet right where it is.'

Another characteristic of the Scottish gangs is their love of knives. The gangs of Glasgow are also atypical in that they are mostly white. The few Asian gangs that do exist within the city tend to fight amongst each other. However, there is an ongoing feud between the all-white Young Shields Mad Squad and a number of the Asian firms in Pollokshields. This is an area where racial tensions sometimes run high.

In October 2005, fifteen-year-old Kriss Donald was abducted, stabbed thirteen times, doused in petrol and burned to death. His killing was racially motivated although, unusually, he was the white victim of an attack by non-whites. He was killed because he was the same skin colour as the Young Shields Mad Squad, a white gang and the sworn enemies of an Asian mob known as the Shielders.

The Shielders first came to police attention in 1998, when they were alleged to have placed a bomb under a rival gang member's car. Imran Shahid, the self-styled 'godfather', had convictions for serious assault and attempted murder. Known as 'Baldy' because of his distinctive haircut – bleached blond and shaven at the sides – he was a figure of fear within Glasgow's Pakistani community; there were rumours that he had cut off a man's thumb, placed it in a glass of milk and forced him to drink it. In 1994, he beat a man with a baseball bat to the point of brain damage and it was rumoured that he had hired a London hitman to deal with anyone who testified against him.

In February 2003, Shahid was jailed for thirty months for assault to endanger life and dangerous driving after punching a female social worker in the face, then driving a car over her as she lay unconscious on the ground. He had been out of prison for only thee months when, in March 2004, he was attacked with a bottle by a number of white youths outside a nightclub. Baldy was furious. When asked by a friend what he wanted to do about his attackers, he replied, 'Pick up a car and go look for them.' His friend asked who he planned to look for.

'Anybody,' he replied.

Seething with anger, Shahid stated that he would 'chop them up and take their eyes out'. He didn't care who he hurt, as long as they were white. The men who had attacked him were white, as were his enemies, the Young Shields Mad Squad. Therefore, he felt justified in killing the first white male he came across.

Kriss Donald was walking with a friend near his home in Pollokshields when he was abducted at random. The Shielders attacked him with a hammer and screwdriver and dragged him into their stolen Mercedes. 'I'm only fifteen, what have I done?' he asked as he was bundled into the back of the car.

But his attackers were merciless. 'You think this is pain? You don't even know pain yet,' Baldy told him.

They drove him two hundred miles across Scotland, before deciding on a suitable location to butcher him. Eventually, he was taken to a secluded spot next to Celtic FC's training ground and ordered out of the car. He was sliced across the chest, stabbed in his stomach, arm, liver, lung, kidneys and intestines, and three of his major arteries were severed. He was then set on fire and left to die. Barely alive, he rolled in a puddle in a vain attempt to put out the flames, but would never recover from his injuries.

Eight months later, Daanish Zahid was found guilty of Donald's murder. He was sentenced to a minimum of seventeen years in prison. Zahid Mohammed pleaded guilty to the abduction but not to the killing, as he claimed that he had left the car before the murder took place. Both of them gave evidence implicating Imran Shahid, his brother Zeeshan 'Crazy' Shahid, and a third man, Faisal Mushtaq.

By this stage Faisal, Zeeshan and Baldy had fled to Pakistan, where they hoped that they would be safe from British law. They didn't know, however, that the British High Commission in Islamabad had agreed to extradite them back to England and an international operation was mobilizing to apprehend them. The fact that the Pakistani authorities had agreed to this one-off extradition was largely down to the efforts of Mohammed Sarwar, the MP for Glasgow Central. There is no extradition treaty between the UK and Pakistan and so the decision was taken at the discretion of the Pakistani authorities, who took a year and a half to be persuaded. Senior officers within Strathclyde Police Force have since stated that without Sarwar's hard work, the killers might have never been brought to justice.

Unfortunately for Faisal and Zeeshan, Mohammed Sarwar was originally from Toba Tek Singh, a city in the Punjab province of Pakistan. He had family living there, many of whom he was still in regular contact with. The two fugitives made the mistake of hiding out in a small village just ten miles away. Word of their location reached Sarwar and before long the Pakistani police were knocking at their door.

Baldy Shahid was pinpointed to an apartment in the affluent Shadhore district of Lahore. He was operating a credit card scam from his rented accommodation and living the life of a wealthy businessman. When police turned up on his doorstep, he was taken completely by surprise. A search of his flat revealed a fake British driving licence under the name of 'Enrique Soprano'. The man who saw himself as an untouchable mafia boss was led away in handcuffs and was flown back to Scotland.

On 8 October 2006, Baldy Shahid and his associates were sentenced to life in prison. He received a minimum tariff of twenty-five years, the longest of the three sentences, as he was deemed to be the ringleader. Zeeshan Shahid was given twenty-three years and Faisal Mushtaq, who raised his middle finger on the way to the courtroom, was given twenty-two years. They showed no remorse for their actions.

'You bastards,' Kriss Donald's mother shouted to them as the verdict was delivered.

Just because their leader was behind bars did not mean that the Shielders were no longer a threat. In reality, a large number of serious crimes are carried out under the orders of convicted prisoners. There are numerous ways of getting a set of instructions across that the guards are unable to pick up on. Coded messages are written in letters, calls are made on illicit cellphones and commands are given verbally on prison visits. Those who are in jail can still be a huge danger to society.

In June 2007, it was reported that Mohammed Sarwar was stepping down from his position as MP for Glasgow Central. He spoke of repeated threats to his family and claimed that the Shielders had warned him that they were going to kill his son and abduct his grandchildren. He added that his quality of life had dropped dramatically since he had helped to locate them.

However, he denied it had any bearing on his decision to leave public office.

Baldy may have been locked away but the remaining members of his gang still regarded him as their leader. In criminal circles, those with the least morals are often the most admired. Although Shahid had been removed from the outside world, he still had a firm grip upon the streets of Pollokshields. The fact that he was able to intimidate an MP was testament to his power.

On 9 January 2008, Baldy exercised his authority yet again in a bid to punish a former gang member for giving evidence against him. Daanish Zahid had been let out of prison for a day to receive treatment at Glasgow Royal Infirmary. Although he was under the strict supervision of the prison guards, he was still at risk of attack from the Shielders. Shortly after his arrival at the hospital, the police received a phone call stating that a group of knife-wielding gang members were demanding to see him. The visit was supposed to have been secret.

The police believed that Baldy masterminded the attack from his jail cell, informing his fellow gang members of the visit. The level of control that he was able to exact over his firm from behind prison walls highlighted failings in the Scottish prison system. It was their job to prevent him from committing crimes whilst behind bars. Although he was unable to punish his enemies personally, he was fully capable of having other people do it on his behalf.

Later that year, the gang struck again. Barry O'Neill was one of the key witnesses in Baldy's trial, having given evidence relating to the fact that the Shielders were looking for revenge after the nightclub bottle attack. In August 2008, he stopped his car at a traffic light in the Springburn area of the city only to find the door ripped open by an Asian male. His attacker leaned into his car and stabbed him before making his getaway in another car.

One by one, the Shielders were taking revenge on everyone who had testified against them, and it was alleged that they were receiving their orders directly from Baldy. There were even rumours that he was continuing to run his credit card fraud operation from jail. Someone close to the gang claimed that they were making up to £1 million pounds a year and that part of this money was being used to pay off other prisoners who had put a price on his head.

Though he was feared on the streets of Pollokshields, Baldy was hated in prison. Inmates offered drugs and tobacco to anybody who could take him out. His offence was seen as the lowest of the low: the killing of a child. He spent the majority of his sentence either on the segregation wing or the vulnerable prisoner unit, and is likely to do so for the rest of his time inside.

On 8 January 2009, Baldy was back in court. He had assaulted a white inmate who he claimed had racially insulted him – ironic, given the nature of the crime that he was in for. He was walking back to his cell when the prisoner shouted abuse in his direction. Not one to suffer abuse quietly, he rushed over and punched and kicked the man before prison guards pulled them apart. Khan was jailed for three months, to run concurrently with his life sentence.

Faisal Mushtaq was equally unpopular inside. The word was that he had attempted to win the favour of the other inmates by handing out free drugs and tobacco. The minute he ran out of bribes, he was attacked.

Far-right groups have touted the Shielders as proof that Glasgow's Asian community are 'anti-white'. However, the truth is that Asian gangs within the city originally sprang up to protect themselves and their communities. The majority of racial attacks in Scotland are perpetrated by whites against Asians. Glasgow is a divided city and prejudice is rife.

In the wake of Kriss Donald's death, some of the city's white gangs spoke of 'revenge' for what had happened and used his murder as an excuse to attack asylum seekers and Pakistani shopkeepers. Gangs like the Toryglen Nazi Circus, the Bowery Wee Mob and the Young Toryglen Toi reportedly developed links with Combat 18 and other far-right organisations.

Leading criminologist Dr Susan Batchelor cites the insular nature of Glaswegian gangs as a catalyst for their racist behaviour. Whilst researching youth gangs in the city, she made the astonishing discovery that some gang members in the Possil area had never even been to the city centre. They remained isolated within their own deprived, predominantly white community. They attacked Asian and Eastern European immigrants, as they saw them as outsiders invading their turf – the area that they rarely left and saw as their property. In their case, racism was a result of ignorance and extreme territorialism.

Sectarianism has long been another driving force behind many of the city's gang feuds. Firms like the Sonnyhills Mad Sqwad, the Gallagate Mad Skwad, the Castlemilk Young Machrie Fleeto and the Young Blackhill Toi align themselves with loyalist paramilitary group the Ulster Defence Association, in order to demonstrate their staunch Protestantism. Other groups, such as the Pollok Bushwackers and the Young Tyre Cumbie Troops daub IRA graffiti on buildings in homage to their Catholic roots.

Religious conflict is further exacerbated by the football rivalry that has such a long and discreditable history in Glasgow. Catholic gangs tend to wear green to signify their support of Celtic F.C., whilst Protestants wear the blue of

Rangers. When the two teams play each other, the fans' enthusiasm for football has often been overtaken by anger and sectarian aggression. Religious hatred within Glasgow harks all the way back to the days of the Brigtonderry.

WHILE RESEARCHING THIS book, I was pointed in the direction of a gangland enthusiast who had collected video footage of hundreds of different Glaswegian youth gangs. He subsequently showed me clips of the main sectarian gangs within the city. Some of the images were the type you would associate with Belfast or Londonderry rather than Blackhill or Pollok.

The Gallagate Mad Skwad's video contained the most extreme imagery. At one point, a swastika flashed up on the screen, with the Red Hand of Ulster emblazoned in the middle of it. Right-wing symbols and union flags were interspersed with pictures of machete-wielding, shaven-headed youths in tracksuits. The footage was captioned 'Stand up for the crown'.

Surprisingly, a large number of teenage girls were present in the clips I saw. Firms from other parts of Scotland, like the North Motherwell Young Team and the Jungle Derry, had equal numbers of each gender and there were several all-female gangs. Whilst some of these were subdivisions of other gangs, others, such as the Derry Burdz and the Gorbalz Burdz, were gangs in their own right.

The Gorbals Burdz are amongst the most feared of Glasgow's all-girl gangs. They fight with lockback knives and knuckledusters and defend their territory from male and female gangs alike. The Gorbals is a rough place, an area synonymous with crime and acute poverty, and the Burdz have been forced to grow up in a district in which the women are often as tough as the men. They are affiliated with an all-male gang known as the Young X Cross Cumbie, one of the more ruthless gangs in the area. The Cumbie boast that they rarely needed to fight anymore because the Burdz are so good at defending their territory, although they are more than capable of sticking up for themselves – and even of killing.

Twenty-one-year-old William Smith was sick of being tormented by the Cumbie. They would sit outside his house drinking and being a nuisance. So one day in December 2006, he ran out and chased them down the street, only for them to charge back at him. He fell to the ground and the mob descended upon him, beating him with sticks and punching and kicking him repeatedly. He suffered fatal kidney damage and died in hospital four days later.

Rather than showing remorse, the Cumbie were arrogant and boastful. They publicly mocked their victim by referring to him as a 'mug' and 'dafty' on social networking sites. Footage filmed whilst William's killers were out on bail showed them brandishing knives and machetes minutes after leaving the courtroom. They were also seen threatening a rival gang by saying, 'Get back to Norfy [Norfolk House, a block of flats in Gorbals] before we murder you like Willie Smith, you dafty, do you want to get put in a box an' all?' The clips were uploaded on YouTube.

On 3 October 2007, six teenagers were jailed for their part in the killing, including Jason McFadden, George O'Connor, Iain Stevenson and Alexander Harvey, who were sentenced to eight years imprisonment for culpable homicide – a lenient punishment, given their complete lack of remorse.

Shortly after their sentencing, a video of the proceedings was uploaded onto YouTube under the caption, 'The troops in the high court fur murder.' It had been filmed on a mobile phone. William Smith's grieving mother described the footage as 'sick'. The gang, it seemed, were proud of what they had done.

So, were the Gorbalz Burdz as violent as their male counterparts?

'The girls are the worst when they get going,' I was told. 'They mainly only fight with other young lassies though. Boys fight with boys and girls fight with girls, although sometimes the girls will jump in if their boyfriends are getting battered.'

My source was adamant that the women could be just as vicious as the men.

Another aspect of the female gang culture is the girls' alleged promiscuity. It is rumoured that the older members of the Burdz insist upon taking out their younger friends, in makeup and mini-skirts, on the premise that they aren't allowed to retain their virginity if they want to be a part of the gang. Regardless of whether this is true, it is evident that there are a multitude of risks associated with young girls aligning themselves with male gangs. Some of them adopt a groupie-like attitude and sleep with older men in order to demonstrate their allegiance. They are often exploited and seen as sexual objects: trophies for the more respected members of the firm.

THE GLASGOW GANG life encompasses all ages, genders and races. There are children as young as six and men in their late twenties involved in the same recreational violence. 'Young teams' are rampant, sometimes with several different gang territories existing within a matter of yards of one another. But how big a problem are these youth gangs? Although innocent people occasionally get hurt, the majority of the victims are willing participants in the feuding. Street gangs create unease and ordinary members of the public are often caught up in the conflict, but there is a greater menace on the streets of Glasgow: a group of men who would laugh at the idea of fighting for 'fun'. They are the firm the Scottish media dubbed the Alien Abduction Gang.

Feral, Buckfast-drinking teenagers pale into insignificance when compared to Glasgow's organised drug gangs, and one man in particular was spoken of in hushed tones amongst the city's large criminal fraternity: Kevin 'Gerbil' Carroll. His gang earned their name when their victims were likened to the subjects of alien abduction, because they professed to have no recollection of what had happened to them. Gerbil was rumoured to be the head of a group of armed robbers, who would kidnap drug dealers and torture them until they agreed to hand over their money. Their victims would endure hours of physical and mental anguish. When it was all over, they were turfed out naked onto the streets, alive, but deeply traumatised.

Carroll grew up in Possil, a centre for Glasgow's heroin trade. The Abduction Gang were renowned for their willingness to resort to extreme measures to extract money and drugs from their targets. They would masquerade as police drug squads in order to gain entry to a house. Once inside, they went to work on the occupants with blowtorches and power tools. The drugs that they stole would be used as bait to lure in more potential victims. One man was sold £60,000 worth of cocaine only to have it stolen back immediately. Another 'customer' was robbed of four kilos without requiring violence; they simply told him that he was 'taxed' and walked away with the drugs.

Some of the gang's victims, however, were not as lucky. A dealer from Springburn was threatened with syringes and locked in a cupboard for two days. The gang stole £30,000 from him. Another of their targets was scalded with boiling water and permanently scarred after they gained entry to his home by pretending to be postmen.

Anyone who was armed but unaffiliated with the gang was seen as a potential threat. Christopher Logan was kidnapped from his flat in Springburn and threatened with a gun and a blowtorch. He had a Heckler and Koch machine gun that had been stolen from from the army, complete with ammunition. As far as they were concerned, this made him their rival. They took his weapon and left him lying in the street; the gun was then used by gang members in a triple shooting, in December 2006. Raymond Anderson and James McDonald marched into the Applerow Motors garage on Balmore Road, Lambhill. They fired a barrage of shots, killing Michael Lyons and injuring Steven Lyons and Robert Pickett. Michael's uncle, David, cradled him as he died. 'Bullets were flying everywhere,' he later recounted. 'My nephew was shot in the back and died in my arms.'

The Lyons family were reputedly one of the city's most feared criminal families, and the killing was thought to be the result of a long-running feud between them and the Daniel family. Gerbil was dating the daughter of Jamie Daniel, the head of the Daniel family, and there were rumours that he had a hand in the shooting. After being accused of four separate offences related to the robbery of the gun, he admitted to a single charge and was sentenced to eighteen months in prison.

Anderson and McDonald were eventually caught after being secretly recorded bragging about their exploits.

'What's the difference between Glasgow and Africa?' they joked. 'You can shoot Lyons in Glasgow.'

Their trial was likened to that of an American mafia family: key witnesses were separated from their friends and families and placed on life-long witness protection. The firm did everything within their power to try and get the two suspects off. The getaway car that they used was set alight to destroy any DNA evidence; a letter was written to the owner of the garage, detailing a fictional drug debt, to try to throw the police off the scent; and perhaps most brazenly of all, Robert Pickett was offered money to say that the 'wrong men' were in the dock.

Pickett was later jailed for two years for contempt of court. He was unable to sway the jury, who found McDonald and Anderson guilty of murder. They were given thirty-five years each in prison: the longest sentences in modern Scottish history. The judge described the killing as a 'cold-blooded, premeditated assassination'.

Shortly after their imprisonment, a number of inmates were offered £50,000 to kill the two hitmen. An Asian man was the first to receive the offer but refused to have anything to do with it: he knew full well that if he were to carry out the hit, he might himself be a dead man. Convicted murderer Jamie Bain was the second choice for the killing, but he too declined.

Anderson and McDonald were furious that anyone had even considered accepting the money. They approached the Asian inmate and demanded that he pay them £50,000 as compensation for entering into a dialogue with their enemies. Scared for his life and his wallet, he went to the guards and told them that he was being threatened. The two gang members were placed in the segregation unit as punishment.

Anderson was particularly feared within the jail. There were rumours that he had inmates cleaning his shoes and cooking his food. Meanwhile, the rest of the gang were going strong: they were robbing drug dealers all over Scotland and making countless enemies along the way.

In January 2010, Kevin 'Gerbil' Carroll was shot five times in broad daylight outside the Asda supermarket in Robroyston. Witnesses saw three masked men fleeing the scene. He had died the way he lived: like a scene from *The Sopranos*.

There are several theories as to why Gerbil was killed. The

most obvious is that it was in revenge for Michael Lyons' death: there was thought to be a £50,000 price on his head. The alternative is that Anderson and McDonald had put a hit out on him, as they believed that he had informed on them. Prisoners in HMP Shotts, where they were jailed at the time of the killing, were reported to have known all the details of the crime within minutes of it being carried out.

Whatever the motivation for Gerbil's murder, the Daniel family were furious. The head of the clan, Jamie Daniel, was alleged to have put up a reward for anyone who could locate the people responsible. Carroll's death would undoubtedly herald a new wave of violence on the streets of Glasgow: it had escalated an already bitter family feud to the point of no return.

And so Glasgow retains its title as Britain's most violent and gang-ridden city. From the teenage tearaways of Pollokshields and Govan, to the likes of the Daniels and the Alien Abduction Gang, it remains a place where men – and women – fight bloody battles over drugs and territory. Lives are being lost over bags of chemicals and sections of dilapidated council estates.

According to Strathclyde Police Force's Violence Reduction Unit, the levels of violence in the city have remained relatively constant for the last forty years. There has been little change, despite the continuing efforts of the local police force to combat the problem. There is no simple solution to the issue of young people engaging in recreational violence. It is an age-old tradition that has terrorized the slums of Glasgow for centuries.

The Violence Reduction Unit was created in order to find a new approach for tackling gangs. It uses techniques gleaned from Boston and Cincinatti in the United States to offer realistic alternatives to the gang lifestyle. Those who are deemed to be at risk are given access to training, healthcare and careers advice in an attempt to wean them from antisocial behaviour. The programme has had limited success, providing activities and vocational courses designed to distract young people from committing crime. Caroline Foulkes, the communications manager for the Reduction Unit, points out that gang make-up is very varied in the different parts of Glasgow. In order to effectively reduce youth violence, prevention techniques need to be adapted to suit the circumstances. 'However,' she says, 'the one common denominator is violent young men.'

Liverpool

RHYS JONES IS a name synonymous with the tragic consequences of teenage gun crime. Rhys was the unintended and innocent victim of a mindless war between two gangs. His murder catapulted Croxteth and Norris Green into the public consciousness as centres for gang violence. But, as anyone who lives in Liverpool will tell you, their rivalry is just one of many that exist all over the city.

Liverpool is England's poorest local authority. It has never fully recovered from the decline of the shipping industry and pockets of deprivation are scattered all over the city. Nearly every area has its gangs: some are merely anti-social, some acquisitive, while others wage war on rivals with guns, knives and even explosives. The Croccy Crew and the Nogga Dogs, whose feud led to the death of young Rhys, are a small, if highly publicised, part of the phenomenon of increasingly well-armed teenage gangs.

Although the exact roots of the conflict between Croxteth and Norris Green remain unclear, a number of events have aggravated the feud. On New Year's Day 2004, twenty-year-old Danny McDonald was shot at point-blank range whilst drinking at the Royal Oak pub in Norris Green. A hooded man walked in and opened fire in front of sixty witnesses. McDonald died from his injuries. Another man, John Cummins, was shot in the stomach, but survived.

The shooting was almost certainly gang-related. McDonald was said to be a boss of the Croxteth Crew, something confirmed when I spoke to Richie, another member of the gang.

'He was our leader,' he said. 'It was Smigger that did it: that's why we did him.'

He was referring to Liam 'Smigger' Smith, the leader of the Strand Gang, also known as the Nogga Dogs, from Norris Green. Smith was himself later shot in the head outside Altcourse Prison in Liverpool. Smith had been visiting a friend when he was spotted by Ryan Lloyd, another inmate. Lloyd phoned two of his friends and they drove to the prison and blasted him. All three men destroyed their mobiles and the cars that they had driven were burnt out to destroy the evidence.

On the day of Smigger's funeral, Norris Green came to a standstill. Shops and pubs were shut and school playtimes were cancelled. The one supermarket that stayed open hired four security guards to keep watch outside the front door, scared that the Nogga Dogs might view it as a sign of disrespect that they had continued trading. There was an atmosphere of fear and tension: ordinary citizens were scared to leave their houses. The words 'R.I.P. Smigger' and 'Smigger ov Nogsy' were sprayed on shop shutters all over North Liverpool.

Ryan Lloyd, Liam Duffy, Thomas Forshaw and an unnamed sixteen-year-old were eventually charged in connection with the shooting. Forshaw and the sixteen-year-old received life sentences with a minimum tariff of eighteen years. Lloyd was given a minimum of twenty-eight years and Duffy, a known drug dealer, was given twenty years for manslaughter. The court heard from a representative of Merseyside Police, who told of the fear that the gangs had wrought upon the local community. He pointed out that the housing association in Croxteth and Norris Green had more vacant properties than tenants wanting to live in them. Residents were being driven away by the threat of gang violence.

'Smigger got the same treatment as Danny,' Richie said. 'They killed our leader so we killed theirs.'

Now that lives had been taken on each side, hatred between the two groups was at an all time high. Both gangs had been deprived of their leader, but both continued their activities undeterred. 'We don't have a leader now,' I was told. 'The older members and the ones that have done certain things are more respected though.'

Richie grew up around gangs, weapons and violence. He saw his first gun at nine years old and fired a pistol at age eleven. He joined the Croccy Crew at thirteen and at fourteen had received his first gunshot wound. He was walking through Norris Green when he was ambushed and shot in the arm.

'Did it hurt?' I asked.

'Nah not the first time – the second did! I was seventeen and they got me in the leg and the belly. I nearly passed out from the pain.'

I asked him what illegal activities the gang was involved in.

'A few of us do robberies,' he told me. 'Not very often though, we mainly just terrorize Nogzy, but when I was fourteen I got done for an armed robbery.' He had robbed an Asian corner shop worker at gunpoint and spent four years in HMP Hammersmith.

'They think they're bad in there,' he said. 'They all think they're 50 Cent. London gangs can't fight for shit. Strangeways in Manchester, that's what you call a proper jail. HMP Polmont in Scotland, one of my mates is in there and that's a rough jail.'

I asked if there were any other gangs that he respected, if the Croccy Crew had any allies.

'Well there's certainly no-one else in Liverpool,' he said.

'Croccy runs Liverpool. Glasgow is probably the roughest city for gangs. London is just a bunch of dickheads. Some London Paki tried to get cheeky with Mercer and look what happened.' He was referring to an incident involving Sean Mercer, the youth responsible for the Rhys Jones killing. He had stabbed another inmate with a pair of sharpened tweezers during a confrontation at HMP Moorlands, a notoriously violent young offenders' institute.

'What was the story behind that?' I asked him.

'He was saying he ran the jail and being a cheeky twat, so Sean stabbed him in the back and nearly left him paralysed.'

Richie and his friends are still in contact with Mercer, despite what he did.

'It was bad, I'm not going to say it wasn't, but he's still our mate,' he said. 'What happened to Rhys was an accident. [Sean] was tryna shoot one of Nogzy and hit him by mistake.'

I asked him whether Rhys's death had made the gang any less likely to use guns in the future.

'Nah,' he said. 'You get such a buzz when you hold a gun. You're like yeah, I'm the man.'

Whilst I was in jail, I overheard a conversation with a member of the Nogga Dogs, who thought differently about Rhys's death.

'It's not what they did that was bad – that was a mistake,' he said. 'It's how they were in court, laughing and joking. They are a bunch of nonces. Kid killers. If it was us, we would have made sure there was no kids anywhere near there.'

This was hardly true. There are members of both the Croccy Crew and the Nogga Dogs who are under the age of eighteen. According to Richie, the youngest member of the Croccy Crew is twelve years old.

'The young kids don't use guns though,' he said to me, 'Just knives!'

He claimed that guns in Liverpool were both ridiculously easy to buy, and extraordinarily cheap. 'Well if you've got thirty quid you can get a 9mm.' I had met people in prison who were selling 9mm pistols for £1,000 and up: £30 is cheap for this type of gun. 'Sawn-off shotguns are £150, MAC-10s are £150, you can get a Desert Eagle for like £500 or an MP5 for £3,000. You can get whatever you want really, my mate's got an AK. I think it cost him a few grand. You can get silencers for £500 too and even grenades and bombs.'

A MAC-10 goes for £3,000 in Sheffield, seemingly twenty times the price of what they are being sold for in Croxteth.

'Why are the guns so cheap in Liverpool?'

'It's cause they've all been used,' said Richie. 'No-one knows what's been done with them. People might have done murders with 'em. Also, it's a port so there's always people bringing guns over. We've got the docks. Guns and drugs pile in.'

Richie's gun of choice was the Heckler and Koch MP5. 'I obviously can't say if I've used one or not, but I've heard that you get a shoulder clip so you can get a better aim with it. Desert Eagles are good too – they would kill you with one bullet.'

MP5s and Desert Eagles are the types of weaponry that the SAS use: the fact that they have found their way onto the streets of Croxteth is particularly disturbing. For the Croccy Crew, firearms and bulletproof vests are a part of daily life. They hide their guns in hedges and gardens and pick them up when they need to use them.

Just as there was no real reason for the feud to start, there is no foreseeable end to it. As well as being a constant source of danger, it is also a major inconvenience: Croxteth's local job centre is in Norris Green. So, in order to claim their jobseekers allowance, the Croccy Crew have to travel into enemy territory.

This means that they have two options: go without their benefits or venture into hostile terrain.

'Normal people can go wherever they want,' I was told. 'It's just the gangs that are at risk. We don't do anything to innocent people.'

Richie had a school friend from Norris Green who he had abandoned when he became involved with the Croccy Crew. Croxteth gang members rarely mixed with people from Norris Green, regardless of past friendships. 'The only time we're in the same place as them is when we're shooting at them,' he said. Neither of the groups would enter into a dialogue with each other, they would just fight: whenever they saw each other, conflict was inevitable.

'Trust me, there's a lot more shootings than you see in the news,' Richie said. 'There's just not many grasses in Liverpool, so you never hear about them.'

There is a strict code of silence held by both sides, which is possibly why the problems in Croxteth and Norris Green were allowed to simmer for so long. It took the death of an eleven-year-old boy to gain publicity for the teenage gang epidemic; but gun crime is nothing new on the streets of Liverpool. There are other places in the city where similar turf wars have received a fraction of the attention.

SEVERAL MILES SOUTH of Croxteth is an area where children even younger than Rhys have been caught up in territorial shootings. Huyton is a district in which six different gangs have been identified: the Moss Edz and the Wimborne Gang from Page Moss, the Longy Boyz from Longview, The Hillside Edz from the Hillside estate, the Bakiez from the Bakers Green estate and the Dovey Edz from Dovecot. The Wimborne gang are centred around muggings and house burglaries, rather than fighting with other gangs. They break into people's houses and steal possessions sometimes while the helpless occupants stand and watch. When there are no suitable occupied houses to target, they raid derelict properties, stripping the lead and copper wire from them and then setting them on fire. They have members as young as twelve years old.

The Moss Edz are renowned for the young age of their gunmen. Their leader is said to be a fourteen-year-old schoolboy and they have several pre-teen members. Nine-year-olds on the estate have access to sawn-off shotguns, 9mm pistols and SA80 assault rifles. In 2008, seventeen-year-old Scott Elliot was sentenced to nine years in prison for shooting at a house owned by the grandfather of the Dovey Edz leader. During the same incident, a younger member of the gang shot himself in the foot whilst waving a gun at the leader's younger brother. These weapons are clearly not just for show.

On 5 November 2009, it was reported that a group of youths were firing indiscriminately at houses in Page Moss. The Dovey Edz were the prime suspects. It was a common occurrence for the residents there; they were used to the sound of gunshots. What was once a pleasant neighbourhood was now being referred to as the 'Wild West'; it was rumoured that the shootings were revenge for a number of similar events that had occurred in Dovecot.

All of the six crews in Huyton are hostile towards one another. It is a place where it is only by luck that there hasn't been another child slaying. Children of the age of Rhys Jones have access to automatic weapons and pledge allegiance to their postcode. Some live a matter of yards from each other but yet they are sworn enemies. In Huyton, crossing a geographical divide can result in death.

The same can be said of estates all over the city. It is paradoxical that the most dilapidated parts of Liverpool often harbour the most territorial attitudes. For the poor and disaffected, sometimes the only thing they can be proud of is the place that they grew up in. Tracksuit-clad youths fight over grey council flats and litter-strewn patches of turf. They are willing to give their lives for places that others are desperate to move away from.

L8 has been Liverpool's most notorious postcode since the Toxteth riots. Although the region has improved since the 1980s, it still harbours a gun culture similar to that of Huyton and Croxteth. There are two main youth gangs in the area: the all-white Park Road Edz from Dingle and the Somali Warriors from Toxteth. The Park Road Edz are mainly concerned with stealing cars and motorbikes, whereas the Somali Warriors are renowned for their use of knives. They are based around the Granby area and are fiercely territorial: anyone who strays onto their turf can expect to get robbed. It is rumoured that they knock their victims out and carve the initials 'SW' onto them with a flick knife. Though this may be an urban myth, it is a measure of the fear that they engender.

Toxteth has one of the largest Somali communities in Britain. The majority of Somali people are law-abiding, but a small contingent have been attracted to the gang scene. Police believe that there is a core group of around thirty Somalis involved in drug dealing and car crime. This is unsurprising, as it is thought that up to seventy per cent of Somali men in Britain are unemployed, and many witnessed wartime atrocities in their home country. Poverty, cultural differences and language barriers make it difficult for them to integrate into mainstream society.

On March 11 2008, Somali student Ahmed Ibrahim was

beaten to death by a group of youths armed with samurai swords, baseball bats, machetes and metal poles. It was thought to be the result of a dispute with a Somali gang. His cousin had been accused of drinking alcohol, a sin within the Muslim community, and he had accompanied him to a 'straightener', a one-on-one fistfight to resolve disagreements. However, they were confronted by an armed gang, who held Ahmed down and laid into him. At one point one of his assailants shouted, 'He's still alive,' suggesting that it was undoubtedly their intention to kill.

Ahmed Ibrahim died of a fractured skull and damage to the brain. His cousin, Abdullah Ahmed, had a finger cut off during the fray. Five men were arrested: four from Toxteth and one from London. It was alleged that one of the men issued threats to Ibrahim's cousin shortly after the murder: he was said to have called him as he sat in the police car and warned him that if he told the police anything he would be killed.

Ibrahim's other cousin present, Ahmed Mahmoud Ahmed, claimed that one of his attackers was armed with a gun and had threatened to kill him if he went to his cousin's aid. He also said that his mother's windows had been smashed and her car vandalised on the day of the murder. Furthermore, he said that the rumour that his cousin had been drinking was completely false. If this was true, the tragedy had been for nothing.

Brothers Khadar Mohammed and Ali Mohammed were eventually jailed for the murder. They were given minimum sentences of sixteen and fourteen years respectively, and their three accomplices were given three years for violent disorder. The judge described the killing as a 'planned and premeditated attack'. It was an incident in which a group of violent youths had used religion as an excuse for bloodshed. Ahmed Ibrahim's only crime had been to stand up to his accusers. What was supposed to have been a fistfight became an act of senseless butchery.

In an area like Toxteth, youth gangs also provide a tool for organised criminals. Their loyalty to their postcode, combined with their desire to prove themselves, makes them the ideal minions for Liverpool 8's numerous drug lords and taxmen. During my time inside, I met countless small-time gang members who had been recruited to deliver drugs and take part in drive-by shootings.

'You start off mindlessly shooting each other and when you get a bit older, you realise how to make money from what you're doing,' one prison inmate said to me.

Gangs like the Park Road Edz and the Somali Warriors act as feeder groups for larger drug cartels. They provide the perfect workforce for professional criminals.

Liverpool is a city where organised crime is rife. It is one of the main entry points for heroin and the control point for much of the UK's drug trade. Drug running firms have links with Spain, Colombia, Morocco and Amsterdam. Some of their wares are sold in Liverpool and the rest are distributed all over the UK through a system of 'runners' and delivery boys.

Indeed Liverpool 8 famously boasts the only drug dealer to have entered the *Sunday Times* Rich List. He was at one time described as Interpol's number one target, thought to be making up to £1 million a week. Curtis Warren was living proof that a Toxteth tearaway can progress to become a multi-millionaire crime boss. With links to the Cali Cartel, the Turkish heroin mafia and various other international crime groups, he was deemed to be Britain's wealthiest criminal. Warren grew up in the Granby ward of Toxteth, where his upbringing was almost a prototype for many members of the new youth gangs. By the age twelve he had already been cautioned for a range of petty offences. At thirteen, he appeared in court charged with burglary and received a sentence of twenty-four hours at an attendance centre. Two years later he was given three months in a detention centre and at the age of eighteen, he was sent to a borstal for attacking a policeman. He was roaming the streets from an early age, 'grafting', robbing and stealing on the streets of Granby.

His rise from there was meteoric as he forged business alliances first with older Liverpudlian drug mobsters and then, crucially, with international traffickers looking to expand the UK market for their products, particularly cocaine, which was about to enjoy a sales boom in the UK. With his tough background, sharp street sense and his work ethic, Warren was soon at the very top of the tree, a druglord extraordinaire.

The fact that he was eventually caught and jailed in Holland for a £125 million multi-drug conspiracy, and more recently was jailed again for thirteen years for a cannabis smuggling conspiracy on the island of Jersey, has done little to dent his notoriety. The authorities have said they are seeking assets of his worth as much as £118 million, an inconceivable sum for a scally from Liverpool 8.

Warren and his crew started off as feral street kids and grew to be one of the most powerful criminal organisations in the world. They were earning more than rock stars or actors whilst at the same time giving the proverbial middle finger to the police and were ultimately Liverpool's equivalent of the mafia.

Liverpool is a port city where crime flourishes at every level, from youth gangs to serious villains. The docks have long enabled guns and drugs to be brought in with relative ease. In some parts of the city, children can never realistically expect to receive a higher education or pursue a professional career, and so they look up to the likes of Curtis Warren. Poverty and lack of opportunity have bred crime and violence, whether it is the recreational violence of the Croccy Crew or the multi-million pound criminal empire of the Granby Gang.

The Croxteth–Norris Green feud has been flung into the public eye, but these areas are the tip of the iceberg. 'There's things like that bubbling up all over the place,' one inmate told me. 'Liverpool's a mad city – even Crosby has its own firms and that's the posh part. Nothing's ever gonna change, it's just the way it is.'

Lancaster

LANCASTER LACKS THE gangland credentials of Glasgow or Liverpool. It is a small city in the north of England famous for its historic cotton mills, its Georgian port and its prestigious grammar school. It is hardly the type of place that you would expect to be a hotbed of gang activity. However, it is also home to the Ryelands, a locally notorious council estate.

Ryelands made national headlines after appearing on an episode of ITV's *Neighbours From Hell*. An Asian shopkeeper was subjected to a prolonged campaign of racial hatred, in which his shop was firebombed six times (once whilst a crew were filming it) and daubed with racist graffiti. He was shot at, attacked with a knife and asked to pay £100 per week in protection money to a man referring to himself as the 'King of Ryelands'.

One of the men responsible for firebombing the shop was a figure known as 'Slasher'. He was a member of the so-called 902 Crew and he was on my wing in HMP Wolds. He rejected the claim that he had a racial motivation for targeting the store. 'He pissed off a lot of people on the estate,' Slasher said of the shopkeeper. 'There are rules you have to live by if you live on Ryelands and he wasn't following them. If you were born there, you know to keep your mouth shut.'

Slasher had been involved in crime from the age of seven. 'All my friends and all of my family are criminals,' he said. 'It's all I've ever known.' As a child he acted as a lookout for car thieves and burglars and was soon committing thefts of his own. At age ten, he discovered marijuana: his babysitter would ply him with it so that he went to sleep quickly. This prompted him to start stealing cars and selling them on to fund his habit. By twelve, he was taking Valium, magic mushrooms, LSD and speed.

A year later, Slasher's father died of cancer. He began drinking heavily and taking drugs every day. By this stage, he was taking ketamine, ecstasy and cocaine and drinking so much that he suffered from the shakes when forced to go without; he was a fully-fledged alcoholic at thirteen years of age.

At fifteen, Slasher was expelled from school for fighting. He was illiterate anyway, having played truant most of the time. It was during this period that he joined the ranks of the 902. The gang allegedly started in the 1940s, when the estate housed large numbers of young evacuees from London, although at that point it had not yet received its name. Teenagers from the rougher parts of London apparently formed gangs based upon what part of Lancaster they had been re-housed in, replicating the gang culture of wartime London.

Teenagers from Ryelands would fight with those from Scale Hall and the Hareruns estate. They fought with knives, sticks and stones. As time went by, they added chains and baseball bats to their collection and shifted their attention towards the 808 Crew from the Marsh estate, the Vale Estate Crew and the 602 Ridge Crew from the Ridge estate. Slasher found the antics of the 902 far more interesting than school. He was smaller than the other children and was regularly picked on but once he was in a gang, no one could say a thing to him. Now it was just a matter of proving himself to the other members.

The first act of violence that he committed was at a night-club in nearby Carnforth. One of his friends was selling ecstasy and a rival dealer tried to steal his drugs. Slasher grabbed a bottle of beer, smashed it on the table and stabbed the unfortunate taxman in the neck with the broken glass. His victim fell to the floor in a pool of blood.

By the time he had reached his sixteenth birthday, Slasher was often drinking ten pints a day. He was permanently drunk and angry and spent most of his time walking the streets looking for a fight. His mother had kicked him out of the house and he had no chance of getting a job, as he still couldn't read or write. The only option available to him was crime.

Later that year, one of Slasher's friends slept with his girl-friend behind his back: he was furious. After sitting in his flat drinking pint after pint and trying to calm himself down, he came to the conclusion that there was no way he was going to let it lie. He grabbed a craft knife and headed over to his friend's house to confront him.

This was the night that Slasher was to receive his name. The second his former friend opened the door, Slasher stabbed him hard in the side of the cheek. 'I only wanted to cut him a bit and scare him,' he told me. 'The blade got stuck in his cheek-bone. I tried to yank it out and it slipped and cut the artery in his neck. I've never seen so much blood. It was like a tap.'

Luckily his victim survived, but Slasher was jailed for four years for attempted murder. It was his first time inside and he was determined that he wouldn't be taken for a mug. As soon as he arrived on the wing, another inmate tried to bully him for his tobacco. Slasher beat him into a pulp. He was getting a taste for violence; gone were the days when he could be intimidated.

When he got out, Slasher had a reputation to live up to. His credibility on the estate had gone up and the 902 embraced him. The rivalries with the Ridge estate and the Marsh estate were still going strong. It was time for him to pick up where he had left off.

Brooks nightclub, Lancaster. He had been drinking since 5 pm. It was the first night out since his release and he had taken three ecstasy pills; all he wanted now was a good punch-up to round the night off. Luckily for him, the 808 were drinking in the same club. At first, the two groups remained blissfully oblivious to one another. Then as the crowds of drinkers were shepherded out of the doors at closing time, they caught each other's gaze.

A mass brawl ensued. Terrified club-goers looked on in shock as they went at each other. Slasher grabbed a bottle of beer, smashed it on the floor and stabbed the nearest 808 member in the side of the face with the jagged glass edge. His bloodstained victim fell to the floor; what had started as a fist-fight had quickly escalated into something more serious. Slasher had a fondness for weapons: he could fight hand to hand, but preferred to cut people – why use fists when he could use a knife or a bottle? Unfortunately for him, the police were there the whole time and were standing close by when he launched his attack, though he was too drunk to realise. He was arrested, remanded and taken to HMP Lancaster Farm.

Whilst inside, Slasher hatched a bizarre plot to stop the witnesses from turning up at court. He found out who they were and arranged for his brother to buy them all tickets to Pontins on the day of the trial, so that there would be no one to testify against him. It might have worked had he not been overheard talking about his plan by one of the prison staff, who reported him to the police. A warning was issued to each of the witnesses stating that they would be held in contempt of court if they were unduly absent.

Slasher was given an indeterminate sentence with a minimum tariff of two years and two months. When serving an indeterminate sentence, the inmates have to be on their best behaviour to be let out on their first parole hearing. The more offences they commit behind bars, the longer they are kept for. When I spoke to Slasher, he said he had served nine years. He was caught with steroids, refused to do a drug test, got into fight after fight, and spoke of his desire to cut off his probation worker's head.

'I've calmed down now,' he told me. 'I converted to Buddhism. Now when I feel like slashing someone up I meditate instead. Well, I've got to get out of here sometime. I'm older now and I can control my temper. It's them out there that you need to watch.'

He was right: the 902 weren't about to come to an end just because one of its members was out of action. In 2005, the gang proved that they were still going strong despite their most notorious member being behind bars. They drove to the Marsh estate in a white van, jumped out and started attacking houses and cars at random. Windows were smashed, fencing was uprooted and a resident had their front door put through with a garden fork. The locals were terrified.

Five years later, reformed London gangster John Pridmore was drafted in to see if he could talk any sense into Lancaster's teenage gangs. 'Many kids in Lancaster are getting sucked into the gang culture and drugs,' he said of his motivation for coming to the city. 'They think it sounds glamorous and cool but it's a violent and dangerous world that only leads to prison or a box six feet under.'

Pridmore, who wrote a book called *From Gangland To Promised Land*, had been an enforcer prior to his reformation. He became a born-again Christian after an incident in which he thought he had killed another man. He reasoned that the youth of the city would admire and respect him more than they would their parents or their teachers but, try as he may, Lancaster's gangs continue to wage war.

'The difference now is that more kids have guns,' said Slasher. 'I wouldn't say that there are a lot of them on the estate but they are just starting to creep in. Things have definitely got worse, not better. There's gangs in Morecambe and Heysham too and all the towns around Lancaster. We fought with the Morecambe lads a few times. Their firm's on the up.'

Morecambe is the second largest settlement within the City of Lancaster District. It is also home to the Morecambe Boys, a thirty-strong gang that fights with rivals from Lancaster and Heysham. Although separate estates within the town have been known to fight with each other, they all come together against their common enemies. They fight with the usual array of weapons: bottles, sticks, knives and baseball bats.

The 902 crew are no great threat to the majority of society. They operate solely within their own culture. Lancaster is hardly on the same level as Glasgow or Manchester, but it has a small core of criminals intent on breaking the law. 'Most of Lancaster and Morecambe is quite nice,' Slasher told me, 'but everywhere has its bad bits.'

He had hit the nail on the head: Lancaster cannot be described as particularly gang-infested, it is no different from anywhere else in Britain. Wherever there is poverty, there are gangs.

Edinburgh

EDINBURGH IS A city of glaring extremes. It is home to some of Scotland's richest areas, places like Craiglockhart and Morningside, which fall within the top one per cent of the country. It is also home to Craigmillar, where thirty-three per cent of the population are unemployed. Wealth and poverty exist side by side. The average life expectancy in Barnton is ninety, whereas in Niddrie it is sixty-one, seven years lower than in Iraq.

Whereas the Edinburgh of popular perception is characterised by historic buildings and affluent surroundings, the youth of the city's poorer suburbs have taken to emulating Glaswegian gang culture. Knife-wielding 'young teams' wage war against their rivals, tanked up on cheap booze and drugs. 'They're like Glasgow's gangs but not as hard,' said my friend from Niddrie, an area heavily plagued by gang violence.

Edinburgh gangs are similar to their Glaswegian counterparts: they dress the same, act the same and use the same slang. Most of the crews are called 'Fleeto', 'Young Team', 'Tong' or 'Derry', and despite the supposed rivalry between the two cities, Edinburgh youths clearly mimic the Glaswegians to an extent. The gang enthusiast that provided me with videos of the Glaswegian 'young teams' showed me a few clips from Edinburgh, so that I could draw my own conclusions.

In the first that I watched, the Young Pilton Derry posed in front of a derelict block of flats armed with baseball bats and metal pipes. It could very easily have been one of the Glaswegian gangs: they wore the same clothes, adopted the same poses and had the same music playing in the background. The only difference was the lack of knives or machetes.

The next clip was more of the same: the Young Niddrie Terror posed with baseball bats and drank Buckfast in front of gang graffiti. Their youngest member looked to be no older than eleven.

'I went to school with some of the YNT,' my Niddrie contact told me. 'They'd steal designer scarves off people or rob their Rockport boots. Then you'd get the people they robbed off ganging up and jumping them to get their stuff back. That's how you got some of the big fights in the city.'

The Young Niddrie Terror have been around since the 1950s and are one of Edinburgh's best-known gangs. Their rivals are the Young Leith Team, the youth wing of Hibernian FC's notorious Hibs Casuals. They are one of the most violent of the 'youth teams' and, as well as fighting with rival gangs, they are involved in low-level drug dealing and street robbery.

On December 15 2006, seventeen-year-old Liam Melvin was stabbed to death in Southhouse, southeast Edinburgh. Months earlier he had been pictured posing with an axe on a social networking site under the initials 'YNT'. The killing was thought to have been the result of a feud with another gang.

Sixteen-year-old Jay Murray was convicted of culpable homicide in relation to Liam's murder. Edmond Reid was convicted of assault, but spared a jail sentence; he had stabbed Melvin in the head, whereas it was a stab to the stomach that delivered the fatal blow. Melvin himself was, at the time of his death, facing charges for allegedly stabbing another teenager.

Melvin had been best friends with James Demarco, another figure with suspected gang affiliations. On 13 May 2007, Demarco stabbed an eighteen-year-old youth in the neck during an argument at a house party in the Burdiehouse area. His victim died and Demarco was sentenced to fifteen years in prison. He was only eighteen himself.

In September 2007, Demarco proved that he was still capable of extreme violence even from behind bars. Whilst talking to one of his friends, James Paxton, on a telephone in the segregation unit at Edingburgh's Saughton Prison, he became aware that Paxton was with a man known locally as 'G'. Demarco mistook this G for another man with the same nickname who had gone on a date with his ex-girlfriend, an act of disrespect that he was unable to let go. He saw this as an opportunity for revenge.

Paxton was the ideal henchman. He was already awaiting trial for two separate stabbing attacks, one in which he had sprayed a man in the face with ammonia; his victim spent nearly three months in a burns unit and received treatments for twenty-two separate wounds. The minute that Demarco heard that G was with him, he ordered Paxton to stab him, unaware it was the wrong man. He knew that Paxton would comply: the two of them were good friends and they were both equally sadistic.

'I'm gonna take a sword to him if he's not out this house in the next five minutes,' Paxton assured him. The phone call was recorded.

Screams and shouts could then be heard, after which Paxton came back on the line to tell Demarco, 'That's me just took the machete tae him. I couldnae find my sword or it was going right through him.'

All the time that the attack was going on, Demarco was

listening in and laughing. 'He's burst wide open,' Paxton announced. 'It's like the massacre part two.'

'Proud of you brother,' Demarco told him. 'I love you.'

'Aye, I love you too,' Paxton told him. 'I'll be joining you soon.'

He knew he was already almost certainly heading to jail for the two previous offences. To him, the possibility of a third serious charge was now almost an irrelevance.

When questioned later by police, Demarco told them, 'You'll know it all. You've heard all my calls anyway.'

Paxton was later jailed for seventeen years and one month and given an additional four years of supervision. The judge described the offence as 'wicked and depraved' and gave Demarco an extra forty-five months on top of the fifteen-year sentence he was already serving. Demarco called the judge 'a fucking prick' as he was led away.

THE SAVAGERY DISPLAYED by Paxton and Demarco was the product of a culture in which life is cheap. Many of Edinburgh's youth gangs come from broken homes and many of them are the sons and daughters of alcoholics and heroin addicts. Loyalty takes the place of conventional morality: it is seen as more honourable to take a life, on the orders of a fellow gang member, than it is to refuse to kill a fellow human being. These groups exist in a world where the norms and values of mainstream society do not apply. They abide by their own code of conduct and follow their own warped morals.

'It's what happens when you get a bunch of poor, violent people stuck in a small area,' my Niddrie contact said. 'The Niddrie and Leith rivalry is one of the harshest but there are similar things going on all over the city. When I was a kid I used to stay in Wester Hailes – it was the same there. All of the different schemes there were at war with each other.'

Wester Hailes is a suburb on the western edge of Edinburgh, home to some of the cheapest housing in the country. 'The main gangs were the Young Mental Murrayburn and Young Sighthill,' he said. 'And then there was the Walkers, the Broomies and Young Saughton all nearby.' Wester Hailes shares its borders with a number of other equally impoverished areas, all with their own 'fleets' and young teams.

'There was wee schoolkids fighting with each other all the time. I went to St Augustine's School. Across the road was Forrester School. There were always gang members sneaking across to fight. The Young Mental Gorgie used to come round our way as well. I used to know this guy Mooch who was with them lot. He didn't really fit in with their riotous image though. He was a big tubby stoner. He probably just hung about with them to buy dope off them.'

The Edinburgh gangs are often just as divided as their Glaswegian counterparts when it comes to religious affiliation. Several of the Wester Hailes street gangs are thought to have links with the Ulster Volunteer Force, the loyalist paramilitary group. Although the UVF deny these links, prominent members within the group have visited the area and spoken with gang leaders.

In March 2003, six men claiming allegiance to a Northern Irish loyalist gang were convicted of abduction and serious assault. The court heard how they had boasted of their UVF affiliations to scare the locals into complying with them. Operating on the rundown Calders estate, they sold class A drugs and dished out punishment beatings to anyone who spoke out against them.

The gang was led by David McLeave, who had crossed the

Irish Sea for the sole purpose of committing crime. He was also sadistically violent. One of his victims was drugged with GHB and burnt between the toes with lit cigarettes. Others were stripped, covered in aftershave and set alight. McLeave used a set of tower blocks as a base for his activities and made it clear that anyone who was late with payments for drugs could expect to be punished. One man was beaten senseless with a wheel brace, whilst others were left to his equally brutal accomplices.

The UVF rejected claims that the Wester Hailes drug gang were in any way affiliated with them, despite graffiti sprayed across the estate declaring it a 'loyalist controlled zone'. The police stated that they could find no direct link between McLeave and any paramilitary organization, despite claims that William Moore, a prominent figure within the UVF, had recently visited him to discuss 'business'. Whether or not he was a loyalist terrorist, he was undoubtedly dangerous. He was found guilty of assault, abduction and supplying heroin, cannabis and diazepam and was sentenced to fourteen years in prison in 2003.

Tom Wood, Deputy Chief Constable of Lothian and Borders Police, described the gang's activities as, 'the most serious attempt of an organised crime gang to infiltrate Edinburgh that we have seen for many years'. He said that they had 'led a reign of terror in the truest sense of the word'. He spoke as if they had relinquished their control of the drug trade; however, the truth of the matter is that, whenever the leader of a criminal organisation is put behind bars, there will always be another waiting in the wings.

Northern Irish gangsters have targeted Edinburgh for at least the past ten years. In 2002, there were reports of two senior UVF members visiting the city to give their blessing to a heroin-dealing operation. 'It's an easy target,' another of my contacts told me. 'It's seen as a rich city so people move in from all over the place to try and get in on the drugs market. Then there's the Festival as well: there's plenty of tourists come down wanting weed and charlie. I guess the Irish are like anyone – they want easy money.'

In March 2005, a fifty-nine-year-old grandmother was repeatedly stabbed in her Edinburgh home. On the same day, a sixty-eight-year-old man was brutally beaten with his own walking stick and stamped on as he lay on the ground, and another woman was robbed at knifepoint. All three crimes were perpetrated by a fifteen-year-old boy thought to be linked to a UVF drug gang. He had been out of education since he was ten years old, was on bail at the time and was suffering from a serious drug addiction.

Ulster gangs are not the only ones to have targeted the city in recent years. On 9 January 2003, Colin Sterling, of Jamaican origin, was jailed for supplying class A drugs. He was part of a Yardie gang that had attempted to take over the crack cocaine market. He was caught with a half-ounce lump of cocaine, nineteen rocks of crack and £1,800 in cash, and was sentenced to eighteen months in prison. His cousin was found with cannabis and three rocks of crack and was sentenced to 150 hours of community service.

Police intelligence suggested that the gang were distributing hard drugs via a network of prostitutes. 'The Sterlings were the men as far as we were concerned,' a senior detective proudly boasted. 'They were a significant take-out for us.'

The Sterlings were thought to have links to other Jamaican criminals in Birmingham and Aberdeen. Yardie drug dealers have flocked to Scotland in recent years, as drugs are typically more expensive there than they are in England. Pushers from Leeds, Liverpool, Wolverhampton, Derby and Birmingham have targeted Edinburgh and Aberdeen, flooding the streets with crack and heroin.

As well as bringing drugs to the city, the Yardies are thought to be a factor in the rise in gun crime. In 2008, a white gang linked to Jamaican criminals in Wolverhampton were reported to be using MAC-10 submachine guns. MAC-10s can fire sixteen rounds in a single second; they are small and relatively easy to conceal. They are the weapons of choice for Jamaican gangsters across the UK.

It is thought that several of these weapons were used during a feud between two rival gangs in the Inch and Granton areas. The so-called Inch Crew draws its members from the deprived council estates towards the south of the city, while the Granton Gang are a group of crack and heroin dealers from equally crime-infested estates in north Edinburgh. The two factions are believed to have co-existed peacefully until a fight outside a nightclub in 2007. Since then, there have been countless shootings, stabbings and beatings across the city.

The Inch Crew are perhaps the more organised of the two. Most of their members are from Gilmerton and the Inch, although they have affiliates in Saughton, Niddrie and Broomhouse. They are involved in drug dealing and taxing rival dealers and are well known for their use of firearms. The Granton Gang are a loose collective of dealers from Granton, Royston and Drylaw and are thought to be responsible for an epidemic of heroin abuse throughout the north of the city.

The feud came to a head when shots were fired at a twenty-year-old member of the Granton Gang in late 2008. He was sitting in his van when a motorbike pulled up alongside and the driver fired three bullets from a semi-automatic handgun in his direction. He survived. Three weeks later, his assailant went on to fire two shots through the windows of an alleged heroin dealer's house in Craigmillar. The Inch Crew thought nothing of loosing off shots at rival dealers. To them, it was a necessary part of the business.

A week later, members of the Granton Gang drove to Gilmerton looking for payback. As soon as word got to the Inch Crew, gunmen were dispatched to find and shoot them. Hours later, an alleged gang member was blasted with a shotgun. He survived, despite having four pellets lodged in his head.

The Granton Gang went into hiding after the shooting for fear of further attacks. They even hatched a plan to shoot up a random taxicab in the hope that it would bring more police to the area. The theory was that if they were constantly surrounded by police officers, then it would be harder for the Inch Crew to get to them. On 8 September 2008, a shotgun was fired at the back of a private taxi on Royston Main Road in Granton. The driver was shaken, but unharmed, and their plan worked perfectly: the police were all over the estate.

Later that week, the Granton came out of hiding to launch an attack on an alleged Inch Crew affiliate outside the Gauntlet Bar in Broomhouse. Broomhouse is home to dealers with links to both the Inch and the Granton. It is a volatile area, in which the local criminals have been forced to take sides. Convicted heroin dealer Sean McGovern fired several shots before disposing of his double-barrelled shotgun in a nearby park and fleeing the scene. He later admitted to pointing the gun at suspected Inch Crew associate Jamie Hyland and discharging two shots to scare him.

Fellow gang member Terry Scott had driven McGovern to the scene of the crime and helped to dispose of the car and the gun once the deed was done. Scott was already under police surveillance as part of an undercover operation by the drug squad. His house had been bugged and he was heard disclosing the location of the shotgun. The police found the weapon dismantled into three separate parts and stashed in a bush in Morningside Park. They also heard Scott telling his friends that he had dropped the pair of gloves used to handle the gun. They recovered the gloves and found his fingerprints all over them. 'It's a schoolboy error,' he had joked to his friends. As it turned out, it was an error that cost him five years and nine months of his life.

On 22 December 2008, there was a drive-by shooting on the same estate. Nineteen-year-old Zach Robinson was shot in the stomach at point blank range as he walked home past a local primary school. He managed to stagger to his mother's house, where he was promptly rushed to hospital. He survived. Robinson was another suspected casualty of the feud, although it was unclear why he was targeted.

In April 2009, shots were fired at the front door of a house in Gilmerton. Inch and Granton were thought to be vying for control of the area around Telford College, which was a local drug hotspot. Although the occupant of the house was not involved in the drug trade, local residents claimed that the attack was carried out as a warning to a dealer who lived nearby. It was the Granton Gang's way of saying, 'Next time it will be your house.'

However, the Inch Crew were more ambitious in their activities than their rivals. As far as they were concerned, the college was a small earner. While the Granton Gang were busy trying to defend their territory, dealers from Inch were transporting large quantities of hard drugs all over the UK. They would deliver packages of cocaine as far afield as Liverpool, through a network of runners and errand boys.

David Togher was in charge of the Inch Crew's drug running operation. He was a former soldier, transferring his combat skills to the streets of Edinburgh. He would give out orders to a team of low-ranking minions, who would distribute the drugs under his close supervision. Drugs were bought and sold on a daily basis: the Crew were a commercial enterprise, rather than just another area-based gang, and were eventually making thousands of pounds a week.

But their feud with the Granton Gang brought unwelcome publicity and provided the local police force with an added incentive to take them down. The longer they stayed on the streets, the more their activities would spill out into the public domain. Selling drugs was an undercover activity: only the people directly involved in each deal were aware of what was going on. Shooting at rival gangs, however, was far less discreet. Steps were taken to put Togher behind bars.

In July 2007, the police mounted an extensive operation aimed at identifying the high-ranking members of the Inch Crew and bringing them to justice. During this period, they highlighted Togher as a 'manager/supervisor/facilitator' and described him as the 'lieutenant' of the organisation. They monitored his every move.

After spending six months gathering evidence, and the seizure of more than £450,000 worth of cocaine, the police charged Togher with conspiracy to supply class A drugs. They described how he communicated with drug dealers all over the country and linked him with sales in Edinburgh, Bonnyrigg and Liverpool. Despite never having handled any of the drugs in person, he was proven to have handed out instructions to a series of underlings, who carried out his orders to the letter. The former soldier was jailed for five years after admitting the charge.

Togher was said to be the Inch Crew's second-in-command. Whoever the leader is, he is still at large. Edinburgh police force have been quick to point out how rare shootings are in the Scottish capital, with Detective Superintendent Craig Dobbie going as far as to claim that there is no evidence of any serious organised crime in the city. This is a surprising claim to make about a city the size of Edinburgh.

The truth is that there have been organised gangs in the city for decades. Even before the Inch and the Granton, rival groups of dealers vied for control. Nor is gun crime new to Edinburgh: on the back streets of Granton and Royston, it has been a way of life for some time.

Before the Inch seized control of the cocaine market, there were already two firms locked in a bloody power struggle. One of these factions originated as a 'young team', a territory-based street gang. They went on to be one of the most violent drug cartels in Scotland. It was the first time a youth gang had taken on established crime bosses. The Young Mental Royston started off fighting groups of teenagers from rival schemes but ended up fighting drug dealers in their own area.

The YMR were led by Marc Webley and James Tant, a pair of career criminals with a lust for power. Webley had over sixty convictions for a variety of offences, while Tant was a convicted rapist. At sixteen years old he had held one of his girlfriend's friends down and violently assaulted her. Whilst on bail, he carried out a second attack, following an eighteen-year-old mother into her house and attempting to rape her. He was sentenced to four years and three months in a young offenders' institution.

Tant was what is referred to in Scottish prisons as a 'beast', a known sex offender seen as immoral even by his fellow criminals. Whereas most other career crooks would have avoided him for fear of tarnishing their own reputations, Webley stuck with him. The pair were inseparable. They would ride on motorbikes, brandishing firearms and striking fear into the heart of the local community.

The Mental Royston wore balaclavas as an unofficial gang uniform. Most of the locals knew who they were, but it made them look sinister and helped them to intimidate the other criminals in the area. They would carry guns, crossbows and petrol bombs and were thought to be involved in everything from burglary to protection rackets. There was only one person standing between them and complete domination of their patch.

Peter Simpson, who was then in his forties, was the alleged leader of a group of older criminals who saw Webley and Tant as usurpers. He was no stranger to drug dealing. In 1993, he was found in possession of Scotland's largest ever seizure of LSD. He was caught with £31,810-worth and sentenced to six years in prison.

However, Simpson portrayed himself as a 'Robin Hood-figure', according to police, and took on the role of protector for the community. 'Webley was very much the up-and-coming criminal who wanted people to think that he ran the area and should be respected,' said a police superintendent. 'Simpson started to clash with him in what I would class as a turf war between around twenty people. There were more individuals on Webley's side and the majority of stuff was instigated by him.'

In May 2004, petrol bombs were hurled at Simpson's flat on Granton Crescent and one of his associates was shot through his flat window. Two months later, a house belonging to a member of the YMR was peppered with gunshots in what was believed to be a retaliatory attack. Another two months later, a YMR member was stabbed outside Simpson's house.

It was only a matter of time before somebody was seriously

injured, and the police were all too aware of this fact. Despite trying their best to keep the two factions apart, Webley seemed intent on taking out Simpson.

On January 24 2005, two hooded figures were seen riding a Kawasaki motorbike away from Webley's house in Wardieburn. They pulled up next to Simpson as he got off a bus and chased him along the street. Tant had a sawn-off shotgun hidden in his sweatshirt and Webley had a .25 calibre semi-automatic pistol. Simpson darted up Granton Terrace in a vain attempt to get away. Shots were fired and he was eventually hit with a single bullet that lodged in his back and narrowly missed a major blood vessel. He was lucky to survive.

The streets around Simpson's house had been turned into a war zone; what was once a quiet, residential area now saw Wild West style shootouts and knife attacks. Worried about the effect of the feud upon the local people, the police decided to apply for a court order banning him from living there, and he was forced to move to a different address.

Later that year, Simpson was on a bus with his ex-wife and daughter when Tant and his pregnant, eighteen-year-old girlfriend stepped aboard. Despite the fact that both of them had their loved ones present, a scuffle ensued and Simpson ended up stabbing Tant and biting a chunk out of his ear. Their families looked on in horror as the two men battled it out in front of other, terrified passengers.

There are two different versions of what happened on the bus that day: one given by Simpson and the other provided by his daughter, Astro. Astro reported that she had handed him a knife to use, whereas he claimed that Tant had pulled it from his waistband. Whoever the weapon belonged to, it was used to inflict two serious stab wounds to Tant's chest. Simpson claimed that he had also bitten Tant in self-defence to get him to drop the knife and that the latter's wounds were suffered during the struggle to disarm him.

During his subsequent trial, Simpson's ex-wife described how her cat had been killed, torn apart and left outside her front window. She said that her house had been petrol bombed and that her daughter had bought a bulletproof vest after receiving death threats. According to her, the YMR were targeting their family and making their lives a misery.

Simpson was convicted and jailed for six years. But in February 2009, his conviction was overturned on appeal after criticism of the way crucial evidence had been presented at his trial.

Whereas Simpson was granted his freedom, Tant and Webley were eventually convicted of attempted murder for the bus stop shooting. They were deemed to be equally responsible and the attack was seen as a joint venture. They were given eleven-year sentences. The police had put two of the city's most violent men behind bars.

In 2006, a single shot was fired through the window of a ground-floor home in Royston Mains Gardens. The occupant was said to be a known associate of Marc Webley. Although the main players were locked up, the Mental Royston were continuing where they had left off. They were still players in the drug trade and they still had a number of powerful enemies.

The YMR are testament to the escalating severity of Edinburgh's youth gangs. In a city renowned for its affluence, groups of young people are fighting with guns and knives. The 'young teams' act as training corps for organised criminals. They start as bands of unruly teenagers and soon become ruthless, drug dealing collectives. Juvenile delinquents progress to full-time drug dealers and racketeers.

A study conducted by the Centre for Law and Society at

Edinburgh University suggests that one in five thirteen-year-olds in the city class themselves as being in a gang. This figure falls to one in twenty by the time they reach the age of seventeen, suggesting that they may simply grow out of their behaviour by the time they reach adulthood. However, the percentage of those within a more serious criminal organisation with a 'well-defined subversive identity expressed through a specific name, sign or saying' remains constant with age. In other words, those who are on the fringes of criminality are likely to settle down and go straight, whereas those at the heart of the gangs will go on to become adult gang members.

The YMR began as a bunch of unruly teenagers and progressed to a group of full-time career criminals. Recreational violence developed into targeted acts of aggression. For those who have few talents to fall back on, an aptitude for causing fear is an incentive to become involved in crime. Edinburgh's young teams aspire to perfect their one area of expertise: violence. For some, it is all they have to rely on.

The youth gangs are the larval stage of the older, more profit-orientated crime groups. They are faced with the choice of either working a low-paid job or harnessing the 'skills' that they have developed throughout their teenage years. Many feel that there is no other choice. Crime pays, or at least it pays above the minimum wage. Niddrie and Granton are the forgotten ghettoes of a supposedly affluent city, the seedy underbelly of a tourism hotspot.

South London

I T HAS BEEN estimated that there are around 200 gangs on the streets of Greater London, making it second only to Glasgow for the sheer volume of gang activity. Many of these groups are divided into smaller sub-sets and they tend to be concentrated in the poorer areas of the city. They encompass an estimated 15,000 young people, mostly between the ages of thirteen and twenty-five.

According to government statistics, more gun-enabled crime takes place in London than anywhere else in Britain. Thirty per cent of these offences are listed as 'violence against the person'. The majority of shootings are carried out using handguns: 'That's so that you can hide them,' a contact from jail explained to me. 'If you're going to blast someone, you don't want to be lugging a shotgun around with you.'

Peckham in south London has one of the highest rates of gun crime in Britain. Despite a substantial programme of urban improvement, including a £290 million regeneration of the entire North Peckham estate, it endures high crime levels and an epidemic of teenage firearm ownership. It became especially infamous for the murder of ten-year-old Damilola Taylor in 2000, a crime that was originally thought to be linked to the Young Peckham Boys, the largest of the area's youth gangs.

'That's bullshit – we didn't do that,' Rokker told me. Although no longer involved in recreational violence, he was once a high-ranking member of the YPB and bears the scars to prove it. 'They questioned me for that. They blamed everyone. They even had some Turkish kids in on it.'

When I met him, Rokker was serving a five-year sentence for supplying crack and heroin, having left behind the world of postcode rivalries to become a professional drug-dealer. Having allegedly been a member of two different criminal gangs, he was able to tell much about the various wars that were going on throughout the city.

Rokker was thirteen when he joined the YPB and was by no means the youngest in the gang; some were only ten years old. 'We were doing minor things back then,' he said. 'Robbing cars, jacking phones, that kind of thing.' At that point, he was still going to school; he was studying throughout the week and fighting with the Lewisham-based Ghetto Boys at the weekend.

The Ghetto Boys are another of South London's better-known street gangs. They rose to fame after opening fire on a rival at the 2004 Urban Music Awards and accidentally hitting accountant Helen Kelly as she was leaving the venue. The bullet lodged in the under-wire of her bra, saving her life. Two young men were eventually jailed for fourteen years for the attack.

'What did you fight over?' I asked Rokker, already aware that the two sides probably had no logical reason for their feud.

'Just area beef,' he replied. 'To see whose ends [area] was the hardest.'

'And which gang actually was the "hardest"?'

'Us of course. They had more members – probably a few hundred – but we put up more of a fight.'

Within a year of joining the gang, Rokker had received his first stab wound.

'These things happen when you are on the streets,' he said. The way he talked about it was almost as if it was an occupational hazard. 'That's when I started going at it hard body. A lot of things were going wrong in my life. My gran had just died and I'd been diagnosed with diabetes. I used to look at all the cats [addicts] around the ends and think, you have a choice – I *have* to stick a needle in my arm.'

Rokker came out of hospital angry at the cards that life had dealt him and looking to rebel. The YPB provided the outlet for his frustration. His hatred towards the Ghetto Boys was stronger than ever, as they had left him with permanent scars. Every weekend he would venture into their territory armed with a craft knife, determined to get revenge.

According to Billy, a longstanding member of the Ghetto Boys, their feud with the YPB has many causes. 'It's all about guns, money, pussy and drugs,' he told me. 'We are taking over South East London. If you ain't blue you ain't true.'

I noticed that he had borrowed this motto from the Crips, a reference to the blue dress code that the infamous Los Angeles gang abided by.

'Ghetto wear blue and Peckham wear black,' he said. 'Straight blue all the way.'

So did the gang really have a few hundred members? Had Rokker's estimate been accurate?

'There's around seventy that I know of in Deptford,' said Billy. 'We've got members aged from twelve to thirty, all different age groups. There's people carrying everything from knives to handguns and fully automatic rifles.'

Although they originated on the Woodpecker Estate in New Cross, they are now spread all across the borough. 'There's certain estates where they dominate,' a source close to the gang informed me. 'You have to wear blue to get by.'

The Pepys Estate in Deptford is one of the Ghetto Boys' main territories. 'Pepys Estate is the main place for violence and guns,' said Billy.

But a well-informed Lewisham resident told me, 'It's died down a bit nowadays. They were at their peak a few years ago. Some Peckham youth got stabbed in the eye on the bus. There was a period where Peckham were going to the Pepys Estate every day in massive groups, with guns and knives and shit. No-one was leaving their house.'

The presence of so many armed gang members descending upon the one estate attracted the attention of the local media. The South London press spoke of a 'fifty-strong bicycle gang' and there were a number of stabbings and shootings in both Peckham and Lewisham.

Eventually, the continual invasion of Lewisham's estates claimed the life of an innocent bystander. Jason Gale-Bent was sat on a wall on Woodpecker Path in New Cross when a group of thirty to forty youths on bicycles cycled up to him. They fired a number of shots before all riding off in different directions. What happened next remains unclear: all that is known is that Jason suffered a fatal stab wound and died from his injuries.

The police were quick to point out that there was nothing to indicate that the killing was part of an ongoing problem. Sources close to Jason's family, however, suggest otherwise. According to a former Ghetto Boys associate, he was the brother of alleged gang member Alex 'Young Kraver' Bent, who had died in a car accident a year earlier. Jason's death was almost certainly a result of the longstanding feud between the Peckham Boys and Ghetto Boys.

Shortly after the killing, Peckham Academy and Harris Girls' Academy were evacuated amidst rumours that they were going to be attacked by the Ghetto Boys in retaliation for what had happened. There were fears that the two schools would be targeted in a drive-by shooting.

'So when the YPB aren't fighting with the Ghetto Boys, what else do they get up to?' I asked Rokker.

'All sorts,' he said. 'Selling drugs, street robberies, car crime... we had beef with other gangs too, not just Ghetto. There was the Brockley Mans and the Brixton Boys as well. Nowadays there's all types of cliques the youths are beefing with.'

It almost seemed as if he had a nostalgic view of his former gang membership. He spoke about it as if he was proud of his past. 'It trained me up well to sell drugs,' he said to me. 'It introduced me to the streets.'

At fifteen years old, Rokker was caught with £60,000 worth of weed and sentenced to three years in a young offenders' institute. He claims to have been making tens of thousands of pounds a week. His time inside marked the end of his stint in the Peckham Boys: when he got out, he was no longer young by the standards of the gang and no longer just a Boy; he was a product of the streets of Peckham.

'I realised how much money I could be making. What's the point of warring with some next area if you aren't making any cash from it?'

His stint behind bars had given him a chance to re-evaluate. It was time for him to join a more profit-orientated outfit: the Stickem Up Klick. 'No-one's going to go out beefing and stabbing people up for fun when they are making thousands of pounds from selling drugs.'

His new firm were more of an organised criminal enterprise

than a postcode gang. As their name suggests, they were mainly concerned with 'sticking up' drug dealers and taking their gains from them, although this wasn't their only lucrative venture.

Soon after joining the Klick, Rokker bought his first gun. It was a used .38 special revolver with sticking tape around the handle. It cost him £500 and it was worth every penny, according to him. 'Everybody's strapped up in London. If you've not got a strap then you are a nobody.'

If he and his friends found out that somebody else was selling drugs, they would kick their door down and torture them until they revealed the location of their earnings. 'They got burned with sugar and water,' he claimed. 'They'd get lines of sugar set out along their legs and a kettle poured along the strips so that the sugar melted into their skin.'

Rokker never directly implicated himself in any criminal activity. Instead, he referred to the gang's activities in the third person, so as not to incriminate himself.

'This one time they did an old white man who was selling weed,' he said. 'His wife was shaking so much she looked like she had some disease. She was drinking shots of Jack Daniels to calm herself. They were in the next room going to work on him and every time he screamed she shook so much that she spilt her drink.'

As well as taxing rival dealers, Rokker was selling large amounts of crack and heroin. 'I was doing what I know best. I'd got a feel for selling drugs while I was selling weed and you can make a lot more off brown and white.'

Peckham has a reputation as an open market for hard drugs. Addicts of all races make the pilgrimage into the hardcore estates to buy cheap, low purity heroin and small, white stones of crack.

There was a major downside, however, to making serious

money from drug dealing and armed robbery. It was impossible for Rokker to bank any of his earnings, for fear of being given a confiscation order. If the police found out how he was making his money they would seize the lot, until he could prove that he had gained it through legitimate means. Instead he spent vast amounts on clothes, women and alcohol.

The Ministry of Sound nightclub was one of Rokker's favourite haunts. 'When you've got money the gyal [girls] dem are on you,' he said. Unwilling to leave his fiery temperament at the door, however, Rokker was soon involved in a brutal attack in an argument over a girl.

'There was this guy getting up in my face 'cause I was dancing with his fish [girl]', he explained to me. 'Someone licked him up with a bottle. Then when he was coming out of the club he got shot in the leg.'

Officers found 9mm shells at the scene of the crime. Two weeks later, Rokker's house was raided by the police; they found a .38 handgun but no 9mm. 'They were saying they found my fingerprints on the clips outside Ministry. They charged me with firearms and attempted murder but they didn't have enough evidence for the attempt murder.'

He received a five-year sentence for the gun offence. Rather than go straight when he was released from jail, he went straight back to the Klick, and this time they were concentrating their attention on selling crack and heroin.

'I got caught with four hundred and eighty wraps of brown, four hundred and twenty wraps of white and five thousand pounds: I got another three-and-a-half years.' He reeled off the numbers as if they were nothing to him. 'I was making thirteen thousand pounds a week; as soon as I got out of jail I did the same thing again. They found a text on my phone setting up a three-thousand-pound drug deal.'

Other gangs had tried to muscle into his operation but received short shrift.

'They didn't last long. We had some Yardies from Nottingham come down to Hull to try and rob us. We used to shot [sell] bare food [drugs] down there. Hull is smack city; it was a good money-maker. They went back to Notts in a bad way and didn't come down again.'

As well as competition from gangs in other cities, the Stickem Up Klick were up against various different drug dealing cartels from all over South London. Rather than recognising the fact that there was a large enough market to merit several different gangs selling on the same patch, the other dealers in the area were fiercely territorial. There are seven known gangs in Southwark, the borough that Peckham falls within. The Klick were jostling for supremacy alongside the Bermondsey Boys, C-Block, the Wooly Road Man Dem, ROC, the Latinos Callejeros Cartel and the Original Brooklyn Youts.

Whereas the majority of South London street gang members tend to be black, Southwark is atypical in that it is home to the all-white Bermondsey Boys and the racially mixed Latinos Callajeros Cartel. Despite their name, the LCC have a number of white and North African members, although their ranks are comprised largely of Puerto Ricans, Colombians and Cubans. They are based in Elephant and Castle and wear black and white bandanas.

Whereas the Stickem Up Klick are a small, tight-knit group, the LCC are a larger collective. Their territories extend into the Heygate Estate in Walworth and parts of Peckham and Brixton. They are one of several Latin American street gangs that exist across South London: such as the boroughs of Southwark and Lambeth in particular, as they have sizeable Colombian populations living there.

The LCC are in direct competition with a larger, international gang: the Latin Kings. The Almighty Latin Kings began as a self-defence group, protecting the Hispanic community from racist white street gangs in 1940s Chicago. Latinos were forced to band together in the face of overwhelming prejudice and discrimination. Over time, the group lost touch with their roots and became focused on drug dealing and street robberies, transforming themselves into a global criminal enterprise. Gradually their membership grew to include chapters in Spain, Latin America, Canada, Italy and more recently the U.K.

There are three British-Latino street gangs with suspected links to the Latin Kings: Los Rolos, Los Del Norte and Los Parceros. Los Rolos are a group of international thieves, moving from country to country using bogus passports. They specialise in house burglaries, specifically targeting expensive jewellery and committing all of their break-ins during the day, whilst their victims are at work. They operate under false names and often use fake documentation so that they are able to pass undetected.

Los Parceros are a group of second-generation immigrants mainly concerned with low-level drug dealing and antisocial behaviour. They have a core membership of around thirty and are the least organised of the three groups. Los Del Norte are involved in drug smuggling and money laundering. They allegedly have ties to Colombian crime syndicates and operate in smaller cells of three to five people.

The Latin Kings and their affiliates demonstrate their loyalty by wearing yellow and black, signifying their allegiance to the colours of the five-point crown: the gang's primary symbol. Their rivalry with the LCC is thought to originate from derogatory rap lyrics, uploaded onto the Internet by members of the Latin Kings Royal Chapter Taino Tribe – a Hackney-based group claiming to a British chapter of the gang. 'Who is these LCC guys? They're not great, I'll shank them in their face,' raps one Latino, dressed in black with a yellow bandana wrapped around his neck.

The LCC have forged some powerful alliances across South London, including the Brixton-based Poverty Driven Children and Money Family Gangstaz crews. The Poverty Driven Children are an all-black gang with their own distinctive brand of clothing: a black T-shirt adorned with a white PDC logo. Although several of the founding members have abandoned their criminal lifestyles to pursue music careers, it is notable that most of their lyrics are still about gun crime and selling drugs. They are something of an unusual choice of associate for the LCC, as the gangs of Lambeth and Southwark are traditionally rivals. The PDC have a number of enemies living within the LCC's home borough, most notably the Young Peckham Boys, Rokker's old crew.

One of the reasons for the PDC's allegiance with the LCC is the two gangs' mutual interest in rap music. Several PDC members have appeared in amateur music videos made by the LCC and both groups have aspirations of making it in the music industry. Elijah Kerr, the founding member of the PDC, has recently set up his own record label and preaches the rehabilitative powers of music. This is ironic, given the lyrical content of his songs: 'Hit the street; jump in a Porsche jeep, so what you got a gun? I've got a whole heap,' he raps, whilst posing as a reformed character.

The Money Family Gangstaz are another Latino firm, modelling themselves on the Nortenos: a Mexican-American street gang. They have borrowed the Norteno symbol of the Huelga Bird and adapted it to include the characters SW2, the postcode for Brixton. The Huelga Bird is the symbol of the United Farm Workers, a predominantly Hispanic agricultural labour union in America. It is a black bird of prey set against a red background. The Nortenos use the image in homage to UFW leader Cesar Chavez, who was imprisoned alongside several members of the gang, when he was locked up for challenging a judicial order against the UFW's decision to boycott California grapes.

The MFG dress in red and wear red bandanas, emulating the Nortenos' dress code. Whereas the Nortenos associate themselves with the roman numerals XIV, as N is the fourteenth letter of the alphabet, the MFG use the numerals XIII to represent the letter M. They are a prime example of a British street gang replicating American ghetto culture. Whereas black British youths often can be seen to copy elements from African American rappers, the Latino population model themselves on Mexican and Puerto Rican gangsters from the States. South London is home to Bloods, Crips, Latin Kings and Nortenos: although the accents may differ and they may refer to themselves by different names, the influence is undeniable.

In June 2006, youth worker Shaun Bailey warned of the subversive influence of American rap music: 'Gangster behaviour and hip-hop music is so powerful that even the word "blood" has now joined the English lexicon from an American gang through hiphop music,' he told the newspaper *The Voice*. The word 'blood' is a term of endearment used amongst London's black community. Youth culture and hiphop culture within the city have become inextricably interlinked, exposing young people to the gangland culture of Chicago and Los Angeles.

Many of South London's street gangs are ultimately attempting to replicate the violence of their transatlantic cousins. Coloured bandanas, graffiti tags and gang affiliated hand signs are becoming part and parcel of everyday life. Although Britain has a far lower murder rate than the States, the rate of firearms offences in the capital is steadily increasing. In 2009, it was revealed that shooting incidents had almost doubled compared with the same period in the previous year. 'Gun crime has never gone away,' the Rev Les Isaac, who works as a street pastor in south London, told the BBC. 'Firearms are being discharged more or less on a daily basis in some parts of London.'

He added, 'Those using the guns have got younger. These children are unpredictable, they have access to guns and they are willing to use them.'

Sixty-five per cent of gun crime in London is carried out by black gunmen, despite only one in ten people in the city being black. Asians are the largest and poorest minority, yet they account for only one in twenty incidents.

As the city's youth continue to emulate the States, South London becomes more and more like inner city Los Angeles. Red and blue bandanas, automatic weapons and Americanised street slang are creating a carbon copy of ghetto America. The gangs of Peckham and Lewisham are becoming indistinguishable from those of New York and Detroit.

'Deptford is like Compton without the weather,' one sardonic South London gang member told me. 'Man can get licked up for wearing the wrong colour clothes.'

West London

WEST LONDON IS the richest part of the city, with the lowest crime rate. It has the country's most expensive housing, with average home prices in some streets topping £6 million. Those from outside of the capital look upon it as the domain of the wealthy and privileged, but this is not necessarily the case. Nestled away between the wine bars and gastro-pubs are some of the poorest and most crime-riddled enclaves in Britain.

Police have identified eighteen gangs operating in West London, six in the City of Westminster, home to the most notorious, the SMG Mozart Bloods. The Mozart Estate in Queens Park was once dubbed 'crack city' for the levels of drug dealing that went on there. In 2007, statistics collected by the Department of Communities and Local Government highlighted the estate as having the worst rate of child poverty in the country. It is a fertile breeding ground for guns, gangs and violence.

The Mozart Bloods are based in the area around Harrow Road. They are involved in low-level drug dealing and street robbery. They have also been involved in a war with the South Kilburn Firearms Cartel Crips, a sub-set of a larger group known as the South Kilburn Mandem. The two gangs were allies until the Bloods turned on their former friends and stole a wristwatch from one of their members. Since the robbery, they have been sworn enemies.

In a bid to try and curb the Bloods gang's activities, the local council took the controversial step of spending £80,000 to send some of them on a six-day abseiling holiday in Ewhurst, Surrey. This received widespread criticism, with many feeling that the group were being rewarded for their criminal behaviour. Whether the 'mentoring' trip deterred them from carrying on with their lives of crime remains to be seen. When a group of individuals are making thousands of pounds a week from selling drugs, it is naïve to think that a few days in rural Surrey will be enough to make them change their ways.

The Mozart Bloods are part of a larger alliance known as the Horror Road Mandem. It is the result of five different smaller firms from the area around Harrow Road coming together. They wear red bandanas and are particularly prevalent on the Warwick and Brindley, Mozart and Amberley estates.

The Street Diplomats are one of the largest of the Horror Road sets, with an estimated fifty members aged between fourteen and twenty-five. They are based on the Mozart Estate and wear a colour code of brown and red to signify their affiliation. Many of the gang wear 'R.I.P. Amro' tee-shirts in homage to a fourteen-year-old teenager who had his throat slashed by another Diplomats member in March 2008.

Amro Elbadawi, known as 'Lionheart', was killed by one of his closest friends. He was play fighting with sixteen-year-old Yusuf Drissi when things got out of hand and Drissi cut his throat with a knife. Amro was a star student with a keen interest in maths and science and ambitions to become a doctor.

Witnesses stated that Drissi stabbed Amro in the leg 'as a joke' and shouted, 'You are weak,' as he ran off down the road. Amro was alleged to have returned moments later with a knife of his own, saying, 'I'm not joking around,' and chasing his friend around with it. Drissi stabbed him through the neck, severing a major artery, and lacerated his right lung.

The spot where Amro was killed was soon festooned with floral tributes and personal messages left by his friends. A packet of Wotsits and a carton of Ribena were left in remembrance of his favourite snacks.

Yusuf claimed that he had acted in self-defence, as Amro had a 'capacity for violence'. His claim was backed up by the fact that his victim had been temporarily excluded from school for an assault earlier that year. The killer was given two years for manslaughter. He hadn't meant for Amro to die, but if he hadn't been carrying a knife then his friend would still be alive.

Amro is one of a number of teenage boys who have been killed in gang-related conflicts in West London. He was of Egyptian descent: his parents had travelled halfway around the world in search of a better life.

London's immigrant communities have some of the highest rates of violent crime. Most of the gangs to the West of the city are second or third generation black British, although there are also several Asian firms in Hounslow and Southall. Descendants of immigrants have been shown to be far more likely to join a criminal group than those of British ancestry. They often live in poorer areas, with fewer prospects, and may feel the need to band together for protection. Many of the original black gangs in Notting Hill and Ladbroke Grove came into existence to protect themselves from the racist Teddy Boys in the 1950s.

Whereas West Indians formed the vast majority of London's migrant population in the 1950s and 1960s, there has been a recent wave of immigration from Eastern Europe due to changes in the European Union. The EU enlargement of 2004 resulted in hundreds of Polish workers heading to London in search of work opportunities. Many of them found employment in the construction industry. Some of them worked in factories or laboured away picking fruit. Others found less labour-intensive ways of earning a living.

Hounslow is known for its sizeable immigrant population. Although Asians are the largest minority group, the borough is also home to significant Jamaican, Somali, Kosovan, Albanian and Polish communities. Whereas the majority of the gangs within the region tend to be South Asian, a group of Polish drug dealers have been giving the Asian firms a run for their money in recent years.

The Polish Unit are a collective of Polish immigrants brought together through their love of drinking, fighting and taking drugs. They are based in the Lampton area and pride themselves on the fact that they never go anywhere in groups of less than eighty.

'I was the first Polish guy to start selling drugs,' founding member Duzy told me. 'After me everyone else started doing it. We grouped together for strength in numbers.'

I was intrigued as to how the gang had come into existence: they were essentially the only Eastern European gang, in an area dominated by Asians. If I was going to find out the reality behind life in a Polish street gang, then he was the person to speak to.

According to Duzy, the Polish Unit originally started out as a group of friends who met at Lampton Park with the sole purpose of getting as drunk as possible. They soon began to realise the power that they possessed through merit of brute force and, within a matter of months, they had transformed themselves from a group of drunken delinquents into a criminal organisation.

'People felt fear when we went through the streets,' Duzy said. 'Imagine fifty drunk Polish guys running through the streets shouting, "We are going to kill you"; even though it wasn't in English everyone knew what we meant!

'We had mad beefs with Asian gangs. The main gang we fought was named Too Many because there was hundreds of them but we were more respected than anyone else in Hounslow because we were big and dangerous.'

Although the main purpose of the group was to make money from selling drugs, they also felt that it was important to prove that they were the hardest in the borough. They were the only all-white gang and they had a lot to prove.

The Unit claim to have over a hundred members, twenty-four of which are higher ranking than the rest, known as the Olders Grup. Although they are not averse to using weapons, they usually rely upon their fists and travel everywhere in large groups in case of confrontation.

In February 2010, former Los Angeles gang member Pablo Johnson warned a local newspaper that Hounslow was becoming like America. After moving to London to escape his gangland past, the ex-MS13 gangbanger complained of the lawlessness that was taking over in certain areas of the borough and spoke of groups of youths adopting different colour codes to display their gang affiliations. Although their Polish nationality sets them apart from the other firms, the Polish Unit are typical of the London street gangs in that they adopt American street culture. They abbreviate their name to 'P-Unit' to mimic G Unit, the gangster rap group that 50 Cent belongs to, and tag their name in graffiti to mark their territory.

Graffiti is an easy way for a firm to designate control of a certain building or area. Many of the estate maps and road signs have had the initials of the local gang written upon. The sign for the Warwick and Brindley Estate has been inscribed with the acronym CRIME, a shortened version of Can't Roll In My Ends – a sub-set of the Horror Road Mandem. The whole of Queens Park is littered with GD, SD and GM tags: Grimiest Movements, Street Diplomats and Grey Daiz. Perhaps the most widely spread tag is that of the Make Paper Regardless gang, another of the larger West London firms.

Make Paper Regardless are spread out across Acton, Hammersmith and Shepherd's Bush. They mark their territory either with 'MPR' or the initials of the smaller sub-sets that comprise the group: MDP for 'Murder Dem Pussies' and CPG for 'Crime Pays Gang'. They are one of the largest gangs in the region, laying claim to the South Acton Estate in Acton and several estates in Shepherd's Bush, including Becklow Gardens, Lime Grove, White City and Emlyn Gardens.

Murder Dem Pussies are the younger generation of Make Paper Regardless. They are sometimes referred to as the 'Murder Blues', a nickname taken from the name of a documentary, chronicling the activities of the London police force. It is also a reference to their blue dress code, perhaps the most commonly used colour amongst London gangs. The group gained notoriety after a spate of vicious robberies throughout 2006. They would beat their victims to a pulp whilst filming themselves on camcorders and mobile phones, then rifle through their pockets to see what they could find.

In November 2006, thirty members of MDP boarded a number 207 bus after attending an all-night rave. They were in high spirits. Part way through the journey, they attacked and robbed a twenty-two-year-old man from Hayes for no discernible reason. He was repeatedly punched, kicked and hit with bottles, leaving him with nine stitches in his eyelid and damage to his eye and nose. He was placed on prescription painkillers for a month after the robbery and needed a series of operations to repair his nose.

The attack was thought to be a ritual to test the loyalty of the gang's younger members. All of the assailants were aged between fourteen and seventeen and many of them were girls. They took £70 and a mobile phone. Unfortunately for them, the bus was fitted with CCTV. A number of youths were arrested and taken in for questioning after being identified from the footage.

In March 2007, the gang struck again. Sixteen-year-old Kodjo 'Kizzle' Yenga was walking with his girlfriend Cookie and her pet puppy when they were confronted by a group of teenagers. Cookie knew some of them from her school and chatted with them for a few minutes, before fifteen-year-old Tirell Davis attempted to pick a fight with Kodjo.

'I hear you want to fight me,' he said.

'No,' Kodjo replied, 'I don't want to fight with you because you're a little boy.'

Tirell was furious and demanded that he fought him. Reluctantly, Kodjo eventually agreed, in the full knowledge that his adversary was renowned for fighting dirty. His friend Seun Adeboyoje had suffered a series of threatening phone calls from the same person and had arranged a one-on-one to settle it; instead he had been ambushed by a group of three youths who punched and kicked him to the ground, stamped on him whilst he was down and threw boiling water over his arm and face.

Sensing that he might end up having to fight more than one member of the gang, Kodjo rang two friends and asked them to help him out. As they turned up, eight more MDP members arrived, armed with knives, baseball bats and a bull terrier. The terrier was unleashed at Kodjo and the rest of the gang advanced on him, brandishing their weapons in an attempt to scare him into submission.

'Do you think you are a big boy because you have a knife?' Kodjo asked.

'I don't care,' the knife-wielding thug replied. 'I want you to respect me.'

As Kodjo struggled to get away from his attackers, he tripped and fell to the floor. One of the gang grabbed Cookie around the neck and threatened her with a knife whilst the others laid into her fallen boyfriend.

'Please don't stab him! Please don't stab him!' she yelled, but her screams fell on deaf ears.

'Kill him!' urged another of the gang members.

One of the youths stabbed him straight through the heart and held the knife in the air triumphantly. The rest of the group laughed and joked.

Kodjo, who was born in the Congo, had attended secondary school in Fulham and did his best to stay out of trouble. Nine months prior to the killing, he appeared on an MTV discussion panel about knife crime. He stated that most young men who carried knives did so for protection and added that it wasn't a particularly good thing to do but that he could understand why they did it. He was averse to longer sentences for knife possession and thought that the problem had been exaggerated by the media.

'Personally I wouldn't [carry a knife],' he had told the panel, 'because I'm not in that type of situation.'

Five teenagers were eventually jailed in connection with his death. Tirell Davis and Brandon Richmond were sentenced to a minimum of fifteen years. Richmond was thirteen years of age at the time of the killing. Three other teenagers were each given ten years' detention. 'You were all part of the gang culture, which casts its dreadful influence and leads to the sort of tragedy we have seen here,' the judge told them. 'All of you come from decent and caring backgrounds, which makes the situation all the more worrying.'

In the course of the trial, it transpired that one of the defendants, Yemoh Kurtis, had been in court a matter of hours before Kodjo's death. He was granted bail despite facing a charge of witness intimidation: had he been remanded into custody then things might have turned out differently.

In the aftermath of the killing, local Labour councillor Marianne Alapini claimed that she had heard of a vicious sexual assault being carried out by members of the MDP. She stated that they had gang-raped a thirteen-year-old girl and branded a number of youths as punishment for perceived acts of disrespect. They were by far the most ruthless of the West London street gangs. Whereas other criminals in the area arguably had limits, they appeared to revel in their own cruelty and lack of compassion.

Kodjo's murder was one of several violent, honour-based attacks that the gang would go on to commit. The more savage and emotionless the members were, the higher they would progress within the hierarchy of the firm. They were willing to kill solely to demonstrate that they were capable of killing; on 3 September 2007, they did so again.

Somali student Yasin Abdirahman had just left his home on the Windmill Estate, in Southall, when he was confronted by up to twenty-five armed youths. They had travelled to the area to fight with the rival Grit Set firm, who had stolen a mobile phone from a fifteen-year-old MDP affiliate two weeks earlier. The Grit Set are an outer-London gang specialising in street robbery and low-level drug dealing. They class themselves as a British chapter of the Bloods, one of America's most notorious street gangs. Yasin was studying pharmacy at London Metropolitan University. He had no gang ties whatsoever.

'You Grit Set! You Grit set!' the youths shouted as they advanced upon their victim armed with broken bottles, bull terriers, knives and a baseball bat. Before he even had time to ask who the Grit Set were, he was set upon and stabbed three times in the head, sending him to the pavement. He managed to stagger back onto his feet and caught the attention of a passing motorist, who rushed him to the nearest hospital. He slipped into a coma and died from his injuries a week later.

Yasin lived a purposeful and law-abiding life, working hard at university whilst at the same time caring for his disabled mother who was suffering from multiple sclerosis. Whilst the doctors at Ealing Hospital were battling to save his life, a number of hooded youths with Staffordshire bull terriers were seen congregating outside. Given their previous involvement in witness intimidation, the reason behind their presence was obvious.

Ten teenagers were eventually convicted of charges related to Yasin's murder, the youngest being twelve years old at the time of the attack. Fifteen-year-old Joshua Williams of Aylesbury, Buckinghamshire, was found guilty of murder and sentenced to a minimum of fourteen years behind bars. During the trial, it was revealed that his MySpace page displayed a picture of him holding a knife under the caption 'me, myself and my shank'.

Nineteen-year-old Sheldon John-Lewis and sixteen-year-old Andre Mason were also found guilty of murder. John-Lewis received the harsher punishment of the two: he was sentenced to fourteen years behind bars. Andre Mason, the younger brother of Olympic silver medallist Germaine Mason, was given a minimum of thirteen years in prison.

Germaine was appalled by his brother's actions and claimed that he had acted out of character. He wrote to the judge pleading for leniency and asking if there was any chance that the sentence could be reduced. The court was told how, like his brother, Andre was a promising athlete who had won a number of trophies at junior athletics competitions. Rather than focusing upon his sporting success, he became involved with the MDP gang whilst attending Acton High School and was soon a fully-fledged member. Had he concentrated on his athletics, he could have avoided spending the next decade of his life in a cell.

Peter Beaumont QC, Recorder of London, expressed concern at the fact that Andre continued to seek support from his co-defendants even in light of what they had done: 'Even after your conviction for murder you continue to regard your co-defendants as a group of supportive friends', he told him. 'It is of even greater concern that you have found comfort in your peer group, who have reaffirmed the acceptability of your behaviour and rewarded you with members of the group giving you protection and status in prison, where you continue to demonstrate no real remorse or shame for your actions.'

Carlos Cyrus was the youngest of the convicted teenagers. He was twelve when the murder took place and fourteen when he was told that he would be spending the next seven years behind bars. His headmaster described him as a likeable pupil and expressed sorrow at the fact that he had become involved with the wrong crowd.

Four more youths were charged with violent disorder and conspiracy to commit GBH, including another fourteen-year-old boy. A group of MDP members congregated outside the court after the sentencing had taken place, attempting to intimidate those who were travelling to and from the building. They had hoods pulled over their faces and they were leering and swearing at passers-by. A fifteen-year-old youth who was allowed to walk free shouted 'MDP' as he was driven away from the courthouse.

Kodjo and Yasin's murders were indiscriminate attacks. The gang claimed that Kodjo was looking for a fight and that they thought that Yasin was a member of the Grit Set: in reality, they needed no excuse to attack them. Their reputation hinged around their propensity for unprovoked violence. They were more bothered about gaining kudos from their friends than they were about the prospect of taking a human life. Money, power and respect were the only things that mattered. When they weren't gaining the admiration of their peers by bullying and intimidating the other teenagers in the area, they were selling drugs to make sure that they profited from their gang allegiance.

The South Acton Estate is one of MDP's main drug dealing territories. The estate, which was used as the location for Del and Rodney Trotter's tower block in the comedy series *Only Fools and Horses*, is home to West London's largest expanse of council housing. It is a racially mixed area with approximately 2,000 residential dwellings, many of them high-rise flats. Like most poor, densely packed areas, it is party to its fair share of crime and antisocial behaviour.

Jacob Emmanuel was one of the gang's main crack and heroin dealers on the estate. It was a dangerous occupation and employees would be treated with disdain, brutal punishment beatings being inflicted on them at the slightest provocation. Whereas those at the top of the chain earned thousands of pounds a week, low-level drug runners were often paid next to nothing. They were seen as willing fools who would sell drugs for someone else, when they could have been keeping all of the money themselves.

Emmanuel made the fatal mistake of losing £300-worth of the drugs that he had been given to sell. Although the amount was relatively small – just a few days' wages for the average dealer earning about £1,000 a week – the gang summoned him to Blackmore Tower, a large tower block on the estate. Rather than giving him more drugs to sell to recoup his losses, they forced him into a lift and set a Staffordshire bull terrier on him. 'Kill him! Kill him!' they shouted, the same words that they had used moments before sixteen-year-old Kodjo Yenga was stabbed through the heart.

This was only the beginning of his ordeal. The frightened eighteen-year-old was stripped naked, badly beaten and left unconscious in a pool of blood. He suffered injuries to his arms, legs, feet, body, lips, back and chest. There were footprints indented into his neck and face where one of the gang had either kicked him or stamped on him. Both the beating and the dog attack were filmed on a mobile phone so that his attackers could watch their handiwork, gaining a perverse satisfaction from the injuries that they had inflicted.

On 5 March 2008, gang members Dorian Henry and Andre Williams were given indeterminate sentences with a recommended tariff of ten years. They were convicted of grievous bodily harm, conspiracy to supply class A drugs and being in charge of a dangerous dog. Their dog, Cash, was put down. Williams had used it in two different street robberies the previous year and it was classified as unsafe to keep as a pet. One of the downsides of recording criminal activities on a mobile phone, they were to discover, is that it is likely to end up in the hands of the police.

'This was a pre-planned attack,' Judge Jonathan Lowen told the pair. 'Your motive was punishment or revenge in the context of drug dealing. The attack was carried out by both of you acting together, with other gang members, and filmed for later viewing. Williams used a vicious dog as a weapon and you both encouraged the dog to savage that victim when he had been knocked to the ground. As the dog was on top of him you shouted to the dog to kill him. In addition to the bites sustained when the dog savaged him, the victim was kicked and stamped on by gang members around him. There was a clear shoe imprint on his face.

'You chose a venue from which there was no escape. There was little chance of anyone coming to his assistance. A number of gang members were present to block any attempt at escape. You then robbed him of his possessions and his clothes. You degraded and humiliated him by stripping him naked and you left him entirely alone, bleeding and unconscious'.

Since the deaths of Kodjo and Yenga, steps have been taken to force the group to relinquish their hold on West London's estates. Youth workers and former gang members have been deployed to try and talk young people out of joining gangs, and the councils in Hammersmith and Fulham have pumped money into extra policing.

Although MDP outdo the other gangs in the region in terms of their viciousness, they are merely a part of a growing trend of increasingly ruthless teenage criminals. Organised crime was once the domain of fully-grown adults: nowadays the youths are the gangsters and the adults live in fear. In a society where a fifteen-year-old boy can earn a £1,000 a week selling crack, there is little incentive for him to stay in school. Large financial rewards, for small amounts of work, are ensuring that gangs and crime will continually plague West London's streets.

Despite falling within one of the more affluent regions of the capital, the Mozart Estate and the South Acton Estate do not appear to have profited from the wealth generated in the surrounding areas. So long as there is poverty, there will be street drugs and so long as there are drugs, there will be dealers. The state of affairs in the capital, where rich bankers co-exist with poor single mothers and asylum seekers, exemplifies the gap between the rich and the poor.

Gangs like the Mozart Bloods and Murder Dem Pussies are a product of their surroundings. They are the children of drug addicts, teenage parents and those with their horizons firmly below the breadline. Poverty breeds disaffection and discontent. Unless the class divide is ever bridged, West London will continue to be a place where two worlds exist in parallel to one another: one prosperous and the other brimming with menace and ill-feeling.

North London

WHEREAS FEWER THAN twenty gangs have been identified in West London, there are over forty different gangs in Haringey alone, a single borough of North London. The north of the city has seen many gun and knife-related tragedies over the past few years, such as the fatal stabbing of Ben Kinsella in June 2008. It is home to some of the country's most crime-ridden areas, with Harlesden, Tottenham, Edmonton and Wood Green all featuring well above the national average for a variety of different indicators of social deprivation.

Brent, Haringey, Enfield and Islington are the four boroughs that have borne the brunt of the area's gang epidemic, along with Hackney (included in the East London chapter). Brent has a large Afro-Caribbean population, which is reflected by its large number of Jamaican and 'black British' gangs; Haringey, Enfield and Islington are multicultural boroughs, with African, Cypriot, Turkish, Kurdish and white gangs all vying for control.

North London's gang wars were catapulted into the public eye after the BBC documentary *Murder Blues* broadcast the activities of the city's anti-gun crime unit. One gang in particular featured repeatedly throughout the series: the Tottenham Man Dem, an alliance of eighteen smaller sets, many wearing red and modelling themselves upon the Bloods.

Tottenham is one of the most culturally diverse places in the country, with approximately forty per cent of the population belonging to ethnic minority groups. Many live below the poverty line. It has some of the highest rates of burglary, firearms offences and violent crime and it has been the site of a number of bloody, drug-related murders over the past few decades.

The Tottenham Man Dem began as a drug dealing collective based on the Broadwater Farm Estate, made infamous by the murder of PC Keith Blakelock during a ferocious riot in 1985. As their reputation spread, they drew followers from all over Haringey and the surrounding areas. They soon had 400 members at their disposal and began to broaden their activities to include kidnap and extortion.

As the Man Dem went from strength to strength, they developed smaller sub-groups all over North London and enveloped a number of the less well-known gangs. They began to adopt American style gang signs and started to refer to themselves as 'Pirus', a Bloods sub-set originating in Compton, California.

Twenty-five-year-old Marcus Cox was a high-ranking member of the TMD. He was chased through the streets of Tottenham by a crazed gunman and tripped and fell in his hurry to get away: he was shot four times as he lay defenceless on the concrete pavement. One of the shots travelled through one side of his head and out of the other, ricocheting off the floor and re-entering his flesh. Another penetrated his shoulder, destroying the main vessel above his heart.

Cox's criminal career began at the age of eleven, when he was convicted of his first burglary. He lived a life of violence and crime, working his way up to become a senior figure within the gang and making enemies along the way. He was a figure of fear within the black community: a known bully with a penchant for robbery and kidnap. A gun was found next to his body, suggesting that he was carrying it at the time of his death.

Over 500 people turned out for Cox's funeral, ranging from close family and friends to those with alleged gang affiliation. However he also had many foes, and the police had difficulty pinpointing which one had pulled the trigger. He had wronged so many people that it was hard to narrow it down to a single suspect. There had been countless underworld figures lining up to shoot him – it was a case of finding out who had got there first.

As the investigation progressed, the same name cropped up over and over again: Syron Martin, an alleged skunk dealer, who claimed that Cox had kidnapped and robbed him six weeks earlier. He had been badly beaten and told that he was going to be killed unless his family forked out £20,000. Martin managed to escape before the money was handed over, but was left shaken by his ordeal and spoke of being paranoid and suicidal in the following weeks. His mother stated that his personality altered so much that he was 'like another person'.

A witness stated that Martin had threatened to get even with whoever was responsible for the kidnap. A search of addresses he was known to frequent uncovered a bulletproof vest and a series of newspaper clippings about the killing. It was beginning to look like Operation Trident, the Metropolitan Police unit set up to combat 'black-on-black' gun crime, had got their man.

Damien Brown, Martin's mother's boyfriend, confessed to being present at the time of the shooting. He said that Martin had accompanied him to Tottenham High Road so that he could show him where a shop was. 'While I was waiting for the order at the chicken shop, Syron said that he could see the person that had kidnapped him,' he said. 'The driver of the blue BMW got out of the car, produced a gun and aimed it at Syron. He pulled the trigger three times and I assume the gun was jammed because nothing came out. I then saw two shots fired in the direction of the driver, who ran across the road followed by Syron.'

Martin was eventually convicted of manslaughter and sentenced to eight years in prison. He pleaded diminished responsibility on the grounds that he was suffering from post-traumatic stress disorder. He also claimed that he acted instinctively, as Cox had pulled a gun on him.

Whilst Cox's friends and family were in a state of shock about his death, others were relieved that his reign of terror had come to an end. So-called taxmen evoke mixed feelings amongst the criminal fraternity; some see them as a more noble class of villain, as their victims are breaking the law and arguably deserve as good as they get. Others believe in honour amongst thieves and view them as the lowest of the low. It is perhaps the most dangerous crime to be involved in: drug dealers are not likely to forget someone who has robbed them. More often than not, they will seek revenge.

For every Tottenham Man Dem member who has been killed, there are lives that they have ruined. Thirty-two-year-old Douglas Mullings was preparing for church when he noticed that someone had bumped a gold Mercedes into the back of his car. The youths responsible were members of the Meridian Crew, a Tottenham Man Dem set based around the Meridian Walk area, who had stolen the car. An argument ensued and Mullings quickly found himself under attack. Rather than apologizing for the collision, the gang armed themselves with bricks and pieces of wood and pursued him into his house.

Moments later, Mullings returned with a long knife and chased the youths away. Infuriated by the fact that their victim was fighting back against them, they called for back-up, telling an accomplice to bring a gun with him. 'Bring your piece,' he was told.

The gunman was driven to the scene in a red Rover. He had a shotgun in his hand and a black bandana tied across the bottom of his face. He ran over to Mullings and shot him in the back of the head at point blank range. Mullings was rushed to the nearest hospital in a desperate attempt to save his life. The man who had made the phone call stood outside the family home, boasting about the shooting. 'I'm glad I did that,' he proclaimed, as his blood-splattered victim lay gasping on the floor.

Mullings survived, despite a hole in his head the size of a small grapefruit. Paramedics stated that he was lucky not to have died from loss of blood alone. There were fragments of bone and brain matter oozing from his wound and he had shotgun pellets lodged in his brain. He was left paralysed down his left hand side, with reduced speech capacity and substantial brain damage.

Residents of Meridian Walk spoke of the gang's reign of terror in the weeks leading up to the shooting. They talked of gunfights in the street and hard drugs being used in full view of the local children. Parties would keep the residents up into the early hours of the morning and any attempt to complain about the noise was ignored.

David Gaynor and Simeon 'Sykes' Szypusz were eventually charged with the shooting, after witnesses identified Gaynor as the shooter and Szypusz as having ordered the hit. Gaynor was taken in for questioning and pleaded with the officer in charge of the case: 'You're a good officer man. I need help. I can give you drug dealers, gun suppliers…' The ease with which he was willing to compromise his gangland values to save his own skin was testament to his lack of morality. Asked where Sykes was hiding out, he immediately surrendered the address of his former friend, hoping that it would reduce whatever sentence he received for the attack.

Gaynor was a professional criminal, nicknamed '1G' after the $1,000 price that New York hitmen are supposedly paid for each job. He portrayed himself as a cross between 50 Cent and Tony Soprano, looking up to both 'Mafioso' wiseguys and black gangster rappers. His involvement in crime began when he was fifteen years old and since then he has had convictions for possession of an offensive weapon, drugs offences and violence. Despite his posturing and bravado, he was seen rubbing his eyes as if crying during the investigation and was all too ready to provide the name of his accomplice.

A search of Szypusz's house revealed a set of three bullet-proof vests and a hat that had been worn during the attack. Like Gaynor, he was quick to shift the blame once he had spent a few hours at the police station. 'Merick Hamilton made the call to David Gaynor,' he wrote in a statement. 'He also said, "Good, I'm glad that was done."'

Despite his efforts to implicate his friend in the shooting, Szypusz was eventually convicted of attempted murder and threats to kill and sentenced to twenty-five years in prison. Gaynor was given twenty years for attempted murder and firearms offences and Hamilton received a three-year sentence for threats to kill. The court heard how Gaynor had boasted about the attack in a rap song he wrote shortly after the shooting, including the lines, 'I'll kill you in front of your family G, I knock down families and family trees.' He also boasted about his use of a shotgun: 'You wanna die like Scarface, I'll be dat mad one dat kill Scarface. Give us a taste of da pump [shotgun] and a scar on your face.'

The judge described Gaynor as an 'evil, callous and dangerous man'.

'You didn't know Mr Mullings,' he told him. 'You never had any contact with him whatsoever. Your only role was to kill him at the request of your friend because he felt disrespected.'

He then told Sykes, 'The same applies to you: evil, callous and dangerous. This case is worse in many respects than pre-meditation. It was simply the casual organisation of a murder.'

Mullings was lucky to be alive, given the extent of his injuries. The shooting was a clear attempt to kill him over what began as a petty dispute. It shows the casual brutality of the gang and their willingness to take a man's life over a minor act of disrespect. Marcus Cox had lived a life of crime and he was killed as a result of a violent robbery. Douglas Mullings, however, was a committed family man; he was shot because he had stood up to a group of people that were making his family's life a misery.

In a remarkable display of compassion, Mullings insists that he has forgiven his attackers. He is a devoted Christian and a believer in the importance of mercy. The Tottenham Man Dem, however, appear to have their roots in a different 'religion' altogether. Mark Lambie, their original leader, was referred to as 'The Prince of Darkness' and 'Obeahman', Obeah being a form of folk magic practised in Central Africa and the West Indies. Some of his followers even believed that he was invincible and possessed supernatural powers.

Tottenham's gang leader gained notoriety after being arrested on suspicion of the murder of PC Blakelock, during the riots in 1985. He was eventually cleared of the killing, but his reputation for violence stayed with him. The accusations that were levelled at him only served to raise his reputation amongst his peers: many of them hated the police with a passion and saw him as something of a local hero.

Lambie was fourteen at the time of the PC Blakelock killing and it proved to be the beginning of a stormy relationship with the Metropolitan Police. As a youth, he was thought to be involved in low-level drug dealing, selling crack and heroin for a group of older gangsters known as the Tottenham Boys. As time went by, he progressed to more and more extreme criminal acts, both at home and abroad, and become Operation Trident's number one target. Intelligence implicated him in several murders but there was insufficient evidence to prosecute him.

The Prince of Darkness added to his invincible image after surviving a shooting by rival gang members, in 1996. He was a figure of fear amongst the Man Dem: many of them thought him to be a voodoo magician or sorcerer and some began to refer to him as 'The Devil Man', the dark lord of the Tottenham underworld.

In May 2000, however, he was convicted of kidnap and blackmail and sentenced to twelve years in prison. He had teamed up with another North London gang, known as The Firm, and abducted and tortured two Jamaican men that he believed were in possession of large sums of money. Twaine 'Tupac' Morris and Gregory 'Beenie Man' Smith were lured to Broadwater Farm where they were bundled into the back of a car and driven to a house. The occupants were ordered to stay downstairs while Morris and Smith were beaten with hammers, burned with an iron and scalded around their genitals with boiling water.

The Firm, based in nearby Edmonton, were led by the equally ruthless Anthony 'Blue' Bourne. Bourne had previously been acquitted of the murder of sixteen-year-old Guydance Dacres, who was shot dead at the Chimes nightclub in Hackney in 1997; Dacres was rumoured to have been caught up in a feud between The Firm and the Hackney Man Dem.

For Lambie, Bourne and his gang were the perfect allies. Both gangs believed that torture was an acceptable way of extracting money from a target. If the victims didn't pay up then it was their own fault if they got hurt: it was unavoidable.

Eventually, Smith cracked under the pressure and gave the address of a house on Wakefield Road. It was in fact a hairdressing salon, rather than a stash house, but Smith knew that if he remained quiet he would be tortured indefinitely. They shoved him into their car boot, before driving to the hairdressers to retrieve the cash.

Upon gaining entry, the two firms proceeded to rob the two women they found inside and a male customer. They were determined to profit from their journey, despite the fact that there was no money being held there. During the commotion, Smith managed to escape from the locked boot and run to Tottenham Police Station, half-naked and dripping blood.

Meanwhile, Morris had also managed to escape and had thrown himself onto the bonnet of a passing police car, in a similarly haggard state. The two gangs were arrested within days of the attack and a quantity of heroin, allegedly belonging to Lambie, was seized.

Furious, Lambie called his victims, demanding £5,000 of protection money and an additional £1,000 a week in order for them to remain alive. To demonstrate the seriousness of the threats, Morris was shot three times as he walked along Park Lane in Tottenham; he survived.

Smith and Morris were placed on the witness protection programme and agreed to testify against Lambie, Bourne and their associates. The 'Prince of Darkness' was evidently not above the law, as he was sentenced to twelve years in jail, as was Bourne.

In the wake of his kidnap and blackmail convictions, Lambie was described as a 'malign and corrosive influence' by a local councillor and labelled by the London police force as potentially responsible for a number of gangland killings, even though he had no conviction for murder. They were ecstatic about the fact that he was finally behind bars, as were the citizens of North London's many council estates. However, without the Lambie and Bourne alliance to keep Tottenham and Edmonton at peace with one another, the two areas were no longer allies. It was to mark a new reign of bloodshed: not only were the TMD at war with the Hackney Man Dem, they were now engaging in shootouts with members of new Edmonton-based firms that were coming into existence.

Following the regeneration of the Edmonton Green area in 1999, some of the larger tower blocks were demolished and new estates were formed. Many of the original Firm members were re-housed and smaller factions began to spring up across Edmonton; what had started as one gang had become at least six, all vying for control.

The TMD also split up into a number of different sub-divisions: the eighteen sets that still exist. Though they came together under the banner of the TMD, they each had their own distinct territories and codes of conduct. Some groups aligned themselves with the Bloods and adorned themselves with red bandanas, whereas others such as the CE Black Gang chose to dress in black from head to toe.

The first sign of trouble between Tottenham and Edmonton arose when two teenage boys, thought to be members of the Tottenham-based Northumberland Park Killers, were attacked by members of Edmonton's Shankstarz gang. An eighteen-year-old and fifteen-year-old were taken to hospital with stab wounds. The Shankstarz hail from an area of Edmonton nicknamed 'Shanktown', shank being street slang for a knife. Whereas most of London's firms choose to use guns, Edmonton's criminals have a reputation for using blades. The fact that they stabbed their victims, as opposed to shooting them, was their way of letting their rivals know that they were willing to get up close during a confrontation.

The NPK wear purple bandanas to signify their gang affiliation. 'We wear purple 'cause we're Bloods and Crips,' one of their younger members explained to me. 'Blue and red combined makes purple.'

Two years later, twenty-year-old Duane Tomlin, rumoured to have been involved in the stabbing, was shot dead as he stepped out of a parked mini-cab in nearby Freezywater. Witnesses stated that a number of shots were fired from a white van moments before the killing took place and that two dark-coloured cars were seen driving away from the scene. The van was found burnt out in a car park minutes from where the shooting took place.

Tomlin's death marked the first fatality in the Edmonton/Tottenham rivalry. It also heralded a breakdown in the unity of the Edmonton gangs. Some followed in The Firm's footsteps, aligning themselves with the Tottenham Man Dem, whereas others remained loyal to their Edmonton friends. The Red Brick Crew from the Silver Street area of Edmonton chose to align themselves with the TMD, whilst the Edmonton Young Gunnerz, Dem Africanz and Young Dem Africanz joined up with Shankstarz to form the Green Gang, named after Edmonton Green.

The Green Gang is a collective rather than a single gang. Each of its component groups feel that they have retained their independence, seeing the Gang as an alliance rather than a merger. They signify their allegiance by wearing green bandanas. The Young Gunnerz and the Shankstarz are predominantly Afro-Caribbean, whereas Dem Africanz and Young Dem Africanz are mostly Congolese. It is a multicultural outfit that places geographical location above nationality.

In November 2007, Northumberland Park Killers associate Yanick Mayavova was attacked with an empty champagne bottle at Club 19, an urban music venue in Forest Gate. Two Green Gang members, Aidan and Liam Palmer, were thought to be behind the attack. Enraged at what had happened, the NPK drove to the Palmer brothers' grandfather's house in Edmonton, to seek revenge. Their plan was to wait until the brothers returned and then ambush them.

However, the NPK were spotted by several other Green Gang members, who quickly alerted the rest of the firm. Mikel Dixon, Jermaine Lewis-Barnes and Rodney Brew were sitting in their car, waiting for their victims to arrive, when they were set upon by up to fifteen Edmonton gang members. Their windows were smashed with wooden baseball bats and Dixon was stabbed in his tongue, mouth, chest, thighs and arms as he struggled to get away.

A second youth, Nathan Mason, was rushed to hospital after being stabbed in the heart. He somehow survived and he was eventually discharged from hospital after spending five days in the intensive care unit. The NPK's plan for revenge had backfired spectacularly.

In the early hours of New Year's Day 2008, the conflict claimed its second fatality. Seventeen-year-old Henry 'Big H' Bolombi was alighting from a bus in Edmonton, when he was confronted by several members of the TMD. He was chased along the street and stabbed through his chest. He was rushed to hospital, where he later died from his injuries. He had a criminal record for street robbery and he was an alleged member of the Dem Africanz firm.

Bolombi's death marked an escalation in the conflict and initiated a vicious spate of revenge attacks. Edmonton's image as a centre for knife crime was slowly substantiating itself: the national press were beginning to refer to it as 'Knife Town', and it would soon become synonymous with gang-related fatality.

Later that month, Dem Africanz member Louis 'Usher' Boduka was stabbed to death, during an argument with Red Brick Crew member Kevin Lewis. Boduka was travelling on a bus through Edmonton when he spotted Lewis outside an Internet café. Having been close friends with Bolombi, he was incensed at the idea that the RBC were still choosing to ally themselves with his killers. Boduka became involved in a scuffle with Lewis and Lewis stabbed him through the heart with a three-inch flick-knife.

Lewis was found guilty of manslaughter and sentenced to five years in a youth detention institute. A flight to Jamaica had been booked in his name, indicating that he knew he would be prosecuted unless he fled the country. He argued that it was not his intention to kill Boduka and claimed that he had acted out of instinct after Boduka had attacked his friend.

'If you had not had a knife that day, a young man would not be dead,' Judge Beaumont told him.

Gang members were now afraid to walk the streets without carrying a weapon for their protection. The RBC were the smallest of the Edmonton firms and knew that tensions would be running high now that they had taken a life. They took their knives with them wherever they went, for fear of a retaliatory attack.

On 15 February 2008, sixteen-year-old Ofiyke Nmczu was beaten with a brick outside a shop on Ponders End High Street. Two weeks later, he died from a fractured skull. His attacker was a high-ranking Shankstarz member whose grandfather's house had been targeted by the NPK the previous year.

Liam Palmer was charged with manslaughter and sentenced to four-and-a-half years behind bars. The killing was the result of a row over a series of violent rap lyrics that Nmezu had posted on the Internet: Palmer claimed they were disrespectful. He was later found to have recorded his own rap songs, boasting about how he had stabbed Mikel Dixon and expressing his deep-seated hatred towards the NPK. He name checked several members of the gang, detailing graphic acts of violence that he was planning on carrying out.

Several direct threats were made in Palmer's song: he said he intended to kill Tion Miller's one-year-old son and spoke of various incidents in which gang members had been punched, stabbed and terrorized by the Shankstarz. 'Your friend called Lips? He's just a little prick,' he rapped, 'cause Stormer banged him up and he ran like a little bitch.' How he could object to Nmezu allegedly disrespecting him, when his lyrics were so full of hatred, is a mystery.

Jerome 'Smallman' Bruce-de-Roche was one of the Shankstarz members who had helped protect Palmer from the attempted ambush at his grandfather's house. Sensing that the NPK would be looking for revenge after Dixon's stabbing, he decided to flee to Trinidad and lie low for a few months. This was a wise move: the TMD were furious that one of their members had been assaulted and were looking to stab a member of the Shankstarz to get even.

On the day he returned form the Caribbean, Smallman was drinking at Bar Ab in Hertfordshire when he was informed that a group of youths were looking for him outside the venue. Fearing for his life, he attempted to sneak out through the back door. However, he was spotted leaving by a friend who called to see what he was doing. Several members of the NPK heard his name being called and advanced towards him, armed with flick knives and kitchen knives. They backed him into an alleyway behind a clothes shop and stabbed him six times, lacerating his liver and collapsing one of his lungs.

Bruce-de-Roche managed to drag himself to a street nearby, where he was found by a friend and rushed to hospital. Though several of his wounds were life threatening, he survived after receiving emergency treatment.

Samson Ogundipe, Tion Miller and Jermaine Nimoh were eventually convicted of the attack after a bandana, a baseball cap, and a small quantity of Miller's blood, were found at the scene of the crime. Ogundipe and Miller were issued with indeterminate sentences and Nimoh was given nine years behind bars. The judge described Ogundipe as the 'ringleader', stating that if he had given him a fixed amount of time in jail then it would have been sixteen years.

On January 21, 2009, the anniversary of Boduka's death, tensions were at an all-time high. The occasion was marred by a series of stabbings, near to a railway underpass in Edmonton. A number of Dem Africanz members were reported to have travelled into RBC territory looking for trouble. They placed bandanas over their faces to disguise their identities and carried out attacks on local youths. In their eyes, the RBC were the ultimate traitors: they were allied with a gang who had attacked one of their fellow Edmonton residents.

Later that day, three men under the age of twenty-three were admitted to hospital, suffering from knife wounds. The police stated that they were keeping an 'open mind' as to the motivation for the conflict, but given the timing and location of the attack it was obvious as to why it had happened. It was an act of revenge for the Green Gang's fallen comrade: on the anniversary of his passing, they felt that they had to avenge his death.

By this stage, the situation in Edmonton was gaining national media attention. It was featured on a BBC documentary and several broadsheet newspapers touted what was happening as evidence of Britain's rising rate of knife crime. In an effort to prove that gangs were not above the law, the London police force launched a complex operation, aimed at taking several of the main players off the streets. They interviewed almost 200 witnesses and secured new legislation, ensuring the anonymity of their six key witnesses. It was time for the police to show the gangs who was in charge.

In May 2009, Liam Palmer was finally brought to justice for his part in the attack on Mikel Dixon in 2007. He was sentenced to eight years in prison for conspiracy to commit violent disorder and wounding with intent. He was the first of a large number of gang members to be convicted for offences related to the failed ambush on the Palmers' house. The police work was finally beginning to pay off.

The court heard how Palmer had once been friends with Dixon; they had played football together as children and their relationship only began to sour when Edmonton and Tottenham developed their rivalry. Similarly to Norris Green and Croxteth in Liverpool, former friends were forced to oppose each other, for fear of being seen as traitors to their neighbourhood.

Shankstarz members Karl Christian-Law, Jerome Bruce-de-Roche and Aiden Palmer were given twenty-two-month sentences for violent disorder committed on the day of Dixon's stabbing. Others were ordered to do community service. The local law-enforcement agencies were doing everything in their power to restore peace to the streets of North London.

Later that year, former gang member Ken Hinds stepped in to try and broker a truce between the two factions. The fifty-year-old felt that young people might listen to him, as he had once thought as they did. However, there was only so much that Hinds could do: he couldn't bring the two sides together, as the situation was still volatile. The best he could do was act as a go-between, relaying messages between the senior figures on each side of the divide. Although his actions may have lessened the animosity between the groups, the conflict still remains unresolved. 'We stabbed up soooo many manz itz nuffin,' boast the Shankstarz on their MySpace page.

East London

THE EAST END has been notorious for vice and petty crime since even before the nineteenth century. A close-knit, densely populated area that has housed successive waves of immigrants, it has retained its criminal subculture throughout the decades. East London has produced more notorious gangland figures than perhaps any other area of the UK, from Dodger Mullins to Jack 'Spot' Comer to the Kray twins and beyond. Its 'old school' gangsters were typically involved in rackets such as protection, long-firm fraud, armed robbery and, in recent decades, the drugs trade.

The Beaumont Gang perhaps typify East London's 'new school' street gangs. In the late nineties, demand for cocaine, crack and heroin was on the rise. Their base, the Beaumont Estate in Leyton, is a drug hotspot, a large estate plagued by unemployment, teenage pregnancy and substance abuse. Before the drug epidemic, it was home to four brothers who specialised in armed 'blags'. They eventually turned their hands to drug dealing and put together a gang of street dealers to sell their wares.

According to a study by Professor John Pitts, of the University of Bedfordshire, in 2001 the Beaumont Gang linked with the Tottenham Man Dem, the Harlesden Crew and Hackney cliques the Love of Money Crew, the Holly Street Boys and

Mothers Square to form an alliance so formidable that it effectively kept the Jamaican Yardies out of much of East London and
made the Beaumont 'the major supplier of narcotics'.

By 2001 the gang was so powerful that none of the other
firms in their immediate area dared to oppose them. This
resulted in a degree of tranquillity on the estate. The burglary
rate was high as there was a constant ebb and flow of crack and
heroin addicts coming to and from the area but gun and knife
crime were relatively low, as there were few, if any, competing
gangs.

In 2002, the gang's status as the unopposed rulers of the
estate came to an abrupt end. One of their dealers was struck
with a bottle after a dispute with a smaller firm known as the
Oliver Close Gang (OCG), named after the Oliver Close
Estate, also in Leyton. They had harboured resentment against
the Beaumont Gang for some time as they felt that they had
muscled in on the narcotics business in their area. They
claimed that they had been robbed by one of their members
and immediately set about rallying round all of the smaller
drug crews to form an anti-Beaumont collective.

The Chingford Hall Boys were the first of these to ally
themselves with the OCG, as they saw an opportunity to gain
a foothold in the drug trade by teaming up and overthrowing
the Beaumont. Gradually, other gangs began to add their name
to the list. Selrack and the Hatch Man Dem pledged their allegiance after becoming frustrated with the power that the
criminals on the Beaumont Estate had over them. M-Block
from the Marconi Road area of Leyton and the BDG Bloods
from Leyton Grange quickly followed suit.

The alliance against the Beaumont Gang was known as Piff
City, 'piff' being the name of a particularly potent strain of
cannabis. Their membership quickly grew to around 100

soldiers, aged between ten and forty. Over time, they merged with a number of other smaller street gangs and grew to the point where they ranked equal with the Beaumont Gang in terms of the threat that they posed. A study conducted by the University of Bedfordshire in 2007 rated both gangs as 198 – the maximum score – on the Harm Assessment scale, a system set up to rate the risk posed by criminals. They were evenly matched: two titans of the drug game battling for supremacy.

Worryingly, the 'soldiers' who were often used to fight these battles were naïve young children with little or no comprehension of the consequences of their actions. One in ten perpetrators of gun-enabled crime in Waltham Forest, the London borough that Leyton falls within, are between the ages of one and ten. Only thirty per cent are over twenty-one. A staggering nineteen per cent of the victims are under eleven. It is a war that is being planned by men and fought by children.

In September 2006, students attending an IT course at the City Learning Centre College on Billet Road in Walthamstow reported that they were being intimidated by members of the Chingford Hall Boys, who claimed that the college was their territory. They stated that George Monoux College was also on their turf, whereas Waltham Forest College belonged to the Beaumont Gang. Waltham Forest College had already been the site of an alleged stabbing earlier that year after an altercation between the Oliver Close Gang and the DM Fam from the Drive and Marlowe estates in Walthamstow.

The DM Fam consists of thirty to forty members between the ages of fourteen and twenty. They came together as a result of a number of members defecting from other gangs to form a firm of their own. They have been implicated in a variety of different crimes, ranging from firearms to murder and they are ranked as one of the most dangerous gangs in the borough.

They are one of several firms that sprouted up after the emergence of Piff City. The fact that they were fighting with the Oliver Close Gang in a Beaumont-controlled area can be explained by their alliance with the Beaumont Gang. With such a powerful group of dealers as their friends, it would have been within their interests to make sure that no-one strayed onto their territory.

On October 26, 2007, a teenage boy was shot in the shoulder whilst talking with a friend on a street backing onto Marconi Road, the home of the Piff City affiliated M-Block gang. Fourteen-year-old Kevin Agyemang was waiting for a bus when a car pulled up alongside him and fired two shots in his direction. He was found by the police and rushed to hospital shortly after 11pm. Local residents stated that they believed the attack to be gang-related.

In August 2008, another group entered the fray, the Priory Court Grey Gang. The Grey Gang were originally neutral towards the Beaumont but the relationship soured over petty squabbles between members. They are a small gang with approximately thirty members but what they lack in numbers they make up for in firepower. Spouting bravado-ridden Americanised mottos ('snitches get stitches' and 'bang bang, all day on the block'), they are thought to be responsible for a number of violent street robberies across Walthamstow and Leyton.

Eighteen-year-old Charles 'CJ' Hendricks was friendly with certain members of the Beaumont Gang, although he shunned the criminal lifestyle, opting to pursue a trainee mechanic course instead. As far as the Grey Gang were concerned, he was one of 'them'. They bullied and intimidated him, attacking him with a metal pole, and he was forced to wear a stabproof vest for fear that he would be knifed.

Then early one Sunday morning, the tables turned. Four members of the Grey Gang found themselves on Beaumont territory on parkland near Walthamstow Central station, and they were confronted by some of Charles's more aggressive friends, angry at the way he had been victimised. Rather than back down, the Grey Gang readied themselves for combat. Charles was unaccustomed to gang violence and was therefore unprepared for what came next. In the resulting affray, he was stabbed in the chest.

Charles Hendricks died from his injuries. Later accounts indicated that his relationship with Beaumont members was one of friendship rather than gang affiliation. The killing drew widespread criticism even from East London's criminal fraternity, who frowned upon the idea of a civilian being attacked for being friends with members of one gang or another. The Grey Gang were completely unfazed by the others' opinions of them; it added to their ruthless image and gave them credibility amongst their peers. To them, it was a notch on their belts.

And so the streets of Waltham Forest are left in the midst of a three-way gang war: the Beamount Gang versus Piff City versus the Grey Gang, with all three having attacked one another at some point in the last few years. Whereas the borough was once 'run' by the Beaumont Gang, it is now a relative free-for-all, with various factions sprouting up all over Leyton, Walthamstow and Chingford. There are the Boundary Boys, an African guns-for-hire gang operating out of Manor Hall Gardens in Leyton; the Red African Devils, a largely Somali gang from Leyton High Road; and the gun-toting Can Hall Crew who have been implicated in numerous stabbings and the shooting of a policeman.

Although Waltham Forest has its fair share of problems, it is by no means the main area affected by gang-related violence.

It is home to thirteen known gangs, compared to twenty-two in the neighbouring borough of Hackney, indeed Hackney has the most independently operating street gangs of anywhere in London. It is little wonder that the surrounding areas are beginning to follow its example. In one twelve month period, 167 instances of gun crime were reported in Hackney compared to 139 in Waltham Forest, despite the latter borough housing approximately 11,000 more people. There were six homicides, whereas several of the more affluent boroughs had none.

Hackney is London's poorest borough. Sometimes referred to as 'Crackney' by the national media, it is a place where cocaine and heroin have invaded society, from the trendy wine bars of Hoxton and Shoreditch to the gritty back streets of Dalston and Clapton. For some within the borough, gangs are a way of life and drugs are the only available source of income.

The rate of violent crime in the area has increased dramatically over the past decade and there was a twenty-five per cent rise in gun crime in the borough between March 2009 and March 2010, a period that also saw 156 more violent crimes reported than in the previous year, with a small but significant percentage of them involving firearms. And like others elsewhere, the Hackney postcode gangs have adopted the 'gangsta' culture, calling themselves names like the 'P-Block' (a derivative of D-Block, a New York based gangster rap group) and the E5th Ridaz (a 'rider' being US street slang for an active gang member).

However, while American street gangs became infamous for shooting rival gang members in drive-bys from the windows of their cars, Hackney is the home of a very British phenomenon, the 'pedal-by'. Teenage gunmen ride up to their victims on pushbikes, open fire and then pedal off into the night.

Bikes are a speciality of the London Field Boys, an area-based gang who gained notoriety after the murder of fourteen-year-old schoolboy Shaquille 'Festa' Smith in August 2008. Shaquille was sitting on a park bench with his sister and his best friend when he was set upon and stabbed by a group of ten to fifteen gang members. They had ridden to the Pembury Estate in search of the P-Block firm but they were unable to find them and so they had decided to take their aggression out on a group of unsuspecting schoolchildren.

Shaquille's friend Tyrell was chased away with a knife so that the gang could focus their efforts upon him and his sister. They punched his sister and slashed her across the face and neck, angry at the fact that they had travelled all the way to the estate for nothing. Shaquille was punched, kicked and then stabbed in the stomach as he scrabbled in the bushes in a desperate attempt to get away.

Shaquille's sister shouted for his mother, hoping that the presence of an adult would bring an end to the attack. The Field Boys mounted their bikes and fled the scene, leaving their wounded victim's mother to find him lying in a pool of blood. She rang for an ambulance and pressed his wound with a towel in an attempt to stop the bleeding.

The teenager was rushed to the nearest hospital. At first it seemed like he was going to pull through. He woke up in the hospital bed demanding to see his baby sister and asking for some strawberry flavoured water. However at 7am that day, he died from his injuries, yet another young victim of a motiveless killing.

Six gang members were eventually jailed for Shaquille's murder. They swaggered into the courtroom, sticking up two fingers and making threatening gestures towards the public gallery. They seemed remarkably blasé throughout their trial and showed no remorse, fidgeting and whispering to each other the whole time. They even had to be transported to the courtroom separately after the prison service expressed concern that they might behave violently. The fact that they had taken a life meant nothing to them. One of them walked out of the dock in protest, throwing a childish tantrum at the fact that he was being punished for his actions.

Godiowe 'Saveloy' Dufeal and George 'Goodz' Amponsah received a minimum of eighteen years for their part in Shaquille's murder. Godiowc had been caught with a firearm four years earlier and he had only been out of prison a week at the time of the attack. Freddie 'Chips' Amponsah, Amisi 'Hidz' Khama, Kadean 'Littlz' Dias and Leon 'Kids' Atwell were given a shorter tariff of fifteen years, as they were below the age of eighteen when the crime was committed.

After the sentencing, a number of gang members attempted to attack Shaquille's family as they left the courthouse. The minute police turned up, they ran away. The judge aptly described them as 'cowards'.

In the wake of Shaquille's death, the various firms from the nearby estates swore revenge. Even though he had no gang affiliations, his murder was seen as a sign of disrespect towards the Pembury Estate, where he would regularly hang out with his friends. P-Block are part of a larger alliance known as E9 To 5, which includes B-Block from the Balance Road Estate in Homerton and the E9 Kingshold Boys from the New Kingshold Estate, also in Homerton. The Field Boys had made a lot of enemies and in June 2009, the head of the Kingshold Play Association claimed that children on the estate needed their own playground as they were too scared to venture into the London Fields Estate to use theirs. Tensions between the two groups were mounting.

The Field Boys were also wary of wandering into the New

Kingshold Estate, although it was the female members of the gang who were the most cautious. And they had good reason to be, as the Kingshold Boys have a disturbing history of gang rape, a crime carried out to demonstrate their power over those who disrespect them.

On April 30, 2007, a fourteen-year-old girl advised a friend to dump her boyfriend in a casual conversation. It was nothing personal; she simply didn't think that he was a good match for her. Unbeknown to her, the boy in question was a Kingshold Boy and he didn't take kindly to her advice. Furious that she had tried to turn his girlfriend against him, he vowed to get her back for what she had done. The next time he saw her, he tried to punch her but another youth intervened.

The following day, he saw her walking home from her cousin's house. This time he had three of his friends with him. He grabbed her in a headlock, slammed her up against a fence, then forced her into a block of flats on the nearby Parkside Estate. One of the gang produced a knife and told her that if she didn't perform a sex act on all four of them then he would use it on her. He pushed the blade against her throat. She was begging and pleading with them that she was a virgin and she didn't want to lose her virginity in a gang-rape.

The girl tried to run away but she was hit in the head and dragged along the road to another block of flats. She was crying and whimpering and clearly being manhandled but passers-by pretended they hadn't seen her. She was taken to the first floor of the flats, where she was raped. One of the boy's friends recorded the incident on his camera phone and the rest of the gang jeered and mocked her, telling her that she was a 'slag' for allowing herself to be raped.

Part way through the attack, a woman walked past the gang, oblivious to what was going on. The Kingshold Boys threw a coat over their half-naked victim and told her to keep quiet. When the coast was clear, they gave her permission to leave, although shortly afterwards, they changed their mind and ran after her, surrounding her and dragging her into a ten-storey tower block.

By this point, the four assailants were ringing their friends up and telling them to come down to the estate and watch. The girl was sobbing and pleading for them to leave her alone. Another woman walked past them and asked her if she was alright. She shook her head and the woman carried on walking, pretending not to register her response.

Soon nineteen youths were crammed onto the crowded landing, laughing and jeering and tugging at their victim's clothes. She recognised one of the boys and begged him to help her but he told her that he was 'with my boys' and a few minutes later, he was performing a sex act on her.

Hours later, an older gang member arrived on the scene and ordered the younger members to stop what they were doing. He helped the girl to break free and told his fellow Kingshold Boys how horrified he was at what they had done. Some things are frowned upon even by gang members.

The brave girl later identified nine of her attackers and they were all eventually convicted and jailed for what they had put her through. The youngest of them had been thirteen years old when the rape took place. Most unusually, the older gang member who had facilitated the girl's escape provided evidence against her attackers. He was clearly disgusted at what they had done to her and made an exception to the 'no snitching' rule so that he could put them behind bars.

It is ironic that the Kingshold Boys are so critical of the Field Boys for killing a fourteen-year-old boy when they have gang-raped a girl of the same age. Meanwhile, the Kingshold Boys are releasing boastful hiphop albums bragging about their crimes, as most of the London gangs appear to do. 'I sell crack plus I'm saving up to buy a big MAC, I've got these peng tings [girls] – laid 'em on their fucking back,' they rap.

Reported instances of rape in Hackney went up 6.5 per cent between February 2009 and February 2010. They rose by eighty-eight per cent in Waltham Forest and forty-four per cent in Tower Hamlets. It is little wonder that the areas with the largest gang populations have all suffered dramatic increases in this type of crime.

The gangs of East London portray themselves as fearsome street soldiers, but most of their victims are young and vulnerable. The limited ethics of the 'old school' gangsters have been replaced with a rejection of any comprehensible code of morality. Murders, rapes and sexual attacks are becoming increasingly commonplace. Whereas the streets of Hackney and Waltham Forest were once run by established gangland figures, they are now controlled by groups of feral children with no limits as to what they will do for respect.

Gone are the days when a firearm would be produced for a specific robbery and hidden away again afterwards. The streets of the capital are becoming increasingly infested with guns to the point where young men are carrying them as a matter of routine. From pockets of deprivation in otherwise affluent parts of West London to large expanses of underprivileged council housing in the South and the East of the city, the breeding grounds are fertile for crime and violence. Guns and knives are more than just a fashion statement, they are a means of gaining respect. Those who have nothing are able to take what they want and have something. For the youth of inner city London, they are the stepping-stone between being a nobody and being a somebody.

Derby

DERBYSHIRE IS A predominantly rural county, a far stretch from the sprawling inner-cities of Greater London or the soaring tower blocks of Strathclyde and Merseyside. The Derbyshire Constabulary website has a section reporting the number of sheep rustled, an indicator of the relatively low crime rate within the region (182 ewes and 220 lambs were stolen between January 2009 and January 2010).

Whilst the majority of the county that it falls within remains relatively crime-free, Derby itself is home to some tough estates with high rates of gun crime and drug abuse. Whereas cities such as Glasgow and Liverpool have seen most gang-related violence in traditionally 'white' areas, most of Derby's firms operate solely within the black community. Normanton has one of the worst problems with firearms, with youths from the area frequently clashing with those from the nearby Austin Estate.

Normanton is home to Derby's largest concentration of black and Asian residents, with sizeable Pakistani, Bangladeshi and Afro-Caribbean communities. Indeed fifty per cent of the city's ethnic minorities can be found in the locality, with more than 180 nationalities making it one of the UK's most culturally diverse areas. It also has the lowest paid workers, highest crime rate and one of the highest rates of prostitution in the country.

The Austin Estate in Sinfin is another low-income area with widespread unemployment and a burglary level that is twice the city's average. Although its population is almost four-fifths white, it is also home to the Browning Circle Terrorist Crip Set, a largely black street gangs.

The 'BCT' developed from a group of friends who hung out together in the Browning Circle area of the estate. When a teenage boy from Sinfin got into a fight with a member of a similar group from Normanton and Allenton, they immediately jumped to his defence. 'That's when younger people started saying they were A1 or BCT,' explained a member of the Normanton/Allenton faction. 'They would get into disputes and fight and eventually, everyone in the area joined the so-called A1 gang.'

Animosity between the two groups increased until there was a clear division between the two parts of the city. They took their gang 'colours' to a ridiculous degree: the A1 even started wearing purple shoelaces and the Crip Set wore blue and black. The local police force reported children as young as nine wearing A1 colours and chanting the name of the gang. Teachers at the local schools became aware of the tension in the area and started sending pupils home for wearing purple clothes. As the months went by, they progressed from fists to knives to 9mm pistols and automatic weapons. Soon the two sides were involved in regular shootouts, meeting up specifically to fight with one another.

It was during one of these organised confrontations that the first death occurred. Fifteen-year-old Kadeem 'Snipez' Blackwood, a member of the 'youth wing' of the BCT, was challenged to a fist-fight after allegedly disrespecting the mother of a senior A1 member. Blackwood weighed seventeen stone and was particularly well built. Knowing that he had no chance of beating him in a fair fight, Michael-Paul Hamblett-Sewell arranged for fellow gang member Callum Campbell to accompany him, and told him to bring a gun.

They were due to fight at Caxton Park, a recreation ground frequented by children in Sunny Hill. Blackwood was armed as well, although he had a knife instead of a gun.

'What's that for?' he asked, as a loaded shotgun was lowered towards his chest.

He was blasted to death.

Kadeem's murder was the first gang killing of its kind in Derby; until then, it had been seen as relatively peaceful in comparison to the likes of Nottingham and Birmingham. Hamblett-Sewell denied everything. He claimed that he had no idea that Campbell had brought a gun to the fight and said that he had left the gang six months before the shooting took place. Nevertheless he was found guilty of murder and sentenced to twenty-three years in prison. He remained emotionless throughout the trial, turning to his mother and shrugging nonchalantly as the verdict was read out.

Callum Campbell was given a shorter sentence of twenty-one years despite being the one who had pulled the trigger. He had acted under Hamblett-Sewell's orders, following the commands of a higher authority within the gang. Kadeem Blackwood's parents wept as the two men left the dock. No amount of jail time was going to bring back their son.

Derbyshire Police took a number of steps to ensure that the killing was a one-off. A special taskforce was set up and officers were sent to primary schools to warn children about the dangers of gang membership. The idea was that the pupils would be taught what the consequences of joining these groups were before it was too late. Targeted patrols were carried out in Allenton and Sinfin, aimed at reducing the amount of guns on the estates there. Until that point, Derby had been considered relatively gang-free. It took the death of a teenage boy to make the authorities sit up and take notice of what was going on.

The A1 continued to make a nuisance of themselves, selling drugs and fighting with other gangs across Allenton, Normanton and Sinfin. One member in particular struck fear into the community. Carlos Grant carried a firearm almost as a matter of principle. Even when he was partying with his friends, he had his gun on him – a state of affairs that would eventually lead to his downfall.

In May 2008, Frank Farrell was at a house party in Allenton when he was approached by Grant and two of his friends. They were in a belligerent mood and demanded to know why he wasn't drinking. They asked him why he was so quiet and they seemed to take offence at the fact that he was keeping himself to himself. Farrell was wary of the three men. He went outside to get away from them but they followed him and continued to intimidate him. He began to argue with them, asking why they refused to leave him alone. Part way through the argument, Grant leaned over to one of his friends and whispered something in his ear. His eager accomplice pulled out a gun and shot Farrell in the leg.

Farrell suffered a fractured thigh bone and was lucky to escape without worse injuries. His attackers fled the scene in a black Volkswagen Golf and drove to Stoke-on-Trent, where they spent the rest of the night. He was able to identify his assailants and they were later arrested and charged.

During the investigation, a number of incriminating photographs were found on gang member Jahvan Gibbons' mobile phone. They showed a group of youths waving guns in the air in what was described as an 'Al Qaeda fashion'. It was not the first time Gibbons had been in trouble with the law.

In August 2007, he was subject to an ASBO (anti-social behaviour order) after residents of a Sinfin housing estate complained about his behaviour. He was accused of intimidating children and vulnerable adults and throwing stones at a Community Watch patrol van. A petition of 119 signatures was handed to Derby Homes, the company responsible for the area's council housing, who gained an injunction against him banning him from parts of Sinfin.

Gibbons' involvement in the shooting is testimony to how vandalism and petty crime can escalate into violence. He was able to bully and harass an estate despite the fact that he was living in Littleover, a separate area of the city, at the time. He had travelled into Sinfin with the specific intention of causing trouble. What had started out as antisocial behaviour quickly progressed to gang crime. Within a two-year period, he went from throwing stones at a van to shooting an innocent man over a petty argument. Judge Hamilton described him as having an 'unhealthy fascination for firearms' and sentenced him to twenty years in prison.

Carlos Grant was found guilty of assisting an offender and possessing a firearm with intent to endanger life. He was given a minimum of nine years and ninety-five days behind bars. A third man, Caleb Alexander, was given six years for assisting an offender. As far as the police were concerned, three more A1 members were off the streets.

I managed to trace Jason, a longstanding member of the A1, and asked him how their activities have been affected by the increasing police attention. 'We're still going strong,' he claimed. 'Carlos was obviously one of the top guys. By him going to prison it just makes people stay in the gang more out of love for him and the rest who are lost in the system. It did cripple the money in the gang though so there weren't as many guns being used but it made the youngers [sic] work harder to be like him.

'We're allied with the 38 Estate from Sinfin now,' he went on. 'We see each other as one. Our top guy is close family with their top guy so we have linked up.' Now that the gang has a foothold in Sinfin, an area the BCT regard as their territory, the conflict between the two groups will no doubt increase even further. 'Well they're our enemies. Some of their youngers call themselves the YBCT – they are our enemies too. We've had a little dispute with A-Town from Alvaston but they're not really our enemies, just some of their people are.'

The 38 Estate gang wear red to signify their membership. They are divided by age, with the younger members of the group forming a separate subdivision known as the 38 Youngers. Their territory is a mere stonesthrow away from that of the BCT. A-Town are a multiracial firm with black, white and mixed race members. They have a reputation for firearms, after two of their members were caught with guns in their car at the site of an altercation outside a pub. They had the safety catches off, indicating that the guns were about to be used.

According to Jason, guns, knives, metal poles, rocks and baseball bats are all used on a regular basis. Derbyshire Police are trying hard to stem the tide of gangland violence in the city, with a number of succesful initiatives making it increasingly difficult for the youths to operate. But is it too little too late? Now that primary school children are claiming affiliation to either BCT or A1, what can be done to divert them from becoming active gang members?

'It has calmed down a bit,' Jason said. 'It could get mad real soon though. All their little friends are getting too happy and trying to start shit with us but it's all talk and no action. They're no threat to us. We showed them what it is...' Was he referring to Kadeem's death? 'Kadeem don't mean nothing to us,' he said flippantly, as if to clarify his exact meaning. 'We didn't really know him so why should we care? We care about Callum. He has spent most of his life in prison. We should kill another one of them pricks. We live a road [street] life. Why get the police involved? They make life hard for us.'

It is a sign of the ruthless nature of these individuals that they are more taken aback by a rival gang member talking to the police than they are at the death of a fifteen-year-old boy. 'If Callum didn't shoot Kadeem then he could have died,' Jason went on, attempting to justify his friend's actions. 'Kadeem had a knife but if he had used it, we wouldn't be talking like this because their whole squad would have got deaded. Their boy died and all they did was get jumpers saying R.I.P. Snipez. He thought he was Superman and that's why he got shot.'

The A1 gang remain unrepentant for their actions. As far as they are concerned, their victim deserved to die. 'He knew the consequences of living like he did,' Jason told me – although it is doubtful whether he actually did. Fifteen-year-olds are irrational and impulsive. They are prone to acting without thinking, driven by bravado and testosterone. When weapons are made available to those who are yet to reach adulthood, the consequences can be disastrous. The gangs of Allenton and Sinfin have no respect for the age of their victims. If they are old enough to bear arms then they are old enough to die.

Although Derby's postcode rivalries are very much in their infancy, they pose a growing threat to the youth of the estates in which they take place. Derby's gang problem is a recently occurring phenomenon. A city with no previous reputation for gang related violence can easily erupt into a sudden wave of bloodshed.

Wolverhampton

WOLVERHAMPTON IS ANOTHER Midlands city with a growing gang problem. During my time inside, I met a Midlands-based gangster serving a sentence for firearms possession. He had a tattoo of a gun on his arm, as if to illustrate the way he lived his life. 'My brother's serving a sentence for gang-related violence,' he told me. 'It's no joke in Wolves. The youths are wearing different colour rags and going on like Crips and Bloods. It's serious things.'

From what I gathered from other inmates on my wing, there were four main gangland areas within the city: Heath Town, Park Village, Whitmore Reans and Pendeford. These are all areas with large black and Asian populations. The Fire Town Crew from Heath Town are the city's best-known street gang, gaining infamy for the murder of twenty-one-year-old Marlon Morris in August 2008.

Heath Town is a large council estate to the north-east of the city with a total of forty-six different nationalities. Its unemployment figures are twice the national average and roughly half of the residents have no qualifications. It is typical of the type of surroundings that gangs spring up from.

The Fire Town Crew have been fighting with the Pendeford Crew for the past few years. Although little is known about the source of the feud, they are both involved in drug dealing and so it is most probably a turf war. Jamie 'Goldie' Price, the son of drum'n'bass DJ Goldie, is a high-ranking member of the gang.

Goldie senior was absent for much of Jamie's early life. He has since stated that he had to move away and abandon him for his own safety, as he could no longer survive on the estate where he had grown up. He claims that he would either be on drugs or involved in a life of crime if he had stayed put where he was. Unfortunately, the lack of parental guidance took its toll. His son became involved in a life of gangland violence, culminating in the loss of a young man's life.

Jamie was protective of his fellow gang members. He wasn't one to stand back and watch them being attacked without going to their aid. He was particularly infuriated when he learned that one of his close buddies had been chased through the city centre by the Pendeford Crew. Luckily his friend had managed to get away but it was still a clear declaration of war. After a brief confrontation with the gang outside a takeaway shop, he was alleged to have taken out a knife and stabbed disabled gang member Marlon Morris in his heart, liver and back. A group of men were seen fleeing the area in a small, red car, followed by the Pendeford gang who were chasing them on foot. 'Fire? I will bring fire!' shouted a Fire Town gang member, leaning out of the door to shout abuse at his rivals as they drove off into the night.

Morris had suffered a disabling injury to his left arm in a biking accident and had no chance of defending himself. He had no injuries to his hands, suggesting that he made no attempt to protect himself. His fellow gang members accompanied him to the hospital but refused to cooperate with staff. They told them that they were unwilling to reveal their friend's identity and seemed more concerned with protecting his freedom than they were about protecting his life.

Marlon Morris died from the stab wound to his heart.

Goldie was devastated. He knew Marlon's father from back when he had lived in Wolverhampton and he found it hard to come to terms with the fact that his son was a killer. He later told the press that he had done everything within his power to change the path that Jamie's life was heading along. He had offered for him to come and live with him and told him that he would pay for anything that he wanted to do. Unfortunately, no amount of money could make up for the years of absence during his son's early life and Jamie Price was now facing the consequences.

In order to shed some light upon the origins of the conflict that had led to Marlon's death, I managed to get in touch with a high-ranking Fire Town Crew member who was willing to talk to me over the phone. He spoke with a strong Black Country accent, with a slight hint of Jamaican patois thrown in every now and again, and he seemed apprehensive about telling me anything that could possibly identify him. 'It's against the codes talking to man dem outside the circle,' he said. 'I could get myself into a lot of trouble doing this.

'Firetown is just the name that we give to our area,' explained 'Davey', not his real name. 'It didn't start off as a gang. We didn't think of ourselves as a gang until the media started calling us one. Firetown was originally just a group of friends from the same estate who would defend our area against outsiders. To cut a long story short, a couple of man from Heath Town ended up falling out with a few man from Pendeford and then everybody else started getting involved. One thing led to another and then, bam, there's people getting shot and bare madness going on. I personally would have preferred for none of this to have ever happened. There's no need for any of this. It brings it on top for us.'

Newspaper articles had portrayed the conflict as a battle over drug turf, but he denied this.

'Nah, nothing like that. It started off as something minor and it just built up over time. Some of the man dem do sell drugs but everybody is their own person. We've all got our own little raises that we do. Some are into shotting [selling drugs], some are into sticking up dealers and some are working regular nine to five jobs. Whatever it takes to get by. Everybody's got their own personal limits of what they will or won't do for money. Me personally I've sold drugs before and I've stolen cars but I don't do either at the moment. The only crime that I'm guilty of right now is backing my bredrins [friends] up if push comes to shove.'

'What would you be willing to do to back somebody up?' I asked, attempting to gauge the extent of his dedication to his friends within the gang.

'Whatever it takes,' he replied. 'Usually it's not guns and things like that though, it's normally kicking in doors of people who have tried to take liberties. If you take somebody by surprise you don't need no straps with you, you can go in with bats and CS gas and that's all you need. If it's somebody who's well connected, you might need to have a strap [gun] on you though. It depends on what type of trouble your peoples is involved in.

'Shooters are a last resort. They're a lot of work. You shoot somebody then there's a good chance that you're going to end up killing them and getting lifed off, even if you do them through the leg. You have to pick up the shells as well and then you have to make sure you clean all of the gun powder residue off yourself. If you don't know what you're doing then you could very easily land yourself in prison. Also if you buy a gun that's got bodies on it you can end up getting sent down for something you haven't even been involved in. It's not like it is in the movies where you can shoot somebody and walk away as if nothing's happened.'

He said different makes of gun were easy to acquire.

'Anything that you can get in Brum you can get in Wolves. We're only a stone's throw away so it's the same as there, really. Most people have got nine millis, they're small and they're easy to conceal. There's a lot of converted guns going around. Some of them are death traps. They'll blow your fucking fingers off when you come to use them. Some people have MAC-10s and things like that but they're the people that have been watching *Scarface* too many times. They're hard to aim and they're expensive. The ammunition is expensive too and it's difficult to get hold of.'

So did he think that the feud with the Pendeford Crew would escalate to the point where there would be shootings going on now that a life had been lost?

'Well what do you think?' he said. 'Yeah, things are going to be at the next level now. They're not going to let something like that lie. How can you? If one of your boys has died, you're going to want to get revenge. There will probably be more people getting killed and more people getting lifed off over the next few years.'

Jamie Price's first trial for murder collapsed after a dispute over CCTV evidence and a retrial was ordered, to be held at Nottingham Crown Court. In September 2010, Price, aged twenty-three, was convicted and jailed for life. 'The background here is gang culture,' said Judge John Milmo QC. 'The refusal of gangs to accept the law of the land, coupled with the desire to impose their own anarchic ways, cannot be tolerated by society. In a case of this kind there are no winners, only losers. Everyone involved here has lost and lost in a very significant sense, whether the sentence is one of life or one of death.'

HEATH TOWN HAS been the scene of several high-profile murders, shootings and robberies in recent years and the Fire

Town Crew are one of several criminal groups that have sprung up on the estate. Although Marlon's stabbing gave them a degree of notoriety, they are not the only gang in the area to have a murder to their name. The Demolition Crew are responsible for a killing that the press likened to a scene from a mafia movie, a gangland execution carried out with a level of professionalism akin to that of a career hitman.

The Demolition Crew started a trend of transporting crack and heroin up to Scotland. A rock of crack that sells for £20 in Wolverhampton might fetch £50 in Aberdeen. The problem was that as soon as the word spread about how much money they were making, a host of other Midlands-based criminals wanted in on the action. The Demolition Crew didn't mind sharing territory with those who they were friendly with. They were connected to a West Bromwich-based gang known as the Raiders, who also had strong links to the Birmingham-based Johnson Crew, and were happy to share their spoils. Both groups would sell drugs side by side without the need for violence.

The problems arose when Kevin Nunes, a Yardie drug dealer from Whitmore Reans, attempted to muscle in on the two gangs' territories. Raiders member Adam 'Chopper' Joof demanded a response. Chopper was a dangerous man, dubbed 'The Godfather' by the media on account of the level of control that he exacted over the rest of the firm. He was earning an estimated £40,000 a week and he was enraged at the fact that another dealer was eating into his profits.

Michael Osbourne was equally concerned about Nunes. He was the leader of the Demolition Crew and felt that only his fellow gang members and their allies should be selling on his turf. What if the rest of the city were to start bringing their drugs across to Scotland? The value would decrease and they would lose out on their cash cow. Something had to be done.

Osbourne thought nothing of killing. He had already been implicated in an attempted murder in which a man was shot in his abdomen at a block of flats in Heath Town. A subsequent trial collapsed, sparking claims that the witnesses were too afraid to give evidence. Chopper was the perfect partner for him and they both commanded fearsome drug crews. And so the two gangs joined forces in a concerted effort to prevent Nunes from gaining a foothold in Aberdeen. Osbourne set about recruiting Owen Crooks, Nunes' best friend, and a plan was hatched with the intention of retiring him on a permanent basis.

On 19 September 2002, Crooks delivered his former friend to Joof and his gang, tricking him into a car and driving him to Glentworth Gardens in Whitmore Reans. It was the ultimate act of betrayal. Once he had reached his destination, Nunes was forced at gunpoint along Bridgnorth Road towards Shipley. He was taken to the Fox Inn pub, where Chopper and his associates were waiting.

The terrified drug dealer was then bundled into the back of a car and driven to a secluded country road in Pattingham, Staffordshire. He was dragged out of the car by his collar and shot five times in his leg, chest and arm. The gang buried their weapons and went back to selling drugs as they had done before. As far as they were concerned, there had been a momentary threat to their livelihood but it was now officially dealt with.

Five men were eventually jailed for their part in the killing. Adam 'Chopper' Joof and Antonio 'A1' Christie were sentenced to a minimum of twenty-eight years. The judge described Joof as a 'danger to society'. Owen Crooks, Wolverhampton's very own Judas, was given a minimum sentence of twenty-five years. Michael Osbourne was told to serve a minimum of twenty-seven years. The fifth man, Levi Walker, was already serving a life sentence for the murder of twenty-year-old soldier Narel Sharpe, who he shot for refusing to relinquish a gold chain during a street robbery in September 2004.

Simeon Taylor had driven the car that was used in the abduction. He denied any involvement in the murder, claiming that he was oblivious to what was going to happen once the vehicle had reached its destination. He was placed on the witness protection programme and agreed to testify against the five gang members, although he complained bitterly about the 'pittance' of £20-a-day living expenses that he was given and requested a laptop computer and some DJ equipment to stop him from being bored.

Taylor told the court that Christie had ordered him to shoot Nunes but that Joof had intervened and prevented him from having to go ahead with it. He was deemed to have had no part in the killing and allowed to walk free.

The media attention surrounding Osbourne's conviction brought about a crackdown on gang activities throughout the city. Steps were taken to prevent another gangland execution from taking place. Police intelligence revealed that at least three bars in the city were being used as unofficial gang headquarters. The Moscow Bar on Darlington Street was highlighted as a specific gang hotspot. A police report revealed that revellers were seen wearing stab-proof vests and that there had been a brawl with knives involving twenty drunken men.

In an effort to disrupt the activities of the various gang members that frequented the bar, the police subjected it to intense scrutiny. They imposed a set of thirteen conditions on the owners and told them that the venue would be shut down if they failed to uphold them. Metal detectors were installed at the entrance and the staff were made to keep a record of any incidents that occurred during their presence. The premises were identified as 'high risk' and glasses and bottles were banned in favour of plastic cups.

The Waggon and Horses in Park Village was identified as another gang rendezvous. Park Village gained notoriety after being featured in the local papers as the home of two of the city's youngest ASBO receivers. Ricky and Daniel Oakley, aged eleven and twelve respectively, terrorised the local residents with stones and knives and hurled racist abuse at anyone who stood in their way.

The Waggon and Horses faced complaints that gangsters and drug dealers had taken over the venue, holding all-night parties and smoking cannabis in full view of the management. There were reports of firearms being brandished inside the pub and a woman claimed to have had a gun put to her head. The premises saw a number of violent incidents in the lead up to their closure. Thirty people tried to rush the doors resulting in a mass riot, guns were discharged on several occasions and hard drugs and a firearm were found close by. On 20 July 2008, a forty-seven-year-old man was shot in the body three times outside the pub. Though he survived, it was the final straw. Local residents started a petition to have the place shut down. The Wolverhampton licensing sub-committee were sympathetic to their concerns and ordered that the venue be shut down to prevent further disruption from taking place.

The Wolverhampton CID Urban Street Gang Unit made seventy-three gang-related arrests in eighteen months. That is either a sign of how effective they are at doing their job or a worrying indicator of how many criminals are members of gangs – or both. The police claim that there are only around 150 people involved in serious gang activity in the city, but if there are seventy-three arrests being made every eighteen months, the figures don't add up. The police are either catching just under half of all gang members or they are grossly under-estimating the problem.

For a city of its size, Wolverhampton has a disturbingly large amount of gang activity. However, as one city councillor accurately stated, 'Gun crime and the use of firearms is not just a problem for Wolverhampton it is a problem for every city/town in the country.' What is going on in Heath Town and Whitmore Reans is typical of what is going on in areas all over the country. The only remarkable feature of Wolverhampton's gangs is their desire to extend their territory beyond the city limits.

An investigation conducted in 2003 into drug dealing in the north-east of Scotland revealed that there were as many as nine different groups from Wolverhampton operating there. As well as setting up shop in Aberdeen, they were also beginning to peddle crack and heroin in the smaller fishing towns in the surrounding areas. Fraserburgh and Peterhead transformed from peaceful coastal towns to the scene of slashings, robberies and aggravated burglaries as hard drugs began to infiltrate rural Scotland.

Whilst Joof and Osbourne were hatching their plan to kidnap Nunes, there were countless other firms encroaching upon their territory. They were wasting their time picking off individual drug dealers; by that stage it was common knowledge that the north-east of Scotland was a lucrative market for crack and heroin and countless other criminals were wanting in on it.

The Flava gang were at the forefront of Scotland's Black Country invasion. They were atypical in that they stayed put in Wolverhampton and only travelled to Scotland when they needed to make a sale. They were another gang operating out of Whitmore Reans, spending most of their time living in Glentworth Gardens, the estate that Nunes had originally been driven to by Crooks. They were selling large amounts of crack and heroin, renting a flat in Abderdeen and taking it in turns to stay there. Rather than run the risk of selling out of their own accommodation, they kept all of their merchandise at the addresses of local addicts who were paid to store piles of narcotics in their houses. They ran a sophisticated operation. Addicts would be used as runners, making deliveries and collecting their money for them so that they never had to meet any of their clients face to face.

Flava were making an estimated £6,000 a day and stashing their drugs in parks and other public areas, including the grounds of the Royal Cornhill Hospital. Any customers that the gang were unfamiliar with were treated with the utmost suspicion. They were required to either have a 'reference' provided for them by another known drug user or answer a series of interrogation-style questions.

In spite of their increased efforts to avoid detection, eight key figures within the group were eventually jailed after a major police operation. They were placed under twenty-four-hour surveillance, despite having set up cameras of their own to warn them of police activity. Richard 'Junior' Brown and Jason 'Rudy' Zajaz were sentenced to three years and nine months behind bars. Brown claimed that he had been recruited to the firm after getting himself into a large amount of debt over crack cocaine. Zajaz gave a similar story, saying that he was a mere 'footsoldier' and that he was trying to work off a large sum of money that he owed.

Justin Bennett was given eight years, Shane Lane was given six years and five months, Darrell Mapp was given five years and eight months, Paul Green was given five years and seven months, Jamie Hill was given five years and three months and Elton Whitter received four years and nine months. Two local drug addicts, used as runners for the gang, were jailed for four years and nine months. They were paid for their services in narcotics and received none of the profits from the drugs that they sold.

According to the local police force, Flava were 'the biggest crack dealers in Aberdeen'. They hadn't used their real names for the whole time that they were north of the border, referring to themselves solely by aliases. They did everything within their power to avoid detection but in the end the Grampian Police force got the better of them. But with a number of Wolverhampton-based crime groups still making the journey over into Scotland to sell their wares, the battle is yet to be won.

Gangsters from Wolverhampton continue to exploit the high prices for crack and heroin in Aberdeen and the surrounding areas. Between 2004 and 2009, sixty-one people from Wolverhampton were charged in connection with drug offences in the Scottish city. In August 2009, three Wolverhampton drug dealers were arrested after attempting to throw £88,000 worth of crack and heroin out of a car window. They were thought to be selling their product in Aberdeenshire. In October the same year, an arrest warrant was issued for another Wolverhampton criminal who was suspected of selling class A drugs in the county. In February 2010, Mathew Seddon was given an ASBO banning him from Aberdeen after he was suspected of bringing drugs across from Wolverhampton. Midlands drug cartels have established a firm hold on the city's narcotics trade, travelling 400 miles to pollute the streets with hard drugs.

Aberdeen isn't the only city that has been invaded by Midlands gangsters. In June 2008, two Wolverhampton-based drug dealers were caught selling crack and heroin in the Welsh seaside town of Aberystwyth. There have also been reports of Black Country firms delivering drugs to Edinburgh. The willingness of the city's drug gangs to travel hundreds of miles to sell their wares means that turf wars are often transferred to smaller towns where drugs are seen as less of a problem. The police in Wolverhampton may have the facilities to deal with gun-wielding gang members. The same cannot be said for Aberystwyth.

The gangs of Wolverhampton have established themselves as major drug suppliers to towns and cities across the UK. They have negated the need to operate from a specific geographical location, choosing to sell their merchandise from wherever they can earn the most money. 'Why sell in Wolves where the beast [police] are on you?' an incarcerated crack dealer from the city explained to me. 'You go to Aberdeen and you don't get any hassle. They aren't at you like they are in the ends, the coppers there don't know you.'

If law-abiding citizens are willing to relocate for better job prospects then it is logical for criminals to commute to places where they can sell their drugs at a higher value. This means that areas where crack and heroin are relatively rare are becoming prime targets for money-hungry drug dealers, as they can gain a monopoly upon the market there. It is a worrying development in the trade. Places where addicts were once few are now becoming riddled with them, and Wolverhampton-based criminals are very much at the forefront of what is going on. Midlands drug cartels are gradually extending their tentacles across the country – and one city in particular is giving Wolverhampton a run for its money.

Birmingham

A SURVEY CARRIED out in 2006 revealed that the West Midlands police area had six of the ten worst areas for firearms incidents. Birmingham city centre was the worst of the bunch: there was one incident for every 207 residents. If London is the capital of gun-enabled crime then Birmingham is a close second. The Labour Government spent £38 million tackling gangs in the city – but has it been money well spent?

Taking their lead from the likes of the Flava gang and the Demolition Crew, Birmingham's drug crews have taken to expanding their operations to towns and cities where they are less known to the police. Whilst I was in HMP Wolds, I met a former Birmingham gang member who had been selling crack and heroin to the residents of a small village in rural Shropshire. 'You don't need a lot of cats,' he told me. 'Maybe like ten of them who will buy some of both every day and then you're laughing.' Asian gangs from the city have been known to travel to Cardiff and Newport, and in 2002 an operation was set up aimed at stopping Birmingham and Bristol-based Yardies from selling in Gwent in South Wales and Dyfed and Powys in North Wales. Just as Wolverhampton-based criminals have infiltrated the drug supply for Aberdeenshire, the dealers from Birmingham are focussing their efforts upon Wales and the surrounding areas.

However, even the most deprived parts of Shropshire and Gwent cannot match the levels of crack and heroin abuse in Birmingham districts such as Lozells and Handsworth. With such a lucrative market on their own doorstep, most of the city's dealers stay right where they are. And they sell cheap. In September 2007, the charity Drugscope reported that the ecstasy in the city had such a low MDMA content that users were turning to hallucinogens instead. Birmingham is the home of massively diluted but ultimately inexpensive narcotics. It is also the home of two of the country's most notorious street gangs, competing for control of the city's cut-price drugs.

In late 2009, critically acclaimed film-maker Penny Woodcock released a controversial gangster film, *1 Day*, based on real-life events. It featured shootouts, drug deals and black youths clad in coloured headscarves. It was set in Birmingham and based upon two real gangs: the Johnson Crew and the Burger Bar Boys. Cinema chains across the city refused to show the film for fear of gang members turning up to the screenings.

The feud between the Johnsons and the Burgers has been going on for well over a decade and has its roots in the distribution of crack and heroin. The two firms were originally part of the same scene, a wide circle of disenchanted young black men who had been prominent in the 1985 Handsworth riots and who often met up at a fast-food restaurant in Lozells. The original Johnson Crew, named after the Johnson Café, was believed to have been set up by forklift truck driver Arthur 'Super D' Ellis. They claimed to protect the black community from far-right groups and racism.

By the late eighties, the Johnsons had abandoned any pretensions of vigilantism and concentrated their efforts on making money. Drugs were big business and they were mostly unemployed and lacking in any formal qualifications. They soon controlled the majority of the city's crack cocaine trade and began to intimidate nightclub owners into paying their members to act as security.

At first they co-existed with the newer Burger Bar Boys, named for a fastfood outlet in Soho Road. Even though the Johnsons regarded their manor as Aston, Erdington and Lozells, while the Burgers claimed Handsworth, Perry Barr and Ladywood, there was little tension between the two and each could move freely in the other's territory. In fact their rivals were not each other but violent Jamaican Yardies who had appeared in the city in the 1980s and who treated the local Brummies – known as homeboys – with contempt.

According to one gang member interviewed by the *Sunday Mercury*, 'The Yardies were running the city and were using us local-born lads to do their dirty work on the streets. They were bullying and intimidating everyone, making youngsters commit – and then take the rap for – their crimes. When the Yardies first came, a lot of us were in awe of them and wanted to be like them. They wore flash jewellery and drove fast cars. They were like role models for us but the relationship soon turned sour.'

Eventually the locals hit back to reclaim their city. The catalyst came in early 1993 when a leading member of the Johnson Crew known as Little Mikey was humiliated and shot as he left a Handsworth club. He had been dancing when he trod on the toes of a notorious Yardie, who later approached him outside and pulled a gun.

'There was no arguing, no shouting. He just pulled the trigger and shot Mikey in the body, and then began laughing while cursing him in patois,' recalled a witness. 'Most of us made a run for it straight away but a few of us hid nearby so that we could pick Mikey up when he left. As Mikey was lying on the ground the Yardie stood over him and pointed the gun at his head. Mikey had screwed his body up into a ball and was wriggling on the floor. His head was covered up by his arms and that is what probably saved his life in the end.

'The Yardie fired two shots and then coolly walked away back to his mates like it was nothing. Luckily for Mikey, he had moved at the last second and the bullet had grazed his neck and hand. It was a major turning point for the local boys. They'd had enough and they began to fight back.'

The Yardies now became a target, particularly for the Johnson Crew, culminating in the murder of Birmingham DJ Jason Wharton, shot dead in his car in Handsworth apparently because he had been seen mixing with Yardies. Another DJ, President Sas, was shot in the leg after he was accused of being a Yardie.

In 1997, police arrested high-ranking members of the Johnson Crew and the ensuing court case was Birmingham's first major gangland trial. Several leading members were convicted. But the war with the Yardies had been merely a curtain-raiser for what then followed.

The Johnson Crew and the Burger Bar Boys now fell out. Over the years, they had been growing cooler with each other. Now former friends became worst enemies.

Arthur Ellis himself had grown out of the gang lifestyle, although his violent tendencies were hard to leave behind. In 1994, he was convicted of manslaughter after fatally stabbing a love rival. During his time inside, however, his sons Marcus and Nathaniel both became involved in gangs. Marcus joined the Burgers and Nathaniel joined the Johnsons. His son Michael remained neutral, although he was close friends with a number of the Johnsons.

The first blood in what would become Birmingham's most

notorious gang war was the murder of Corey Allen in 1999. Allen was reputed to be a senior figure within the Burger Bar Boys. He made the mistake of attempting to leave the gang, sparking rumours that he was passing on information to the Johnsons. He was shot with his own shotgun outside a community centre in Handsworth. A subsequent trial collapsed after key witnesses began to mysteriously retract their statements. The Burgers took this as an indicator of their untouchable status. They could kill a man and get away with it simply by applying pressure to anybody who was likely to open their mouth.

And so began the murderous spiral of tit-for-tat killings. By the start of the new century, West Midlands Police's rate of armed call-outs rose to be the second highest in the country. There were stabbings and slashings on an almost weekly basis. And in the midst of the violence, two names cropped up over and over again: Yohanne and Nathan Martin.

The Martin brothers had done well for themselves. They owned their own promotional business, Dynamite Entertainment, booking comedians and musical acts and making a healthy profit from their shows. They were also allegedly involved in the drug trade. They were both senior members of the Burger Bar Boys and neither brother was a stranger to crime.

Yohanne was implicated in the murder of twenty-two-year-old Christopher Clarke, a man with Johnson Crew links, in March 2000. Clarke was punched, kicked and stabbed until he was unable to get up. Once again, the case collapsed after witnesses were too afraid to testify.

Two years later, Johnson Crew affiliate Ashi Walker was blasted with a machine gun. His death was soon avenged.

On 6 December, 2002, Yohanne Martin hired a Mercedes SLK and took it to West Bromwich to show it off to friends. He was sitting in the car outside a restaurant when a BMW pulled up alongside him. Six shots were fired, two of them hitting him in the head. He died instantly. He had avoided legal retribution for Clarke's murder but the Johnsons were less reliant upon evidence. As far as they were concerned, if there was even the smallest chance that he had been involved in the killing then he deserved to go.

A post-mortem revealed that it was not the first time that Yohanne had been shot. He had lived a short yet ultimately destructive life, throwing himself wholeheartedly into an existence centred around guns and gangs. One of his killers was a well-known member of the Raiders, the West Bromwich based firm that Adam Joof had once led. She was also an eighteen-year-old girl.

The Raiders have a business arrangement with the Johnson Crew and demonstrated the strength of the bond between the two groups by killing Yohanne on their behalf. Chantella Falconer was one of the few female gunmen within the gang. She carried out a gangland hit upon a man that she barely knew, aided by two male accomplices. Judge Justice Hughes described the killing as 'clinical and merciless'. It changed the way that female gang members were perceived. The taboos surrounding killing them were removed. If they were going to act like men then they would be treated like men.

Nathan Martin, by this time a seasoned criminal with a total of six convictions ranging from attempted robbery to escaping police custody, was furious. Although it was the Raiders that had carried out the hit, he directed the brunt of his hatred towards the Johnsons, who were an easier target: their members lived closer to him and he knew which pubs and clubs they frequented. He set about recruiting a hit squad to kill a member of their gang as payback for his brother's death.

By this stage, Marcus 'E-Man' Ellis was the second-in-command. He had four convictions, including one for violent disorder in connection with Christopher Clarke's murder in 2001. He was in charge of collecting the weapons needed for the killing.

Michael 'Chunks' Gregory was given the task of driving the car. He was Nathan's best friend and his sister was the mother of Yohanne's child. Unlike the rest of the gang, he had no previous convictions and he had just applied for a loan from the Prince's Trust to set up his own car-washing business. It is likely that he took part in the murder to avenge his friend's death rather than out of loyalty to the Burgers.

Nathan sent two of his associates, one black and one Asian, to buy the car. They bought a Ford Mondeo from a Northampton car dealer. Anthony Hill, a member of staff at the dealership, told the police that there were a number of factors that stood out about them. They had told him that they had travelled down from Birmingham but yet they appeared to have no car. It was parked out of sight to avoid anyone seeing it and using it to identify them. They handed over £1,850 without asking for a test-drive and their mobile phones rang continuously while they were there.

Hill was suspicious of the two men and asked them what they did for a living. They didn't answer. They had brought just enough money to buy the car with, neglecting the fact that they would need some left over for petrol. He gave them £10 back and they sped off back to Birmingham, closely followed by Nathan's silver Vauxhall Vectra.

Rodrigo 'Sonny' Simms was the final member of the hit squad. It was his job to act as a spotter, going along to the New Year's Eve party that the Johnsons were attending and reporting back to Nathan at regular intervals. He was a spy in the midst of the enemy.

Meanwhile, Marcus Ellis's half-sisters, Charlene and Sophie, were standing outside the Uniseven Salon in Aston. They were with their cousin Cheryl and their friend Letisha Shakespeare. There was a party going on inside but it was too hot for them and they had come out to get a breath of fresh air. There was a strange atmosphere in the salon. It was unlike any party they had been to before; there was an unmistakeable air of tension. It was as if it could go off at any time.

Nathan and Ellis were planning on shooting Jermaine 'Wooly' Carty, an aspiring rapper and alleged member of the Johnson Crew. He was thought to have publicly mocked Ellis at the Rosie O'Brien's nightclub in Solihull earlier that night. Armed with a MAC-10 and a Spanish Llama 9mm pistol, Martin and Ellis leaned out of the window of their Mondeo and fired a number of shots in Wooly's diection. Whereas Ellis was aiming at their pre-selected target, Martin sprayed bullets randomly into the crowd of partygoers. He was well aware that most of the people he was shooting at were women.

The eighteen-year-old Charlene Ellis was the first to get hit. The first bullet buried itself deep into her left arm, the second shot struck her in the shoulder and the third hit her in the face before embedding in her brain.

Her friend Letisha, aged seventeen, was shot in both arms, her pelvis and her chest. One of the shots went straight through her heart and her lungs and came out of her back. Cheryl put her hands up to protect her face. She was shot in the hand but managed to run away. Sophie was hit in the arm and chest.

Michael Ellis was asleep at the time of the killing. He was woken up by a phone call from Wooly telling him that his sisters had been shot. 'It was the Burgers,' he was told. Ellis rushed to the salon and accompanied his surviving sister to the hospital, where she was given a life-saving operation. As the medical staff did their best to treat her injuries, he rang the only member of the Burger Bar Boys that he was in regular contact with, his half-brother Marcus.

Marcus hung up. He was able to shoot a group of defence-less partygoers but he was less capable of facing up to what he had done. Michael rang him again a few hours later to inform him that Charlene was dead. Once again, he hung up – and went on the run. He cut off all contact with his family and went into hiding, hoping to avoid both the police and the Johnsons, who would inevitably be looking for him.

The police recovered forty separate cars for forensic analysis and interviewed one thousand three hundred different witnesses. They were determined to catch the killers before they stuck again. The only way that they could get any of the witnesses to testify was by assuring them that their identities would be kept secret. They were allowed to give their state-ments behind a special screen, using voice distortion equipment to ensure that they remained completely anony-mous.

After a long, drawn out court case, Ellis, Martin, Simms and Gregory were all found guilty of murder and sentenced to life behind bars. Tafarwa Beckford, the step-brother of R&B singer Jamelia, was cleared of all charges.

On 1 August 2003, the police received reports of shots being fired outside a block of flats on Lodge Road in Winson Green. A Vauxhall Vectra and an Audi 80 pulled up alongside Tafarwa Beckford and opened fire. He was hit in the head and driven to hospital, where he recovered. The attempt on his life gave a clear message that the Johnson Crew was out for revenge.

The violence shown in the film *1 Day* is a reflection of the real-life conflict on the streets of Birmingham. The cinemas had good reason to be cautious. Members of both gangs are still very much at large and they are baying for each other's blood. Asked if the conflict would ever end, one source told the *Sunday Mercury*, 'Only if science can manage to bring the dead back. Because these guys aren't ever going to forget the loved ones already lost in this war.'

THERE WERE 556 gun-related incidents in Birmingham between 2008 and 2009. Although the rate of firearms offences has slowly declined, the Johnsons and the Burgers are still very much at war. 'It's worse than ever,' a source close to the two gangs informed me. 'There may not be as many shootings but there's more division amongst the youth. Kids are claiming either Johnnies or Burgers without even knowing the origins of it all. Then you've got beef between different sets of the Burgers; it's not just one gang any more, it's split up into lots of different cliques.'

Out of a single firm came a plethora of different subsets. Arthur Ellis's original Johnson Crew divided into two separate factions, which in turn divided into a number of smaller gangs. The Burger Bar Boys gave rise to the Handsworth Town Crooks, the Blood Brothers, the Ghetto Hustla Boys, the Raleigh Close Crew, the Small Heath Mans and Birmingham's Most Wanted. The Birmingham police force claim to be on the verge of eradicating gang crime but in reality, the gangs have ripped themselves apart through internal power struggles. They have destroyed the unity that existed within the two original cliques.

So what does founding member Arthur 'Super D' Ellis make of his creation? It has torn his family apart. One of his sons is serving a life sentence and his daughter and her friend are now dead. He is now a born-again Christian and he has renounced the life that he once led, urging anyone who is considering joining a gang to think hard about whether it is what they really want to do. With their original leader denouncing their organisation, the Johnsons are left with even less purpose. They are soldiers without a cause, fighting in a war that has no foreseeable end. The Johnsons and the Burgers are symptomatic of a generation of disaffected youth who crave the power and status that they have been denied by society. Fuelled by a hunger for fear and respect, they continue to wage war.

Birmingham's gang problem is far from over. Although the names of the gangs have changed over time, their overall aim has remained the same: the acquisition of power within a world where they have none.

WHEREAS THE JOHNSONS and the Burgers used to be the only gangs in the city that made the headlines, two new names have entered the public consciousness in recent years: the Slash Crew and Bang Bang. The rivalry that exists between them is thought to stem from the fact that the latter are an offshoot of the Burger Bar Boys whereas the former are affiliated with the Johnson Crew, although the two factions are also split along racial and cultural lines. Most of the Slash, also known as the Slash For Money Crew, are black, whereas Bang Bang tend to have more Asian members. This has led to them being nicknamed the 'Bang Bang Taliban', a title that several of the gang's members have recently embraced, with some of them even claiming to harbour an extremist agenda and speaking of their desire to be 'martyred'.

According to a 'spokesman' for the Slash Crew, although all of the founding members are affiliated with the Johnsons it was originally intended to be a music group rather than a gang in its own right. 'Slash was formed by two Johnson members, one who passed away and another who is currently incarcerated,' he told me. 'It was a group of seven artists and in our spare time we used to get together in the studio to see who had what skills. Now everyone has started saying that they're Slash and that it's a gang, which is okay but it's not the true facts. All the bad publicity has forced people into the mind state of thinking that Slash is a gang, which was never our original intention.'

Slash was soon hijacked by a younger generation of self-styled gangsters, who used the name to refer to the youth division of the Johnson Crew. 'Because Slash was associated with the Johnsons, a lot of young kids from Aston and Newtown started saying that they were Slash. The kids from the Burger Bar territories in Handsworth and Winson Green responded to that by forming Bang Bang, which is just the younger version of the Burger Bar Boys.'

This younger Slash Crew have been responsible for a number of violent attacks over the last few years, including the killing of seventeen-year-old Bang Bang member Odwayne Barnes in March 2007. He was walking along New Street with a friend when he was set upon by a pair of rival gang members, who chased him to a bus stop outside Matthew Boulton College and plunged a knife into his heart. What started out as a rap group has quickly become one of the city's most notorious street gangs, although the founding members are adamant that they are tired of the bloodshed and maintain that they want the violence to end.

'There have been gang feuds in Birmingham for well over fifteen years and people have passed away on both sides,' my contact told me. 'Everyone would be happy for it to cease but to tell the truth I can't really see that happening.

'I personally think that the main reason that young people join gangs is because they might have been attacked or their friends or family might have been attacked for living in a certain postcode. A gang is like a big family and it will protect them against their rivals, plus it makes life easier and they won't get any bother from people who live in their area once they say what gang they're in because gangs tend to have control of the areas where they live. Then there's other factors like the money that's involved and peer pressure due to the fact that they have a friend or a family member who's involved in gangs so they feel as though it's the right thing to do.

'To be honest with you, there is more of a problem in the black community when it comes to gun crime than there is in your average white area. We've only got ourselves to blame as well, although it does seem like the Government would rather contain it in the lower-class black areas rather than having it spreading out in to the middle class and upper class areas. They put shootings in Birmingham in the news but they don't really care about them. As long as we fight amongst ourselves it's okay to them. The only thing that worries them is that there's a Premiership stadium in areas that each of the gangs control. West Brom's ground is in the heart of the Burger Boys territory and Aston Villa's ground is in the heart of the Johnsons turf. The fact that the gang violence is bad for the football business is their only concern.'

Birmingham is a large city and it comes as no surprise that it has seen the rise of criminal gangs. What is surprising is the level of violence that these groups are willing to resort to in order to defend their territory. Guns have embedded themselves deeply into the fabric of the black community and gangs like Slash and Bang Bang represent a younger, more trigger happy generation, willing to shoot first and ask questions later.

The legacy started by the Johnsons and the Burger Bar Boys has been passed down to a group of teenagers who have no idea how the feud began and even less idea of what the consequences of upholding it may entail. The West Midlands Police Force claim that they are on the verge of eradicating the two main gangs in the city but in reality, the names may change but the conflict will remain the same. Until the cycle is broken, teenage boys will carry on killing each other and lives will continue to be lost on both sides of the divide.

Manchester

MANCHESTER HAS BEEN referred to as the 'Chicago of England'. It saw forty-two gun-related fatalities between 1999 and April 2010, thirty-seven of them in the south of the city. The Moss Side and Longsight districts were the worst affected areas, with Longsight accounting for nearly a fifth of all fatal shootings.

The victims of gun crime in Manchester are typically young, black males living in council accommodation. Most of the shootings are carried out using semi-automatic pistols, although there is an increasing trend towards submachine guns. Although the majority of firearms offences are committed within the city itself, parts of neighbouring Stockport, Bolton and Salford have also had their share of gang-related violence.

Manchester gained its reputation for gangland violence after a series of conflicts, firstly between rival gangs from Cheetham Hill and Moss Side and then between two gangs within Moss Side itself: the Gooch and the Doddington. Named after the streets where the latter two gangs originally congregated, they caused havoc on the streets of Moss Side and Hulme, areas synonymous with drug dealing and gun crime. They were responsible for shootings, kidnaps, stabbings, slashings and beatings, and at the height of the feud the national media dubbed the city 'Gunchester', 'Gangchester' and the 'Bronx of Britain'.

Both the Gooch and Doddington survived both their own conflict, clashes with newer gangs such as the Pitt Bull Crew and the Longsight Crew, and waves of police action, until in April 2009, eleven key figures within the Gooch were jailed for a series of charges ranging from drug dealing to murder. It was hailed, perhaps prematurely, as the end of the war between the two groups. Gun crime in the city fell by ninety-two per cent and the streets of Moss Side were deemed to be as safe as they had been for three decades. It was one of the most successful gang-busting operations that Greater Manchester Police had ever carried out.

By then, however, the city had seen an expansion of gang activity to areas previously immune from it. Drug dealers and gangbangers from surrounding suburbs sided with either the Gooch or the Doddington and there were eventually different sets linked to each gang in Old Trafford, Whalley Range, Longsight, Cheetham Hill and Rusholme. The Old Trafford Crips, the Fallowfield Man Dem, the Rusholme Crips, the Young Cheetham Hill Loccz and the Whizz Crips allied themselves with the Gooch gang, whereas the Longsight Crew, Haydock Close Crew and Moss Side Bloods teamed up with Doddington.

During my time behind bars, I met a former affiliate of the Gooch gang who had left the city after narrowly escaping an armed robbery conviction. He was eventually arrested for supplying crack and heroin on the streets of Leeds. He was able to fill me in on a few of the new gangs that have come into existence in recent years.

'Fallowfield is bad,' he said. 'There's some real badmen there nowadays. People think it's just students there but my cousin lives there and there's a lot of shootings. The gangs there are serious. Gooch and Dodington are still going strong as well and you've got people calling themselves Bloods and Crips nowadays.'

Fallowfield is a surprising location for an armed gang. Although it shares its borders with both Moss Side and Longsight, it is home to a large population of university students, although it also contains areas that are within the five per cent most deprived in the country. The Fallowfield Man Dem are a predominantly black street gang, another odd development in an area that is only seven per cent black.

Until recently, the FMD were led by a set of twin brothers, one of whom was already in jail. Michael Berkeley was unwilling to let the fact that he was behind bars prevent him carrying on with his life of crime. He was in regular contact with his brother Marvin, who he would pass on orders to via an illicit mobile phone. The Berkeley twins were involved in everything from firearms offences to kidnap, threatening to chop their victims 'into pieces' if they failed to comply with their demands.

On 12 February, 2006, two men were driving along a road in the Gee Cross area of Hyde when they became aware of another car following closely behind them. The driver was staring straight at them. They stopped the car and opened the door, ready to get out and see what was going on. The next thing they knew, they were staring down the barrel of a gun.

'Better do what we say or you're both going to get shot', the gunman told them.

The terrified victims were taken to a car park behind a Kwik Fit tyres store and interrogated about what they did for a living. Their captors were under the impression that they were rival drug dealers, selling on their turf. Their mobile phones were checked and they were asked a series of questions.

After rifling through the two men's phone books, the Man

Dem told one of their victims to arrange to meet a man that appeared on his contact list. They made it clear to him that he would end up riddled with bullets if he refused to do so. Frightened for his life, he dialled the number and told his unsuspecting friend that he needed to meet up with him straight away. He told him to wait for him round the back of the Frames snooker club in Hyde. Moments later, Marvin Berkeley turned up in a Nissan Primera to discuss what they would do with their latest victim when he arrived.

As soon as he showed his face, victim number three was confronted by gang member Marcus Smith pointing a gun at his head. He had come with a friend, as they hadn't mentioned anything about him needing to come alone. The two of them were forced into the back of a car and driven to a road junction, where Berkeley ordered the driver to stop. Fearing the worst, they flung open the car door and ran for their lives.

One of the men was lucky enough to make it to a local chip shop. His friend was considerably less fortunate. He was shot in the back, kicked in the head and thrown onto the back seat of the car. Unsure of how to react, the gang then agreed to drop him off at a local hospital but made it clear to him that he would be killed if he told them how he had received his injuries. They allowed another of their victims to accompany him to make sure that he made it inside.

The remaining victim was taken to an undisclosed location and threatened with a gun before finally being let go. The abduction was thought to have lasted around six hours. The man who had been shot in the back underwent an operation to remove the bullet and all four abductees counted themselves lucky to be alive.

Three days later, the gang struck again. Two men were sat in the front two seats of a Mazda in the Gorton area of the city when a screwdriver-wielding carjacker opened the rear door and got in. Panicking, the driver put his foot down on the accelerator and attempted to drive away. His attacker, Fallowfield Man Dem member Kane Snowden, grabbed the wheel and wrestled him for control of the vehicle.

As the terrified driver grappled with the now-enraged gang member, a speeding Honda slammed into the Mazda, jolting it into a parked car. A gun went off, blasting out the rear windscreen and leaving glass strewn across the street. The victim jumped out of the car and ran, fearing that the next shot may be for him. He managed to make it into a garage forecourt before Marvin Berkeley caught up with him and grabbed him. Berkeley said that if he put up any more resistance then he was almost certainly going to shoot him.

Snowden fastened the man's hands behind his back and bundled him into the back of the car. He drove him to Sale Water Park, an area of parkland in nearby Trafford, where the gang accused him of selling drugs. 'You're going to work for us,' they told him. A mobile phone was put to his ear and Michael Berkeley issued a series of threats from prison. 'Do what my mate says,' he warned him. 'Anything they need, give them. It will be easier for you to do what they say.'

The man was then shoved back inside the car and taken to another location, where three masked gangsters drove him to Kingsway and set him free. Although his attackers took every precaution to avoid being identified, they had made several elementary mistakes. One of the cars used in the abduction was left with firearms residue and traces of Kane Snowden's DNA in it. A more adept criminal mind would have either burnt it out or made sure that it was unrecoverable. A loaded firearm was found in Levenshulme; it was thought to be the gun used in the kidnap. A search of the suspects' houses revealed photographs of them posing with an array of handguns. The gang had been sloppy.

Duane Edwards of Gorton was shown pointing a pistol at the lens of the camera. He pleaded guilty to conspiracy to kidnap, conspiracy to commit robbery and conspiracy to possess a firearm with intent to endanger life and received a minimum of six-and-a-half years behind bars. It was not the first time he had been involved in a kidnap: at just sixteen years old he was convicted of false imprisonment, kidnap and wounding. He had clearly learnt little from his previous incarceration. He was a dangerous man and the police were relieved to have him off the streets.

Lee Dilnut, of Moss Side, the only white member of the gang, was pictured posing with a revolver. He was jailed for four years. Marvin Berkeley, of Little Hulton, Salford, was given seven years. Curtis Todd, of Withington, was another of the gang caught on camera. He was pictured pointing a black revolver skyward, clad in a hooded top and a gold chain. On another of the photos, he was featured grinning next to a gun-wielding Lee Dilnut. He was jailed for four years. Kane Snowden was given a minimum of just under seven years.

'Manchester as a city is thoroughly fed up with you and your like, terrifying the living daylights out of decent law abiding citizens,' Judge Goldstone told the guilty youths.

Rather than dissuading the rest of the gang from committing crime, the jailing of their key members seemed to spur them on. The Man Dem seemed determined to put Fallowfield on the map for gun crime, along with the surrounding suburbs of Moss Side and Longsight.

The FMD have singled out the older Longsight Crew as their main rivals. Whereas the taxing of rival dealers is a purely economic activity, their feud with Longsight has overtones of racism and nationalism. There is a perception amongst the Man Dem that most of the Longsight Crew are African, whereas most of their gang are of Afro-Caribbean origins. Whilst it is true that Longsight does have a large West African community, the Longsight Crew draw their members from an eclectic mix of racial backgrounds. There are African, Jamaican, Asian and white gangbangers; all are equally entrenched in the criminal subculture.

The feud between the two factions reached its peak with the death of sixteen-year-old Louis 'Lippy Lou' Braithwaite in January 2008. He was an alleged member of the FMD and, at the time of his murder, was busy placing a bet at a William Hill betting shop in Withington, south Manchester, oblivious to the fact that a gun-wielding Longsight Crew member was on his way to shoot him. A gunman walked in through the front door and fired five shots. A bullet struck Braithwaite in the abdomen and he was rushed to hospital. He was kept alive for twelve days but eventually succumbed to his injuries. He should never have been there in the first place; he was too young to legally place a bet.

Soon after his murder, several of his friends had the initials 'LBR' tattooed on their bodies, allegedly standing for 'Louis Braithwaite Revenge'. Tee-shirts and hooded tops emblazoned with his likeness were printed off and worn as a sign of respect. A green bandana was draped over the cross marking the spot where he was buried. To the rest of the Man Dem, he was Fallowfield's Tupac Shakur: a martyr to the mean streets of Manchester.

Braithwaite's childhood friend Hiruy Zerihun was unwilling to let the death of one of his closest buddies go unpunished and set about assembling an assassination squad to kill the man who was responsible. He enlisted the help of Njabulo

Ndlovu, an Old Trafford Crip member from Newton Heath, and hid a 9mm Tokarev at a secret location in Crumpsall ready to carry out his revenge.

A young man was sitting in the front seat of a Volkswagen Golf when two figures emerged from the bushes clad in dark balaclavas. The rumours were that he was responsible for Louis' death. Eight shots were fired into the car. There were four people in the vehicle. Three of them were unharmed but sixteen-year-old Giuseppe 'G-Sepz' Gregory was less fortunate. He was hit in the head and began to make a spluttering sound, as if his throat was clogged up with blood. 'He's been shot!' screamed the driver, panicking and slamming his foot down on the accelerator. He sped to the nearest hospital, checking his wing mirror at regular intervals to see if the gunmen were in pursuit.

Giuseppe died two-and-a-half hours later. His family were devastated and insisted that he was an innocent victim but it was the second time that he had been shot: when he was thirteen he had been hit five times in a drive-by near the Apollo Theatre in Ardwick. The police had been concerned about his safety and handed his mother a letter warning that his life was in danger. He was associating with known gangsters and he had been arrested on suspicion of possessing heroin with intent to supply. There were rumours that he was a junior member of the Longsight Crew.

Zerihun and Ndlovu were taken in for questioning and denied everything. Ndlovu claimed that he had been playing the computer game *Grand Theft Auto* at the time of the murder and said that he only found out that Gregory had been killed after reading a comment about his death on Facebook. Despite their protestations of innocence, the court heard how Zerihun had threatened a man with a handgun at the pub directly oppo-

site the spot where the shooting took place. A teenage girl testified that she saw Ndlovu getting into the taxi that was driven
to Crumpsall to collect the murder weapon. The
Gooch/Fallowfield alliance was about to lose two more of its
members. They were jailed for life, with Zerihun receiving a
minimum of twenty-three years and Ndlovu twenty-one years.

Soon after Gregory's death, a video was once again posted
on YouTube showing hooded youths wearing 'R.I.P.' jumpers,
with blood-red letters flashing up on the screen warning that
'revenge is promised'. 'Somebody's going to see death,' an
angry rapper shouts in the background, 'because they took my
little homie, the one and only G-Sepz'.

It was another sad reminder of the dangers faced particularly by young, black youths in inner-city Manchester. Two
thirds of the city's gun crime victims over the last eleven years
have been either black or mixed race. Just over one in ten of
them have been below the age of eighteen. Those living in
South Manchester are far more likely to be murdered than residents of nearby Altrincham or Stockport, although those are
hardly crime-free zones.

WHILE THE RECENT history of Manchester's gang crime would fill
several books, its close neighbours Salford and Stockport have
also experienced major problems. Stockport, which borders
leafy Cheshire, was even said to have had an affiliate of a gang
called the '503' based across the Atlantic in Portland, Oregon,
while Salford has been described by police as a 'school of
excellence' for armed robbery and has seen a number of
gangland 'spectaculars', not least the shooting to death of two
Doddington hitmen when they entered the Brass Handles pub
in Pendleton in March 2006 and opened fire, only to be

disarmed and killed themselves. More recently, black and Asian gangsters from Moss Side became embroiled in a turf war with white criminals on Salford's Langworthy Estate.

The Greater Manchester area, with its industrial past, has a long history of gangs, starting with the so-called 'scuttlers' in the 1870s, territorial mobs who fought on street corners with knives, belt buckles and hob-nailed clogs. This book is primarily concerned with charting the phenomenon of the new, post-2000 breed of 'young guns', but I also thought it important to get the perspective of someone involved in gang conflict from an earlier period, to see how things had changed.

Gorton, to the east of the city centre, has had problems with teenage violence since the days of the scuttlers. In the mass unemployment of the Thatcher era, it was home to a street gang known as Gorton The Business. They waged war on rival groups from the neighbouring areas of Levenshulme and Reddish. One of them was 'Frank'.

"When I was involved, it was a lot different,' Frank told me. "You used to have fifty-strong mobs bowling around the estates but nowadays you get smaller firms of around ten to fifteen people and there are no visible signs of the gangs being there. You might see a small group of lads about and think nothing of them but that small group could be made up of people that are likely to shoot you if you say the wrong thing to them.'

On June 14, 2008, sixteen-year-old Sophie Finucane was enjoying a sleepover at a friend's house when she was shot in the head at point blank range by Gorton gang member Wayne Bryan. She hadn't said a word to provoke him; the gun had gone off by accident whilst he was dancing around the room with it in his hand. After spending the next ten days in intensive care, Sophie was eventually discharged from hospital with damaged vision and a loss of the use of her right arm.

Wayne claimed to have found the gun in the house and told the court that he had not intended for his weapon to go off. His attempts to portray the shooting as a tragic accident failed to impress the judge, especially considering the fact that he had grabbed his weapon and fled the scene immediately after the shot was discharged. He was a member of a local street gang known as the West Gorton Crew and he had convictions for a range of different offences, including a number of violent assaults.

According to Frank, West Gorton, a separate area from the rest of Gorton, has been a centre for gang activity as far back as he can remember. 'Their main gang was the West Gorton Reds back when we used to fight with them. A lot of them used to support Man United, you see. They wrote "WGR" all over the place with a marker. They were allied with a gang from Beswick and they were one of our main enemies. Neither of our mobs used guns back in those days though, not many people did. They would carry knives and bats with them and that was it, really. A few would carry pool balls in a sock and that type of thing. I remember when a mob from Chorlton came down and caught me off guard with a pool ball. It hurt like fuck.'

Frank had watched the inexorable march of gun culture, and had his own view on why it was becoming so prevalent.

'People who have got nothing thrive on their reputation. The same way that an athlete will strive for a gold medal, a street kid will strive for a better reputation. To get that medal, the athlete will obviously have to strive harder and harder as his competitors get faster and faster as time goes by. In the street kid's life, they have to get more and more violent to shock people. There was a time when you could stab somebody and it'd be all over the papers. Nowadays you have to shoot someone. Soon it'll be at the stage where you have to chop their fingers off and post them back to their relatives!

'With a gun, anyone can get themselves an instant reputation,' he added. 'Anyone can get a gun; you can get hold of one in an hour, at a push. You can get hold of anything that you could possibly imagine as well, as long as you've got the right amount of money. You can go out and shoot someone and make a name for yourself. I've even heard of a few grenades and rocket launchers going about. A guy I know was trying to get hold of an anti-tank missile to shoot at the police vans a couple of years ago. I think he settled for a flare gun in the end though. All of these things are a way of people elevating themselves from nobody to somebody. The more extreme the weapons they use, the more feared they will become.'

Were there really people selling rocket launchers or was he having me on?

'No you really can get them,' he assured me. 'Things like that are very rare but they are out there. For the right amount of money you can get whatever you want. There's always somebody somewhere who will have the right connections. There are a lot more weapons about on the streets than you'd think but the police try to cover it up because they don't want it to seem like they're on their toes.'

In August 2009, a rocket launcher was uncovered by the Greater Manchester Police during a series of raids. A month later, a woman caused a stir by handing a live hand grenade and two rounds of ammunition in at the local police station.

'It's another example of how things are getting more and more extreme,' said Frank. 'It's like my old gang, GTB. They started out sniffing glue and fighting with other gangs and now some of them are doing armed blags, some have become professional shoplifters and others are travelling all over the

UK doing burglaries. Some got into car crime and started ringing the cars and selling them on and a lot of people became involved in the drug trade as well.

'A lot of the guns that are about are there because of drugs. Poor people might not be able to get a loan from a bank but they can get a loan from a dealer. When somebody gets a loan from a dealer, the dealers don't have the resources that the banks have to get the money back and so they have to use force. Also all of the post offices have screens over the counters and there's CCTV everywhere nowadays so who do you think is doing all of the wham, bap, wallop types of crime? It's the addicts. They don't put any thought into what they do, they just use the easiest available method to get what they want. At the end of the day, crime should be done quietly and calmly with no-one raising the alarm and nobody getting hurt but as long as there are crack and heroin around, there will always be somebody desperate enough to do whatever it takes.

'When they knocked all of the old terraced houses down and shipped people over to [overspill estates] like Hattersley and Gamesley, they destroyed the sense of community in the area and then they started moving all of the ASBO families in who had been disruptive in other parts of the city. All of this coincided with a period of high unemployment where people who had worked all their lives suddenly found themselves out of a job and so the attitude became, "You can take our jobs but you can't take Gorton." We started to become proud of the negative way that other people saw us because at that point, it was the only thing that we really had.

'People couldn't take pride in their material possessions because they didn't have any so they started feeling proud of the fact that the police thought twice before coming on the estate and that was when the residents started rebelling against the authorities. What the fuck could they do for us? As far as we were concerned, they'd already failed us so we became self-governing. We decided who could walk the streets and anything that upset anybody was sorted out in the community. At the end of the day if you're a law-abiding citizen and you were brought up in Gorton then you don't have a problem there. Most of the violence is against other criminals or against outsiders poking their noses in. There are idiots within the gangs that will rob off their own and it's them that cause the friction but generally there's certain rules that all of the local villains will respect.

'There's nothing for anybody in Gorton. You have to make the best of a bad situation though and people do better themselves and people do get out of there but when your range of experience is limited to the one estate, you're not bothered about what you do because you don't know any better. It's like food; if you're brought up on Pot Noodle then how will you ever know that there's other things out there? Until the kids are shown the options that are available to them, things will always stay the same. For the situation to improve, a lot of work needs to be done and people need to be made aware of what lies beyond Gorton. They need to get out in the world and see the things that they could be doing with their lives.'

Frank's description of the situation in Gorton seemed to mirror what had gone on in the more notorious parts of south Manchester and Salford. Teenage street gangs were transforming themselves into organised crime groups as they grew into adulthood. Postcode rivalries can only be observed for so long before those upholding them will choose to put their combat skills to better use. The fact that the Gorton The Business gang had been fighting with knives and sticks from their early teens meant that they were the ideal candidates to be recruited by drug dealers and armed robbery cartels. Their recreational violence had slowly transformed into profit-orientated acts of crime and for a select few, hand-to-hand combat had been replaced by guns.

Yet the streets of Greater Manchester are, at the time of writing, enjoying a relatively crime-free period. Many of the most active and dangerous gangbangers are behind bars and the levels of violent crime have decreased dramatically. Rates of burglary, robbery and firearms offences are still well above the national average but the police have made modest inroads into racketeering and organised crime.

A report commissioned in 2010 by Manchester City Council's Resources and Governance Overview and Scrutiny Committee commended the city on its dramatic reduction in gang-related violence and pointed out that gang-related firearms use had decreased by more than ninety per cent throughout the previous year. This fall was described as 'unprecedented in the recent history of gang culture'. But it is not at all clear whether these statistics represent a momentary blip or a genuine triumph on the part of those working to solve the problem. Perhaps the best that can be said is that, for now at least, the city that was once referred to as Gangchester and Gunchester, is simply Manchester once again.

Middlesbrough

BY THE DAWN of the twentieth century, the north-east industrial town of Middlesbrough was responsible for a third of the nation's iron output. The salt-extraction industry was going strong and employment was at an all-time high and the town was enjoying an economic boom. The Bell Brothers ironworks alone provided jobs for 6,000 people.

A century later, Britain had endured a period of massive industrial decline. Iron and steel were heavily hit. Middlesbrough's economic success had been dependent upon a small number of large companies, resulting in reduced levels of entrepreneurship. As the main sources of employment in the town faded away, the lack of new opportunities became alarmingly apparent. Unemployment soared, along with feelings of unease at the uncertain future faced by the local people.

Modern Middlesbrough contains some of the poorest areas in the country. It has twenty-three wards, thirteen of which are in the bottom ten percent most deprived in England. It is the ninth most deprived district out of a total of 354. It has one of the highest rates of arson, with children as young as twelve joy riding cars around their estates before burning them out and attacking the firemen. The levels of assault, domestic violence and alcohol abuse are well above the national average. It is a shadow of its former proud self.

While the traditional industries associated with the town have dwindled, there are still numerous ways of making money. Figures released by Drugscope in 2007 highlighted Middlesbrough as the cheapest place in England to buy heroin. There were reports of addicts travelling from all over the country to purchase cut-price drugs. The local dealers were undercutting the competition, creating a sudden wave of 'drug tourism' to the area.

Organised crime was quick to follow. Heroin was big business and lone dealers would often find themselves being taxed for their income. The only way to prevent this from happening was to join a larger criminal network. Gangs began to spring up across the town, with a distinct hierarchy ensuring that the main suppliers never had to come face to face with their clientele. They were left with the sole responsibility of letting their customers know when and where the sales would take place.

One gang leader, Habib Khan, made a concerted effort to retain a low profile. He dressed casually and shunned recognisable signs of wealth. Rather than moving into an expensive home in an upmarket part of town, he continued to live in a modest family house in the deprived Middlehaven ward, where life expectancy is the lowest of anywhere in the country.

Habib was small and physically unimposing, quiet and mildmannered, choosing to reject the stereotype of how a drug dealer should act. Behind his unassuming demeanour lay the ruler of an expansive criminal empire, distributing heroin as far afield as Scarborough and Northumberland. He was in charge of a network of 180 different dealers, operating under the self-deprecating name of 'Pakidom' and flooding the streets with hard drugs.

Although the gang's activities were co-ordinated from Middesbrough, they had workers all over the north of England.

Each member had a specific role within the organisation. Tabrez Khan was the telephonist. He had two mobile phones: Line A and Line B. Line A was used to take orders from other dealers. His customers would ring him up requesting wholesale quantities of heroin and he would direct them to a secluded spot where there was little chance of detection. This would be done on Line B so that A was kept free for other customers to ring. Buyers would be met by one of five runners whose job it was to deliver large amounts of drugs divided into wraps of one-sixteenth of an ounce.

The runners were racially mixed: three of them were white and two of them were Asian. They met their clientele at diverse locations, varying their meeting places in order to avoid the police becoming wise to their drop-off points. Popular delivery sites included the car park of the James Cook University Hospital, Teesside Law Courts and Zetland Place in Middlesbrough town centre.

Once the drugs had been exchanged, the money was passed along to Najid Hussain, who counted the takings to make sure that they tallied up. If the figures were correct then the delivery boys would be paid their wages from the total amount. If they were down then somebody had landed themselves in a whole lot of trouble.

Kerry Marie Bogan was charged with weighing the drugs out and passing them on to the runners. She had to divide mounds of heroin into individual deals and wrap each deal using the corner of a plastic bag. She was the only female member of the gang and she had been given the riskiest job of all. Her house was constantly filled with class A drugs and she had a continuous stream of delivery boys travelling to and from her address.

The fact that the Pakidom gang were able to operate at such a high degree of sophistication was even more remarkable given that Habib was thought to be suffering from brain damage. He received a two-year sentence in April 2002 for a dangerous driving incident in which his passenger was killed and he was injured. A consultant neuro-psychologist deemed his thought capacity to be within the bottom one per cent, yet he was clever enough to invest the vast majority of the gang's income into legitimate overseas businesses. They were thought to have earned an estimated £8 million, selling to dealers in Newcastle, Scarborough, Spennymoor, Seaham, Darlington, Durham, Middlesbrough, Bishop Auckland, Redcar, Stockton, Hartlepool, Chester-le-Street and Blyth. If Habib Khan was mentally impaired then he was coping remarkably well with his disability, running a multi-million-pound criminal empire and successfully laundering his earnings.

Habib regularly checked his workers' phones to ensure that there were no suspicious numbers being stored on them. He was determined to safeguard against police informants and rival drug dealers attempting to steal his contacts. Pakidom was run like a military operation. Every precaution was taken to guarantee that the upper hierarchy of the group remained impenetrable. He had very little contact with his workers and only a select few were aware of his position as the leader of the gang. Those who were in the know were made fully aware of what would happen to them if they were to reveal the identity of their boss.

Despite his continued efforts to remain low key, one of Habib's drop-off spots eventually attracted the attention of the local authorities. There were always dodgy-looking characters loitering outside the Job Centre but now that Pakidom had chosen it as a delivery point there were some particularly unsavoury people lining the streets. Sensing that something was amiss, Cleveland Police set up an operation to infiltrate the gang. Undercover officers posed as heroin addicts and traced the network of dealers back along the chain. Line A and Line B were seized and the call records were examined. Tabrez Khan had received a total of 10,000 calls over a four-month period, many of them from known drug dealers. Habib's empire was about to come tumbling down.

As soon as he found out that the police were onto him, Habib booked a flight to Pakistan. He had done well for himself given his supposed brain damage. He had amassed millions of pounds and controlled a large proportion of the north-east's heroin trade. The rest of the gang were heading to prison, as there was little chance of them avoiding a custodial sentence for a drug-dealing operation of this magnitude. His best bet was to hide out in Pakistan for the next few months and enjoy what little freedom he had left.

Tabrez Khan was jailed for six-and-a-half years for conspiracy to supply class A drugs. He was thought to have earned £12,710 from his part in the racket, although only twenty-nine pence of it was ever recovered. The vast majority of his earnings had been moved out of the country to avoid confiscation. The only money that was left to recover was the collection of small change that he had in his pocket on the day of his court case.

Kerry Bogan received a five-year sentence. When the police turned up at her house to arrest her, they stumbled across a room full of discarded carrier bags, all of which had been used to prepare deals. A search of moneyman Najid Hussain's house uncovered £1,300, along with a calculator and a notepad that were believed to have been used to work out the gang's expenses. He was sentenced to three-and-a-half-years in prison.

A drug courier and former Teesside university student was given three-and-a-half years. He claimed that Habib had approached him whilst he was serving a sentence at HMP Holme House in County Durham and asked him to deliver heroin on his behalf.

Paul French skipped bail so that he could spend Christmas with his family. He was jailed for four years for conspiracy to supply and an additional six months for failing to attend court. Several others also received jail terms for a range of offences, including witness intimidation and delivering wraps of heroin.

Habib Khan, after sixteen months on the run, was arrested at Manchester Airport foolishly attempting to re-enter the country. He brazenly claimed that he had heard that the police were looking for him and returned to Teesside 'to sort this out'. He denied any involvement in illegal activity, stating, 'I was not involved in drugs at all.'

The court heard how Habib's accident had left him with impaired reasoning, planning and judgement. The defence portrayed him as a helpless invalid who was unable to read the oath at the beginning of the proceedings. Judge Whitburn remained unconvinced. 'You are the Pakidom,' he told Khan. 'You are the organiser and the head of the hierarchy. For a conspiracy of this size, this length and deception, the very least sentence I can pass on you is one of fourteen years.' He saw Habib for what he really was, the leader of one of the most sophisticated heroin dealing operations in the country.

Whitburn described Pakidom as 'a small tip of a very large iceberg'. They were the top tier of a criminal network that extended across at least four counties. Habib and his gang were thought to have been making up to £4,000 a day. With the main drug cartel suddenly out of commission, those sales would now be available to someone else.

Albert 'Papa' Thoms was another entrepreneur of sorts. He

saw a gap in the market and he filled it. He did not seek to fill Habib's shoes – there was too much competition and heroin dealers were ten-a-penny in Middlesbrough. Crack cocaine, however, was still relatively hard to come by. There was little point in competing in a market that was already over-saturated. Given half a chance, most heroin addicts would take crack as well. It was time for Papa to set up shop.

Lloyd Ormsby was his right-hand man. They were part of a gang of London-based Yardies who were looking to expand their operation. Middlesbrough was ripe for the picking. The fact that there were so many heroin users in the town meant that there was a strong customer base for crack. They set about recruiting a team of couriers to transport their wares across from the capital.

Papa's firm became known as the Donna Network, named after the alias that his girlfriend used when she was taking orders for drugs. Customers would ring her up and tell her how much crack they wanted delivering and Thoms would buy train tickets and top-up cards for his runners and send them up to Middlesbrough. Although the majority of the gang were black, there were also a number of white and Asian members.

Ormsby's girlfriend, Neisha Hemmings, was responsible for looking after the money. She was provided with an address on Essex Street in Middlesbrough where the gang would store large amounts of cash along with the list of dealers that they sold to and a small quantity of crack. Paul Lynch's house would be used as a main storage centre. A network of couriers and street dealers picked up bags of narcotics from his address and distributed them all over the Northeast, using Middlesbrough as a base. They had customers across Teesside, County Durham, Northumbria and North Yorkshire.

Thoms was directly responsible for cooking cocaine into crack and would even transport his own wares across when he was unable to find a courier. He kept a close eye on his stock and made sure that he had a constant supply of drugs coming in. Ormsby was given the task of supervising the couriers and arranging accommodation for the firm to stay at when they made the journey north. He spent his time travelling between London and Middlesbrough, making sure that everything went to plan.

When Thoms and Ormsby were in London, fellow gang member Wycliffe Clarke would stay at their address in Middlesbrough to make sure that their affairs were in order. He was a gangland caretaker, minding their headquarters for them while they were away on business. The Donna Network was similar to Pakidom in that each member had a distinct role to play. There was a clearcut hierarchy: Ormsby and Papa were at the top, the Jamaican nationals were the next step down and the local street dealers were at the bottom of the pile.

'Donna' was the only link between Thoms and the low-level dealers. She was an integral part of the operation, as she enabled her boyfriend to liaise with his workers without him coming into direct contact with them. As far as she was concerned, there was no way that she could be traced, as none of her customers knew her real name. The police were fully aware of the fact that she was operating under an alias and mounted a special operation to find out who she was. They searched through her phone bills and made a note of all of the numbers that she had dialled.

Claudine Neil, also known as Donna, made the mistake of calling a London-based estate agent using her work phone. This gave the authorities a good idea of where she lived and her anonymity was busted. The net was closing in.

'Donna' was traced to an address in Ilford, where she was arrested on suspicion of conspiring to supply class A drugs. She was given the choice of either serving a lengthy jail sentence or providing the names of her fellow gang members. Faced with up to fifteen years' imprisonment, and deportation, she was quick to betray her former friends.

Now that Neil was no longer manning the phones, Thoms was forced to deal with his customers directly – but not for long. In April 2007, a series of raids were carried out across the country aimed at toppling the network once and for all. All of the key figures within the gang were taken in for questioning.

Thoms' barrister later claimed that he had undergone a 'deeply religious conversion' since the day of his arrest and many of his thirteen co-accused provided similar sob stories. Some told the judge that they were dealing to feed their habits, others claimed that they had given in to temptation after suffering from financial difficulties. Whereas Judge Les Spittle accepted the unfortunate circumstances of some of the low-level street dealers, he described Thoms as the 'overall adminstrator' and sentenced him to fourteen years behind bars. Lloyd Ormsby received eight years and ten other gang members were jailed.

The levels of street robbery and shoplifting in the town declined dramatically in the wake of Papa's arrest, as the availability of crack plummeted. It was the fall of yet another criminal empire, although Thoms has profited immensely from his wrongdoing. He was thought to have earned over £300,000 but was ordered to pay back a mere £4252.

Pakidom and the Donna Network are examples of how an illegal activity can be run like a legitimate business. Others are quickly learning that lesson. The war against crime is a two-way battle and the more sophisticated the police become at catching drug dealers, the cleverer the dealers become to counter their moves.

Crack and heroin continue to be bought and sold on the streets of Middlesbrough on a daily basis. It is one of Britain's most lucrative drug markets, with almost double the average level of substance abuse. It is little wonder that the town has been targeted by two such major organised crime groups. Criminal gangs are the product of mass unemployment and lack of opportunity.

Cleveland Police hailed the jailing of the Donna Network as a step towards keeping guns and gangs out of Middlesbrough. Although the rate of gun crime in the town is still relatively low, heroin abuse has brought about an emerging gang culture that is growing increasingly difficult to ignore. In the Linthorpe area, children as young as eleven have been known to bring drugs into school. Business cards advertising crack, heroin, cocaine and cannabis have been found on the deprived Grove Hill estate. In a town with such a serious drug problem, gangs are an inevitable part of life. Strength in numbers is essential for protection against rivals groups of dealers. Pakidom and the Donna Network may have been taken off the streets but they are just two of many. Where there is demand, there will be supply, and where there are desperate people searching for a means of escape, there will be cocaine and heroin dealers roaming the streets.

DURING MY TIME inside, I spoke to an armed robber from the neighbouring town of Redcar, who was able to provide me with an insight into the availability of firearms in the area. Although he looked the part, Micky wasn't at all how I would have expected a violent criminal to be, prior to my incarceration. He came across as amicable and easy to talk to, although I was still careful not to ask him anything overly intrusive that might have led to him mistaking me for a police informant.

'On the Lakes Estate where I live, there's a lot of guns about but it's mainly shotguns,' he said. 'If you want a nine or something like that then you can get hold of them but they are a bit rarer. Again, there are a few people with machine guns and things like that but they are even rarer and they will set you back a fair bit. There's not many people getting shot round Middlesbrough and Redcar, it's mostly stabbings. The people that have shooters mostly use them for robberies or for intimidation. You can't go around being trigger happy or you'll end up getting lifed off. It's not the way we do things.'

Surprisingly, Micky doesn't entirely buy into the view that Teesside's crime problems are due to poverty and lack of opportunity. He found his criminal career exciting.

'Crime is an addiction,' he said. 'You can try and say that it's down to poverty and drugs but I'm still committing robberies even though I managed to kick a two-hundred-pound-a-day heroin habit. I guess the blags are more addictive than the drugs were. I get so hyped up after doing a graft that I get a comedown and my hands start shaking. It's like when you've done a gram of sniff and you end up on a low from it once the buzz has died down. It's the exact same feeling.

'Then there's the bonding and the camaraderie. When you've been out grafting with the same set of people year after year, you develop a sense of trust that it's impossible for you to create from anything else. I've been doing all of my raises with the same firm ever since I robbed my first car at thirteen. When you've been with the same outfit for that long, you end up being like family and you always back each other up no matter what. Every firm is the same, they will have the muppets that they use to do their dirty work for them but the inner circle will always be a tight group of friends. If you've never experienced it then it's difficult to explain. All I can say to you is go and get a group of mates together and run up in a post office with a shotgun and then you will understand what I'm talking about.'

Micky's firm were a classic example of a medium-level street gang. They weren't at the top of the pile like the Donna Network or Pakidom but they were a step up from the various disorganised postcode-based gangs that operated in the area. And they were totally committed to the way of life they had chosen.

'I've been doing crime since I was six years old and it really is a passion. That's the only way to describe it. First it was just shoplifting, stealing sweets from shops and that, then when I reached my teens I started robbing cars and motorbikes. I was just doing it for a laugh back then. It was a way of showing off. I started doing it for a living when I turned sixteen. By that stage we had a couple of years of TWOCing under our belts and everyone in the firm knew that they could trust each other. I reckon that's when most criminals start getting serious about what they do. You need a tight-knit firm. It makes it easier to go through with something when you've got a couple of mates that you know will be there with you.

'The first proper job we did was on a clothes shop. We chipped a roof panel out, cut the alarm wires and went in through the roof. It went without a hitch and ever since then, I've never looked back. One thing led to another and within a couple of years we were going into places with guns and machetes and doing tie-ups on people.'

He talked about the robberies that he had carried out as if they were nothing out of the ordinary, even though taking from drug dealers is a very hazardous activity.

'There are a couple of different firms that are into that kind of thing. A lot of them will only ever rob dealers' houses though 'cause they think that it's not worth doing shops and that. Some will only do big mansions out in the countryside. It takes the coppers a long time to get to them and they're usually full up with antiques. Post offices are another good target. Someone I know stalked a Post Office worker for two weeks and learnt the times that he came and went. He waited for him to open up the office and then three lads with a sawn-off shotgun tied him up and robbed him. They got fifteen grand from it.

'One of the things that pushed me deeper into crime was when my brother got murdered back in 1996. I started taking heroin to numb the pain and I guess the rest of the firm helped me to cope with his death. Obviously they could never replace him but they were always putting me onto opportunities that took up all of my concentration and took my mind off what had happened. I think if he was still alive I would probably still be going out grafting but it'd be on a much smaller scale than what I'm doing now.

'There's not many people from where I live who end up being doctors or lawyers,' he summed up. 'You've got two options available to you if you've grown up on the Lakes: you can either stay on the dole your entire life or you can bally up and earn yourself some money.'

The decline of industry in Teesside has created a distinct underclass. Unemployment has transformed the area and not for the better. For those on the margins of society, crime is the only form of work that is available. It is their one hope of getting rich and for a small but significant minority, it is an obsession that they will pursue regardless of the consequences. Illegal activity comes above everything else in their lives.

Preston

I N MAY 2008, Chief Constable Steve Finnigan of Lancashire Police warned of the corrosive influence of Manchester's gang culture on the small county city of Preston. Mancunian criminals are often made to stand trial at Preston Crown Court, rather than in their home city, to reduce the likelihood of witness and jury intimidation. Although this allows those who are providing evidence to do so in a safer environment, it has been known to evoke copycat tendencies amongst the city's criminals.

Finnigan commented that Preston's street gangs were becoming increasingly embroiled in turf wars. He spoke of rival cliques battling for control, often fighting over drug dealing territory. There are at least twenty known criminal gangs operating within the city, encompassing an estimated 100 total members. Parts of Preston seem to be emulating the more notorious parts of Manchester.

In September 2007, the *Lancashire Evening Post* visited several of Preston's poorer suburbs in the wake of a recent spate of gun crime. Neighbours spoke of gunpoint robberies and drive-by shootings. Residents of the troubled Callon estate warned of a definite gang culture in the area. They complained of a lack of faith in the police force and expressed concerns that the authorities were attempting to downplay the issues that they brought up.

Callon has been the subject of significant media attention over the years. In July 2008, locals complained that they were terrified of leaving their homes after dark. Earlier that week a taxi driver had been threatened with a gun. The area was becoming increasingly lawless, with groups of delinquent youths roaming the streets at night. There was talk of a local gang fighting with rivals in Farringdon Park. One name in particular cropped up over and over again: Andrew Walch.

Walch was the leader of the Callon Gang, the group responsible for the majority of the trouble in the area. They were involved in everything from small-time drug dealing to serious firearms offences. Their feud with the Farringdon Park gang was thought to revolve around the sale of class A drugs. Both sides had access to guns and there was police intelligence to suggest that Walch had accidentally shot a member of his own gang with a 9mm pistol.

In February 2007, the residents of the Callon estate decided that Walch and his gang had gone too far. In an effort to make it harder for him to conceal his face, the local authorities issued him with an ASBO banning him from wearing hoodies, scarves and baseball caps. He had already been prohibited from entering the areas of Fishwick and St Matthew's after similar complaints from residents there. He was becoming something of a pariah, with his fellow gang members the only people who would give him the time of day. The rest of the community saw him as a menace.

Walch was serving a ten-month sentence for racially aggravated assault at the time when the ASBO was issued. He had been involved in an incident in which three Asian men were attacked with a weapon as they walked through a park in the Ribbleton area. The restrictions that were placed upon him evoked mixed reactions from the public. Whereas neighbours felt that it was a necessary measure to protect their community from vandalism and petty crime, others believed that restricting him from wearing hooded tops impinged upon his civil liberties. It was a controversial move but it had little effect upon his behaviour. He continued to break the law at every given opportunity.

That November, Walch was back in court, this time for handling stolen property and committing a bizarre public order offence. He was suspected of stealing a mobile phone belonging to a priest at St Teresa's Church in Fishwick. After searching through the contents of the phone, he came across a number of images that he found apparently objectionable. Although all of the pictures that he uncovered were perfectly legal to own, he confronted the priest in the gardens of the church, threatening to 'come back with twenty people with placards' and telling him that he was 'against the Bible'. The police advised the priest to leave the church for fear of further harassment. He was granted compassionate leave by the Bishop of Lancaster and decided not to return to the parish.

Whilst the 'scourge of Callon' was serving the remainder of his sentence, Lancashire Police were gathering evidence that he had failed to abide by the terms of his ASBO, in an attempt to ban him from the city. They later told a court that there was intelligence to suggest that he was responsible for a samurai sword attack in June 2007. He was said to have been involved in the supply of drugs and had entered the zone that he was supposed to be barred from on three separate occasions. The level of crime on the estate had fallen dramatically the minute he was put behind bars.

Defence solicitor Greg Earnshaw described the proposed exclusion as, 'akin to ... some sort of Western movie where the sheriff is saying you have got until sundown to get out of town'.

Walch's sister Rachael also complained about the way he was being treated. She claimed that she was going to put together a petition containing the signatures of all of the local shop-keepers, as they had never had any trouble with her brother. She insisted that the samurai sword was an 'ornament' and added that the 9mm pistol that he had allegedly shot his friend with was actually a shotgun – and that he didn't do it. She said that if his appeal against the conditions of the ASBO ended up being unsuccessful she was going to contact the European Court of Human Rights in an attempt to have it overturned.

In the end, the terms of the order were deemed to be unduly restrictive and the ban was lifted. Walch was still prohibited from entering Fishwick, St Matthew's and Farringdon Park but as far as he was concerned, he had come out on top. Judge Dodds told him to count himself lucky that he was being allowed back into the city and added that he had 'done well enough'. Callon's one-man crime wave was about to return.

Liam Cromie was another of the estate's resident trouble-makers. Whereas other children might dream of being footballers or astronauts, he had aspired to be a criminal from his early teens. He was small for his age and he had a complex about his height. This made him all the more determined to prove himself as a hardcase.

By age thirteen, Cromie was smoking heavily and attending a special needs school. He had little interest in education and although he was good at football and pool, he had no desire to take his talents any further. He believed that the only way that he could gain respect was through violence. By his early adult-hood, he was associating with drug dealers and gang members on a daily basis. In order for him to gain entry to the inner circle of the Callon Gang, he would have to prove to them that he was just as wild as they were. Infamy was a step above fame.

David Cornall was walking home from the pub when he was approached by an aggressive eighteen-year-old with a chip on his shoulder. It was 10.30pm. Cornall had gone out for a quiet drink with his friends and here he was being confronted by a knife-wielding maniac. He turned to run away but his attacker was too fast for him and he felt a sharp pain as the blade was plunged deep into his back. He managed to stagger home, bleeding profusely the entire way, but the wound was too deep for him to have any chance of recovery. He was driven to the Royal Preston Hospital, where he died at 3am on February 13, 2008.

A knife bearing traces of Cromie's DNA was found close to the scene of the crime. He denied all knowledge of the killing and claimed that he was at his grandmother's house at the time of the attack. Little did he know that listening devices had been placed around his home on Waldon Street in Callon and the police had heard him confessing to the stabbing. He had mistaken his victim for a police informer who had provided evidence against him. In reality, it was the first time that their paths had ever crossed.

Convicted carjacker Michael Kiley testified that Cromie had confessed to the killing during a period of remand at HMP Manchester. 'He said when he first saw him he saw red,' he told the court. 'I told him if you stab anyone above the leg you will kill him. He said he was not bothered but just wished he had got the right guy.' The knife had penetrated Cornall's lung and severed several vital arteries.

'For some time you have terrorised this community in Preston,' Mr Justice Flaux told the teenage murderer. 'You have shown little, if any, remorse either in conversations recorded by the police or at the trial. I make every allowance for your learning difficulties and other intellectual shortcomings but having observed you throughout the trial it seems you were devoid of normal emotions about the enormity of the trial.'

He sentenced Cromie to life imprisonment with a minimum tariff of eighteen years.

Many of Cromie's pals on the estate continued to claim he was innocent. A Facebook page was set up in his honour. The 'get liam cromie out ov jail' group soon had nearly 100 members. Some call themselves the Young Callon Soldiers. 'Cromie is a tru member 4 life,' asserted convicted gang member Danny Dinning. 'Keep ur head up g 1luv.' Dinning was one of five conspirators who were jailed in connection with a gangland shooting in January 2008. He was sentenced to thirty-nine weeks in prison for perverting the course of justice.

The Callon Gang exist within a cocoon in which their deviant lifestyles are seen as socially acceptable. They are surrounded by the amoral and the immoral. Many of Cromie's friends have multiple convictions and, in his world, the only opinions that matter are those of his mates. One of the reasons that Callon has developed such a strong counter-culture is the insular nature of the estate. There is an attitude amongst the residents that the local people should be supported no matter what they have done. The tendency for the population to band together and refuse to co-operate with the authorities has made the area difficult to police. The emergency services are faced with an angry mob whenever they attempt to intervene. Firemen are pelted with bricks and bottles and the police are treated with hostility.

What is going on in Callon is happening in similar communities all over Preston. Shootings, stabbings and daylight robberies seem increasingly common. In an effort to stem the flow of gangland violence, Lancashire Police mounted an operation aimed at identifying the main offenders and taking them off the streets. They highlighted six main organised crime groups operating in the division that Callon and Farringdon Park fall within. Although the Callon Gang feature highly on their list of priorities, their rivals in Farringdon Park are seen as equally important to apprehend. The Farringdon Park Original Gangsters are involved in everything from antisocial behaviour to drug dealing and firearms offences. They are one of the city's most dangerous street gangs, using guns, knives and CS gas to bully and intimidate the law-abiding citizens of the surrounding estates.

The Farringdon Park estate, locally referred to as 'Dodge City', is home to just 210 family dwellings and sixty one-bedroom flats, most of which are council accommodation. Burglary, criminal damage and fly tipping have resulted in the estate becoming increasingly unsightly and rundown. A study conducted as part of a crime prevention initiative highlighted the Original Gangsters as one of the area's main perpetrators of criminal acts. In an effort to reduce the levels of offending, police made a concerted effort to control the gang's leaders. Several were issued with ASBOs and sixteen-year-old Tony Hamer was evicted from his house after allegations that he was using it as a base to sell crack cocaine and heroin. He was thought to be involved in a dispute in which four different houses were petrol bombed, including his own.

A search of Hamer's family home uncovered fourteen rocks of crack, £2,600, a CS gas canister and a truncheon. His mother Maureen denied that drugs had been dealt from her property but was accused of allowing her son to do as he pleased just as long as he was able to provide her with enough money to pay the rent.

The day after the Hamers were forced to leave their house, 140 of their neighbours added their names to a petition in favour of them staying put. The police claimed that the local residents had felt obliged to provide their signatures, although the truth was that the family were actually surprisingly popular. Tony Hamer evoked mixed feelings within the community. Whereas his mother and father were seen as relatively easy to get along with, he was regarded as a troublemaker and had been implicated in a number of violent incidents in the build-up to his arrest. The house of a man he was accused of stabbing had been bombarded with a series of petrol bombs.

Hamer was remanded into care whilst his case was pending. He managed to escape from the court precinct and ran off back to the estate, where he continued to make a nuisance of himself. Rather than lie low in the hope that he could pass below the radar, the young fugitive chose to carry on exactly as he had done before. He was aggressive and unpredictable, attempting to intimidate the other residents into doing as he said.

Within a day of his escape, Hamer had stabbed a teenage boy in the neck during an argument in which his victim was alleged to have pulled a gun on him. He was eventually rearrested and sentenced to eighteen months detention. The judge described him as particularly 'physically aggressive' and drew attention to his lengthy criminal record. He was still sixteen years of age; violence had become a way of life for him before he had even reached adulthood.

On July 30, 2007, Hamer was back in court on assault charges. He had been involved in a brutal robbery in which a sixteen-year-old boy was kidnapped, robbed and beaten before being taken to a second address where he was forced to tell the owner of the property that he was a friend of his captors. Three gang members were eventually apprehended in relation to the attack, including Hamer. All three received custodial sentences. Hamer's involvement with the Original Gangsters had eaten away at large chunks of his life. He may have gained the warped admiration of his peers on the estate but he had missed out on a substantial section of his teenage years.

When released from a young offenders' institution, he was again up to his old tricks within a matter of months. He was stopped in a taxi with a stolen £150 satnav and took it upon himself to run from the police. Fellow gang member Peter Killeen was caught nearby and Hamer was eventually arrested and charged with handling stolen property. He was given a twenty-six week sentence, suspended for two years – although he was also on an ASBO at the time and received twenty-eight days custody for breach of his terms. Killeen was sentenced to community service.

Both were repeat offenders and the trouble that they got from the law was nothing compared to what the other gangs in the area would do to them when they got hold of them. They had made a lot of enemies, and Killeen had come to realise that the police were a lot less scary than the other criminals in the city. Some of the episodes that he had been through were like a scene from a horror film.

Killeen was thought to have stolen a large amount of cocaine from a Fishwick-based drug gang. He had rubbed a dangerous group of people up the wrong way – but that was what being in a gang was all about. If anyone came looking for him, he would always have the rest of the firm to back him up. No-one would dare to go against the Original Gangsters – and if they did then they were either very brave or very stupid.

What the naïve young gangbanger had failed to take into account was the fact that revenge has a tendency to present itself at the most inappropriate junctures. He was enjoying a romantic night in a hotel with his girlfriend when two masked men burst through the door, intent on making him suffer. Nathan McManus was the type of person that lived for violence. He was already being investigated for incidents in which his ex-girlfriend was stabbed in the thigh and the girl-friend of another gang member was brutally assaulted. Anthony Butler was a similarly intimidating character. He had been involved in crime from his early teens. They were clad in balaclavas and wielding an axe. Karma had finally caught up with Killeen.

The couple awoke to the sound of raised voices and heavy footsteps. Killeen raised his hands to protect his face as McManus swung his deadly weapon towards his head. He felt a sharp pang of pain as it cut through the muscle in his arm and chipped his bone. Blood gushed from his open wound and within a matter of minutes, the hotel floor had become a dark shade of crimson.

Killeen survived the attack and told the police that it was probably a result of the drugs that he had stolen. The incident was caught on the hotel's CCTV cameras. Nathan McManus was convicted of two counts of wounding, aggravated burglary, possession of a prohibited weapon and common assault. He was given a fourteen-year jail sentence. Butler was sentenced to seven years in a young offenders institution after pleading guilty to aggravated burglary. His father spoke of his deep distress at the fact that his son had become involved with drugs and gangs. He claimed that Anthony's descent into crime had started at twelve years old when he was kicked out of school for bullying. By age thirteen he was smoking cannabis and he soon began selling drugs of his own so that he could afford his habit. 'After he tried it, another lad started giving him packages to deliver to pay for his cannabis,' Mr Butler told the *Lancashire*

Evening Post. 'It frightens the life out of me that these drugs are so easily available to kids.'

Within a short period of time, Anthony had started delivering shipments of drugs for the older youths on the estate. His lifestyle was becoming increasingly erratic. He was constantly running away from home and sleeping rough in the local park. He was reported missing on numerous occasions and his parents were worried that his behaviour would have a negative impact upon his younger sister.

At age sixteen, Butler was asked to leave home and move into a place of his own. He signed up for a business course at Preston College and made a half-hearted attempt to turn his life around but the lure of the streets soon proved strong and he began to nip out of the college to deliver drugs. Meanwhile, his long-suffering parents were subjected to two separate police raids. The pressure was too much for them to take and their relationship slowly disintegrated. Anthony's selfish lifestyle was tearing his family apart.

Nathan's mother Mandy claimed that her son had 'lost his way'. She said that his aunt, his cousin and his grandma had all recently died and added that he was drinking heavily and taking drugs to deal with his loss. She denied that he was in a gang and told the papers that he had only known Butler for a few weeks before the attack. The local police force painted a different picture altogether. Their intelligence suggested that he had joined the Fishwick gang despite growing up in the suburb of Ribbleton on the outskirts of the city. He had deliberately involved himself in the criminal culture of an area that he could have easily stayed well away from.

McManus continued to make the headlines even while behind bars. His half-brother, Kyle Bruney, was found in possession of a silver ME38 compact revolver. It was originally manufactured to shoot blanks but it had been modified so that it was capable of firing .38 rifle ammunition. He told the detectives that he had brought it home after discovering it in a field. The weapon contained traces of Nathan McManus' DNA. He had hidden it in Kyle's bedroom before being sent to jail for the axe attack and informed him of its whereabouts during a prison visit. Unfortunately for Kyle, his cousin Karl had threatened a man with an imitation firearm and his house was subjected to a lengthy police search. The revolver was discovered hidden at the back of his wardrobe and he was given a five-year jail term.

Guns are now a substantial problem on the streets of Preston. Speaking on behalf of the residents of another crime-infested part of the town, a councillor for Deepdale, Terry Cartwright warned that there was an increasing trend for carrying firearms. 'We never used to have guns,' he told reporters, seemingly taken aback at the speed at which the area had become unsafe. White and Asian street gangs were competing for territory, using an arsenal of deadly weaponry to defend their turf.

DEEPDALE, THE AREA from which Preston North End's football ground takes its name, is a multicultural suburb with a fifty per cent Asian population. The cultural makeup of the area is reflected in the membership of the three main firms that operate there. The Deepdale Youth Defenders are all Asian, whereas Deep Twisted Youngaz and Deep Cut Connections both contain white and black youths. And figures released in 2006 by the Racial Equality Council revealed Preston to have the highest ratio of racist incidents per population of anywhere in the country.

The Deepdale Youth Defenders came together in response to the abuse that the Asian community were suffering at the hands of teenage gangs from Callon. The latter is only a few hundred yards away from Deepdale but the residents of the two localities rarely mix. In July 2006, the Callon estate was home to a mass brawl between white and Asian youths. Shezan Umarji was stabbed fourteen times and his heart and major arteries were punctured. He died from his injuries, sparking a new wave of hostility between the two communities.

'Muslims and non-Muslims may live in the same town, but they move in different worlds,' a member of the Deepdale Youth Defenders explained to a *Daily Mail* reporter in October 2006. 'If the two sides speak, it is only by chance, and rarely by choice.' The Asian population have been forced into a state of relative apartheid by the attitudes of their racist Callon estate neighbours. The Defenders are there to ensure that none of the offending youths can enter their territory and expect to leave unscathed.

Not all of the Asian street gangs in the area are as community-minded as the Defenders consider themselves. Rival crack and heroin rings are becoming increasingly hostile towards one another. Drugs are big business and only a finite number of dealers can set up shop at any one time. The local crime bosses settle disputes over sales territory in the modern way: by shootings, stabbings and beatings.

One of the area's most prolific drug gangs was a collective of well-armed Pakistani heroin dealers selling to addicts all over Deepdale. They had been having trouble with rivals in nearby Fishwick and the situation was about to come to a head.

Mohammed Beg was driving his BMW along a residential street in Fishwick when members of the Deepdale gang deliberately crashed a white van into the side of it, bringing him skidding to a halt. A number of masked men jumped out and bundled him into the back of the van. He was taken to an address in Burnley where he was severely beaten around the head and torso. Three hours later, his unconscious body was dumped in a children's playground near Fishwick Road in Preston.

The Fishwick crew hit back. That same day, Dilbag Singh was chatting to a friend outside the Beer Busters off-licence in Deepdale when he became aware of a Renault Clio being driven nearby. Two gunmen jumped out of the car, walked over to him and shot him in the neck. He fell to the floor, where he was immediately set upon and beaten with a baseball bat. Blood was gushing from his wound and he was struggling to draw air into his lungs. He was rushed home to his family, where his panic stricken mother screamed in terror at the prospect of losing her son. A section of his neck had turned black and he was gurgling and choking.

Armed police escorted Singh to the hospital, fearing that his attackers would return to finish what they had started. Fifty-six shotgun pellets were removed from his flesh. He was lucky to have survived but was reluctant to name his attackers, although he eventually caved in and pointed the finger at Fishwick gang members Kyle 'Maj' Parvez and Zainul James.

By the time of the court case, Singh had become increasingly anxious about identifying his assailants. 'They put names there without my consent,' he told the court, blaming the police. 'They put names in the statement.' In a desperate attempt to avoid being labelled as a grass, he went on to claim that the signature at the bottom of the statement was a counterfeit and that the police had pressured him into providing evidence. Despite this, Parvez was sentenced to ten years behind bars after being found guilty of attempted murder and possession of a firearm with intent to commit murder and James was given a five-year sentence for arson, having been spotted burning the car that was used to drive the shooter to the scene of the crime. Dilbag was jailed for seven-and-a-half months after being found guilty of perjury.

Parvez's friends and family were determined to prove that the police had got the wrong man. They took his victim's sudden change of heart as proof of the two defendants' innocence. A Facebook group was set up proclaiming that the jury were biased because 'there was not one single mixed race person ... the judge may as well have gave them white hoods to put over their heads!' The group eventually attracted nearly 1,000 members, many of them leaving messages of support and expressing sympathy that Maj was 'falsely' imprisoned.

The Fishwick/Deepdale rivalry continues to threaten the peace of both localities. Members of the Fishwick faction are still enraged at the fact that Dilbag Singh provided evidence against them, whereas those within the Deepdale gang are angry that Singh was shot when he had nothing to do with the kidnap. The feud is testament to the manner in which a violent incident can evoke an even more violent response.

But what draws young people to join these gangs in the first place? Why do so many of the city's residents feel the need to arm themselves? During my time inside, I encountered Paddy, a Preston armed robber. He was a young, stocky inmate who seemed too laidback to have been involved in any form of serious crime. He was in his early twenties and he came across as polite and softly spoken, but said he had 'been involved in violence ever since I was a kid ... I've used knives, hammers, guns, whatever'. Behind his easy-going exterior was yet another man for whom crime was a way of life. He had spent the majority of his few adult years behind bars and had convictions ranging from petty assaults to threatening a police officer with a samurai sword.

At the age of fourteen, Paddy had been caught running around the street with a handgun and the police had let him off with a caution and a fine. He had told them that he found the gun by the side of the local canal and they had believed him and allowed him to walk free from the station. 'Nowadays I would have got five years. The funny thing was that I was actually telling the truth as well. That's how common guns are in Preston – I found one lying on the floor, fully loaded. These days it's even worse though. It's like a mini Manchester. There are gangs and guns all over the city.'

One reason that Paddy relied on crime was that he was completely illiterate prior to entering the prison system. 'I couldn't even write my own name. I never went to school when I was a kid. I was hanging about on street corners, drinking and robbing cars instead. I got my first supervision order for a TWOC at fourteen and I've never looked back since. Robbing and stealing has been my only form of income.'

In between stealing cars and breaking into shops, he had hung around with a local street gang, who would go out on the town looking for a fight every Friday and Saturday night. 'A drink and a fight, that was all there really was to do. We used to rob a load of cans and go out causing trouble. The same year I got done for the TWOC, I got another charge for throwing a drainpipe through a pub window. It hit this fella in the face and he ended up with seventeen stitches. I got another slap on the wrists for it.'

Paddy became more and more out of control, until the night of his sixteenth birthday, when he went too far and ended up with a custodial sentence. 'We had broken into a pub cellar and drank all of the beer the night before so we were still pissed up from then. One thing led to another and we ended up fighting with the bouncers outside this club that we'd been in. My mate had a hammer on him and the bouncers got the living fuck beaten out of them but what we didn't know was that the whole thing had been caught on CCTV. I ended up doing nine months on remand for it.'

One of the first things that struck him about the young offenders' institute where he remained until his court date was the extreme territorialism of the other prisoners on the wing. 'Everyone was split up according to what area they were from,' he said. 'It was Mancs versus Scousers 'cause they were the two main groups in there and the other towns and cities were forced to take sides. The Preston lads allied with the Mancs and we were fighting with the Scousers nearly every week. The Mancs don't fuck about, they weren't into fighting with hammers and bats like we were, they had connects for pretty much everything. They put us onto all sorts and by the time I got out I knew how to do ramraids, armed blags, you name it.'

Paddy had walked out of the prison a different person. 'When you come out of jail, you're a better class of criminal. I'd met people who could get hold of guns, drugs, whatever, and on top of that, I was mates with some proper naughty people who were all getting out at round about the same time as me. I was fucking made up.'

Now that he was in with professional criminals, Paddy's 'TWOCing' days were over, although his driving skills still came in handy. 'You need a decent driver for nearly every type of crime that you can do and I was the best of the best,' he boasted. 'We started off with cash machines. We'd cut the alarm wire, saw the hinges off with a still saw, pry the door off and then drive away with the cash. They usually had around seventeen grand in each machine and we'd have three different getaway cars positioned around the city so that we could keep changing our vehicle. There were normally four of us involved in each graft so I got around four grand a time. Obviously this is what the rest of the firm did, not me. I'm not going to confess to anything they haven't got me for.

'The next thing they got into was armed robberies. I'm not saying whether I had anything to do with them or not but I can tell you how the rest of the lads got into them. We used to hang about in a derelict flat above a betting shop and one of my mates accidentally put his foot through the floorboards. There wasn't a big hole there but it was big enough to see down into the bookies and it gave him an idea for a graft. He waited until six o'clock on a Saturday, the busiest day for betting, and then he smashed through the floor and a couple of lads went down with him to tie the staff up and take their money from them. All of the lads were ballied up so that no-one could tell who they were. A few of them had bats with them and the rest of them had lump hammers. They wrapped the workers up in gaffer tape and tied their arms and legs with tie-wraps and once they were satisfied that they couldn't get away, they loaded the money into a carrier bag and that was that. They ended up getting a grand odd each from it.'

The betting shop robbery had given the firm a taste for armed blags and it wasn't long before they struck again. This time, they targeted a post office on a nearby estate, kicking the door off the owner's house and forcing him to open the safe for them. 'The safe was on a timer. We kept his family tied up in case he refused to co-operate and then we waited until eight in the morning when we could get at the cash. Well when I say "we" I mean the rest of the firm... I was asleep at home, obviously.'

This time, the gang weren't taking any chances. Several of them had knives and one had a gun and in order to make sure that they were able to make a clean getaway, stolen motorbikes were positioned at strategic points around the city. 'You can out-run the cops more easily on a bike. You can go up the pavements and even take them off road if you need to. They're a lot better than cars for stuff like that. Saying that, it didn't even get to that stage. We left everyone tied up so that there was nobody to call the cops on us. We ended up getting off with eight grand, a load of commemorative coins and a binbag full of stamps. We couldn't find a fence to shift the coins and the stamps on to so we binned them all in the end. It was a bit of a waste, really.'

Paddy was still only seventeen at this stage and, despite the fact that he was involving himself in serious crime, he was still making less than an average armed robber might expect. He had progressed from being part of a gang that fought with other groups of youths to being a member of a gun-wielding armed robbery cartel but I couldn't help feeling that he had retained the same thrill-seeking mentality. 'Well yeah, there is that to it,' he confessed to me. 'When you're a kid, you get your thrills from fighting with other kids. Sometimes you will use knives and bats and it will give you even more of a thrill. Then you get used to the buzz that you get from it and you need something else. We were doing the robberies as much for the rush as we were doing them for the cash. I think if they're honest, any other blagger [robber] will tell you exactly the same thing.

It seemed as if Paddy had moved on to post office robberies as a way of attempting to recreate the buzz that he had gained during his time as a teenage gang member. 'It's the way most people go,' he told me. 'Most criminals are in gangs when they're younger then when they get older, they end up going to jail and realise that they can carry on having the same bond with their mates by going out blagging or selling drugs as a firm. The prisoners from Manchester and Liverpool show them a couple of things and by the time they get out, they're ready to go back to their estates and teach their mates how to do stick-ups and proper commercial burglaries. I think that's the problem. If you lock kids up for scrapping with each other then you really will turn them into crooks. There's gangs and then there's *proper* gangs, if you know what I mean, and it's pretty easy to turn a group of inexperienced street kids into a proper outfit.'

Paddy had confirmed what the Chief Constable had said about the crooks from Preston emulating Manchester criminals, although he went further by asserting that they were being exposed to Mancunian gang culture behind the prison walls. Rather than drawing their influence from the handful of Gooch and Doddington members that they had seen outside Preston Crown Court, the local tearaways were being placed in young offenders' institutions where a large percentage of the overall population hailed from Manchester. It is impossible to spend a year or more locked away on a wing with a group of people without adopting some of their characteristics. Just as trends in clothing and music are transported from city to city by people travelling from one location to another, trends in crime are passed along from prisoner to prisoner. Gang culture is slowly spreading throughout the country's institutions and it is creating a series of identikit street gangs all over the UK.

Preston is atypical in that the police are open about the emergence of criminal gangs within the city. Whereas the authorities in other parts of the country have often downplayed the reality of what is going on, Fishwick and Deepdale's rising tide of teenage gun crime has been acknowledged and acted upon by the local constabulary. In 2007, one detective warned that he was using firearms warrants on a daily basis and spoke of the escalating intensity of violence in the town. Rather than sweeping the problem under the rug, a number of steps have been taken to reduce gang membership. Officers have implemented a policy of targeting antisocial peer groups before they develop into gangs, attempting to disrupt their activities at the earliest possible stage. Various sporting events have been set up to provide a diversion for the city's youth. Certainly great efforts are being made, yet media reports of drive-by shootings, punishment beatings and stabbings continue to make the people of Preston increasingly fearful.

Leeds

MY PERCEPTION OF Leeds prior to my own arrest was of a vibrant, multicultural city with a laidback, student-friendly atmosphere. Then again, I had only ever seen the parts of the city where my fellow students lived. I had never been to any of the large, deprived estates where the majority of the crime took place. The Leeds that I saw during my time at university was a world away from the Leeds that my fellow inmates in Armley Gaol had seen. I had been cocooned in a small pocket of respectability.

Although I was still fairly naïve back then, there were always certain parts of town that I would avoid. Chapeltown, for instance, had a reputation. There seemed to be drug busts there every other week and every now and again there would be a shooting as dealers jostled for control of the area's lucrative crack and heroin markets. Then there were places like Seacroft and Halton Moor, which were reputedly filled with teenage joyriders and grizzled drug addicts, and Swarcliffe, a part of the city where crime and antisocial behaviour had been a way of life for generations.

Swarcliffe is a poor, predominantly white estate to the east of the city, nestled away within the 'Golden Triangle', a term used to describe an area of largely affluent suburbs in West and North Yorkshire. It is one of the few localities within this district that fall firmly below the poverty line, with levels of unemployment and benefit-dependency way above the national average. It is also home to a violent street gang known as the Swarcliffe Warriors, who have terrorised the local population since the mid-nineties.

During my time inside I became good friends with one of the founding members of the Warriors, who was able to describe how the gang situation on the estate had first come about. I shall call him Chris.

'I was thirteen when it all started,' he explained. 'The whole "Warriors" thing was a bit of a joke really. We saw that film *The Warriors* and we took the name from there. We had a lot of different names though and we changed them all the time. Most of the other areas knew us as LS14, which is the postcode for Swarcliffe and Seacroft, where most of our members were from. They probably don't even call the Swarcliffe firm "the Warriors" any more, although the estate's still got a gang there and we paved the way for what's going on today.

'We started out doing stupid things like picking fights with random passers-by. We had an initiation where you had to kick off on somebody harder than you, just to prove that you were game enough to knock about with us. That was when we were still just kids, messing about. In the beginning it was just fist-fights. Then when we got a few years older, the knives started coming onto the scene.

'When there's other mobs using guns and knives, you're not exactly going to want to take them on with your bare hands. Times changed and things moved on and a couple of years down the line, we were using knives, machetes, crossbows, you name it. Pitbulls as well – if one of those things gets a grip of you then you really fucking know about it.

'Leeds is bad for knives and bats and stuff like that.

Chapeltown and Harehills are bad for shooters as well. I remember going down there in a TWOC [stolen car] when I was fifteen. One of the lads wanted to buy some crack. I don't personally touch the stuff but a few of my boys did. We were on an estate called the Hamiltons in Chapeltown and we'd just bought some rocks off this black fella when I heard a loud bang and shots started ricocheting off the bonnet of the car. Let's just say we didn't hang around the place to see who was firing at us. They had a firm round there called the CPT Crew who were always firing shots off. It was a scary place to go to back in those days.'

Were there, I asked, any other areas that he was wary about going to?

'To be honest, everywhere had its naughty bits,' he said. 'Little London could be bad, there were a fair few shooters going about round there. Crossgates had the Poole Estate Boys, who were a tidy little firm, and even Chapel Allerton had its own gang. They were nearly all girls but they fought better than most of the lads did.'

Chapel Allerton is one of the richer, more desirable areas of the city. I was curious to know how a violent gang had sprung up from such a well-to-do part of town.

'Well all it takes is a couple of rough estates,' said Chris. 'You get a group of ten lads together and arm them all up with blades and then, bam, you've got a gang. The Chapel Allerton Crew were just a load of big, burly fighting birds really though. They weren't anything special but they stood out 'cause they were all female. Our biggest rivals were the Halton Moorers, we had more trouble off them than we did from all of the other estates put together. They were a firm and a half. It was them that gave me this.'

He lifted up his prison issue tee-shirt to reveal a scar

stretching from one end of his stomach to the other. 'A carload of them jumped out on me and then they beat the fuck out of me and slashed me with a Stanley knife.'

Halton Moor is another poor, largely white council estate to the east of the city. It is notorious for car crime and the feud between the Halton Moorers and the Warriors originally started out as an argument over which area had the best TWOCers, or joyriders. As the years went by, the animosity between the two groups intensified to the point where it became dangerous for anybody from Halton Moor to walk through Swarcliffe. There were tit-for-tat stabbings and slashings on either side of the divide and youths on the two estates quickly developed a hatred for one another.

Chris and his friends took great pride in sleeping with girls from Halton Moor as a form of one-upmanship. The ultimate coup was to pull a girl from their rival estate and then burgle her house once she had nodded off to sleep. 'If we hadn't fucked about with their women then I wouldn't have ended up doing my first sentence,' he told me. 'We knew what pubs their birds drank in, they were always in Delaneys and Ford Green in town, and one of our lads ended up shagging a lass that was going out with one of their main lads. Two carloads of them came down to have it out with us and I ended up punching one of them in the head and fracturing his skull. I didn't mean to kill him. His mum even stood up in court for me and told them that it was an accident. I ended up doing four years for it.'

It seemed to me that Chris had got off fairly lightly, given the severity of the crime that he had committed. 'Not really though,' he sighed, his eyes fixed firmly upon the floor as he spoke. 'Just before they banged me up, I found out that my girlfriend had a kid on the way. I missed out on the most important period of his life. I was going to go to college as well. As it is, I ended up in YPs [a young persons' centre] instead.'

So had the Warriors been involved in any more profit orientated forms of crime or did they exist solely to defend the reputation of their area? Chris had sacrificed four years of his life for the gang but had he gained anything from his affiliation, other than a criminal record and the guilt of taking another man's life? 'Well we went out thieving together as well,' he said. 'We were mainly into house burglaries. There's nothing like being where you're not supposed to be to get your blood pumping. You feel so alert and alive when you're robbing someone's house, it's like the best coke you've ever had.'

He usually chose to commit burglaries during the day. 'Well if you get caught during the night it's classed as aggravated burglary,' he said. 'Plus people are normally in at night. The best time to strike is whilst they're out at work. It's easy really. You knock on the door to see if there's anybody there and if somebody answers it, you just ask for a made up name and then fuck off. If we were sure that there was nobody home, I'd kick the door in and we'd help ourselves. I had a really strong kick so I was always the one that got us in there.'

It seemed like a heavy-handed approach to burgling a house. The Warriors didn't seem to care if anybody caught them in the act. After all, what could they really do about it? Any home owner who confronted them would have been in grave danger. 'Nine out of ten times, a burglar will have a weapon on them. Most people aren't going to risk getting stabbed or slashed just to stop somebody from thieving from them. They'll usually just let them take their stuff and then ring the police afterwards. Don't get me wrong, I wouldn't like it if the shoe was on the other foot and somebody burgled my house, but then again I'd say that there are more people in

Seacroft and Swarcliffe who make their money through crime than there are that work. When you're from them types of places, you've got no other option but to go out robbing for a living.'

The city's bareknuckle boxing scene was another lucrative source of income for Chris and his fellow gang members. The Warriors would take part in illegal fights in which the winner and the loser were both paid £100 and DVDs of the action were sold to the spectators. The events were held in Hunslet in south Leeds and were run by the local gypsy population, who would frequently attack the competitors and take their money back from them whilst they were attempting to make their way out of the estate. 'The second time I got stabbed up, it was by a gypsy,' Chris told me. 'I won the fight and the relatives of the fella that I beat weren't too pleased about it so they jumped me and stuck a blade in my belly. The estate that the fights were held in was controlled by a firm of proper hardcore pikeys and they didn't fuck about. The police were afraid to get involved because a lot of them had shotguns on them. It was always risky going there but it was a good way of getting a reputation. All of the kids from the area would see the DVD and if you did well for yourself, you'd end up as a local hero.'

'So didn't you ever have any gang fights with the gypsies?' I asked him, wondering whether he had ever tried to get revenge for the fact that he had been stabbed.

'Do I look like a dead man?' he laughed. 'Nah, you mess about with those cunts and you'll end up in a pine box. I'd rather have it out with the blacks in Chapeltown! You can't have a fight with a single group of blacks or a single group of pikeys without them all getting involved. It's the same with the Pakis, you fuck about with one of their gangs and you'll end up with a fucking army of them breathing down your neck.'

This was the first time that I'd heard him mention the existence of Asian gangs within the city. Were they as prolific as the white and black gangs were?

'Well most of them are in Beeston and Holbeck,' he said. 'I couldn't really tell you because I never went there that much. All I know is that there's a mob called the Beeston Massive Crew who are always scrapping with the white firms from round there. You want to talk to Stevie from Beeston, he was in the Paki Hater Crew, the main white gang from round that way.'

Stevie was a hard-looking white drug dealer who hung around with the black prisoners on the wing. I found it odd that an inmate who had an almost exclusively Afro-Caribbean circle of friends was a member of a gang that was based around hatred towards another ethnic group. Still, there was only one way to find out what had caused him to join.

I was careful not to approach Stevie whilst he was with any of his black friends, as I wasn't sure how they would react to the news that he was part of a group that attacked people based on their ethnicity. I waited until he was on his own in his cell and then I spent the next half an hour quizzing him about his reasons for joining the gang. Like all of the other inmates that I had spoken to, he seemed eager to talk about his life and he made no bones about the fact that he had grown up in an environment where violence was the norm.

'I've been involved with gangs since I was twelve years old,' he said. 'I spent my childhood in Meanwood which was fairly quiet and trouble free and then when I was eleven I moved to the East Grange estate in Belle Isle, which was rough as fuck. Lads from the West Grange estate were always kicking off with us so I ended up joining a gang called the East Grange Boys, who would go into their estate and play fuck with them. That was when I first developed a taste for fighting and I've loved to have a do [fight] ever since then. When you're alongside your mates and you're fighting for your area, you feel on top of the world.'

Belle Isle is another of the city's poorer suburbs. Crime amongst young people is rampant and children as young as eight have been known to set up trip wires for passing motorists so that they can incapacitate their vehicles and attack them. Still, according to Stevie it was never a difficult place for him to fit in. 'I've always had that wild side to me,' he grinned. 'Almost as soon as I moved onto the estate, I knew that it was for me. At twelve years old I was going out TWOCing with the rest of the firm and then at thirteen, I got caught in a stolie [stolen car] and ended up with a supervision order. It didn't put me off in the slightest though. The fact that I'd been in trouble with the police made me feel like I was a proper rebel and it spurred me on to do something more serious.'

At fourteen, Stevie decided to up the ante by committing his first burglary. 'I didn't do houses. Just shops and factories and places like that. I was getting at least seven hundred pounds a week, which is a lot of money when you're that age. I was robbing cars and bikes as well, only by that point I was selling them on. I've always been a grafter. Whilst you were busy playing with toys, I was probably out trying to make a raise. That's just the type of person that I am.'

Stevie spent the majority of his earnings on weed, alcohol and cocaine. He lived a hedonistic lifestyle of drugs, drink and violence and his perfect weekend consisted of a bag of white powder and a fight with a rival firm. Now that they were all a little bit older, the gangs from Belle Isle had decided to put their differences aside in order to team up against the Miggy Boys from the neighbouring area of Middleton. 'Middleton had a much bigger firm than us,' Stevie explained. 'We still had the odd bit of trouble between the two estates but most of the time we just fought together against the Miggy lot. Sometimes they'd come into Belle Isle to have it out with us and other times we'd go to their estate. It was a bit of a laugh really. No-one ever got badly hurt, as far as I can remember.'

Stevie was not your average fourteen-year-old boy. He was in constant trouble with the police and by the time he reached his fifteenth birthday, he had racked up a lengthy list of criminal offences. 'The first major thing I got caught for was a burglary,' he told me. 'I broke into a car show room and drove all the cars away. Then I got an ASBO for theft and commercial burglary, then I got caught stealing a car and then eventually I ended up getting sent to a borstal for robbing somebody's bike. By that stage I'd already been expelled from school for driving a car onto the playground so it wasn't like I was missing much.

'Borstal was shit. It's not like adult prison where they let you live, if you don't stick up for yourself, the other kids will take everything that you've got from you. Saying that, I was still exactly the same when I got out, only I was more clued up.' After hearing what the other criminals had been up to, he had decided to start stealing the stock from delivery vehicles almost as soon as he was set free. He would slash the fabric at the back of the wagons and load the goods into the back of a stolen truck, ready to sell them on to a fence. It was far more profitable than the burglaries had been and he made over £2,000 a week.

By the time he was nineteen, Stevie had already served ten separate jail sentences. 'I was doing my best not to get caught but things just kept coming on top for me. That was when I realised that something had to change. I had some family in Beeston so I decided to move there in the hope that it would take the heat off me. The idea was that I was going to lie low for a bit but things didn't exactly work out how they should have done.'

Beeston was even rougher than Belle Isle and there was tension between the white and Asian communities there. Stevie didn't like the Asians. 'People like to make out that it's white versus Asian in Beeston,' he said. 'It's not like that though, it's white and black versus Asian. Nobody likes them. In fact the reason the PHC [Paki Hater Crew] came into existence was because they killed this black lad, Tyrone. They've brought everything that's happened to them upon themselves.'

Sixteen-year-old Tyrone Clarke was beaten and stabbed to death by a group of up to twenty youths after being chased through Beeston by an armed gang. He was sprayed with CS gas, struck with baseball bats, hit with metal scaffolding poles and a knife was plunged into his heart three times. Although the killing was thought to have taken place as a result of a fight that he had been involved in with a group of Asian teenagers, Tyrone's friends were convinced that there was a racial motivation for the attack. 'If it was the other way around, they would have all gone down for race hate,' Stevie told me. 'As it was they just got standard murder charges. A lot of people weren't happy and that's when we decided to do something about it.'

On the day of Clarke's wake, a crowd of white and black residents descended upon an Asian-owned corner shop. They chanted racist abuse at the terrified shop workers before causing £5,000 worth of damage and assaulting several of the employees. Four men were eventually convicted of violent disorder but by the time they had been identified, two of them were already serving sentences for supplying heroin and one of them was in prison for an unconnected manslaughter.

Whereas the white and Asian populations had once coexisted relatively peacefully with one another, Beeston was now a divided community. There was talk of two new gangs patrolling the streets: the all-Asian Beeston Massive Crew and the ultra-racist Paki Hater Crew. 'That was when I got sucked back into my old way of life,' said Stevie. 'Tyrone was my friend and I couldn't just sit back and do nothing. I've always hated Pakis anyway. I don't mind the westernised ones, we had a few of them hanging about with us. It was the ones from Beeston Hill that I hated.'

In 2009, an Asian worker at a mosque in Beeston warned a newspaper reporter that the population in the area was becoming more and more segregated. 'PHC, Paki Hater Club, is here,' he said. 'They are organised, Combat 18, people like that.'

'They were right to be worried,' said Stevie. 'It's a different level to what was going on in Belle Isle. It's not just a bunch of kids scrapping with each other. There's knives and CS gas being used and it will only be a matter of time before somebody else is killed.'

Several of the PHC were also heavily involved in the drug trade. Beeston had no shortage of addicts and when it came to matters of money, the gang were suddenly a lot less bothered about the colour of a person's skin. 'It's not about whether they're white or brown, it's about whether they're buying white or brown,' said Stevie. He was willing to peddle his wares to anybody, regardless of their ethnicity, just so long as they had the right amount of money and they didn't look like a cop.

Stevie was soon earning a minimum of £2,500 a week from selling drugs. He travelled all over Beeston and Holbeck to deliver his product and he would pass through BMC territory on a daily basis. 'Beeston's not one of these places where there's areas that you can't walk through. You just have to be a bit more careful in the Paki areas. Saying that though, the only time that anybody ever tried to tax me, it was another white lad. It was one of my regular sales as well. He asked for four brown and four white and then when I went to meet him, he hit me with something and knocked me out. When I came round again, he'd taken my drugs, my money, my phone and my trainers. I don't know how he ever expected to get away with it. I almost killed the fucker the next time I saw him.'

Selling drugs could be a risky business. It wasn't only people attempting to steal his wares that he had to worry about. Addicts are untrustworthy and the slightest disagreement can result in information being passed on to the police. 'You've got to keep on people's good sides when you're in that kind of business but at the same time, you can't let anybody take you for a muppet. That was my downfall, I wasn't willing to let things slide with them. One of my sales kept turning up at my house night after night, begging me to sell him drugs. He was bringing things on top for me so I cracked him with a bat a couple of times. A few days later, he rang up apologising and asking to meet me so that he could buy some brown off me. I was just handing over the gear when a copper jumped out and slapped the cuffs on me. I ended up getting three-and-a-half years for it.'

So was he likely to carry on selling drugs when he got out of prison? Surprisingly, the answer appeared to be no. 'I found out that my girlfriend's sister was a heroin addict just before I got sent down,' he said. 'Her kids were so mistreated and neglected. They were completely forgotten about. It's sickening to think that something that I sold did that to people. When I get out I'm probably still going to have it out with the Pakis but I'm not going to have anything to do with crack or heroin. They ruin people's lives and I don't want any part in it.'

In a place where crime and antisocial behaviour are rampant, it can be difficult to remain on the straight and narrow once you have sampled the rewards of criminal activity. Much as he may have intended to stop selling drugs, I suspected that Stevie might eventually lapse back into his old habits. After all, he had moved to Beeston in order to start again and he had soon become involved in exactly the same activities that were getting him into trouble in Belle Isle.

'What do you think would have dissuaded you from becoming involved in crime?' I asked.

'Well if I'd have carried on living in Meanwood then the opportunity wouldn't have been there,' he said. 'At the end of the day, certain people are always going to have a side to them where they will want to get into trouble. It's a matter of whether they can find enough people to go along with them or not. There's only one way to stop the violence on the streets: Don't shove us together on the same estates and expect us all to live in harmony. If you put all of the biggest madheads right next door to each other then it's obvious how it's all going to end. You can lay the blame on us but do you really think that you would have turned out any better than me if you grew up where I grew up?

'Let's put it this way. If you think that Leeds is bad, you want to go to some of the estates in Bradford. Go to Holme Wood and then try and tell me that most of the people there aren't crooks...'

Bradford

HOLME WOOD IS one of Britain's largest council estates, with a population of 10,000. It is also renowned for being at the centre of the city's crack and heroin trade, a fact that was attested to by the numerous different drug crews that I met from there during the course of my prison sentence. Indeed the number of prisoners on the wing who were originally from Holme Wood was staggering; I was surprised that there was anybody left living there. If there was ever a place where more people made their money through 'grafting' than through working then it was definitely a strong contender.

Stevie, the hardman from Beeston, pointed me in the direction of a high-ranking villain from the estate. 'Kenny's the guy you want to talk to,' he told me. 'His lot had things on lock, from cars to drugs.'

Kenny was a young, well-built inmate who seemed to relish the opportunity to tell me about his firm. The moment I approached him for information, he immediately started reeling off a long list of offences that his gang had been involved in during the course of their time together. 'I'll tell you how we do things Holme Wood style,' he said. 'You name it, we've done it. Smash-and-grabs, burglaries, drugs, guns, everything.

'I started off with car crime. TWOCing is like a tradition in Holme Wood. When you're a kid you do it for the crack but then when you get a little bit older, you realise how much money there is to be made from it. If you've got a reputation for being a good driver then there are always older faces who will approach you and tell you what cars they want you to get. At first I was going for whatever I could get my hands on, but when I got a little bit older I started targeting high-powered sports cars. What's the point in wasting time on bangers when you can get the top of the range vehicles to sell? It made more sense to go out and hunt for the cars that I knew would sell for a lot rather than just getting anything that was to hand.

'You need a firm with you if you want to be a pro,' he went on. 'If you're earning money from crime, people are going to try and take it from you so you need some people that you can call on to back you up. We didn't class ourselves as a gang or anything like that, we were just a group of mates, really. Other people might have thought that we were a gang but most thieves will work as part of a team so it was never anything particularly out of the ordinary.'

Kenny's 'group of mates' provided him with a certain level of protection but there were always people on the estate who were willing to try their luck, regardless of how many of the other local criminals he had on board with him. 'There's only one way of truly guaranteeing that nobody messes with you and that's with a strap,' he said. 'I was sixteen when I bought my first gun. Well guns, actually; I got three of them. I bought a sawn-off .410 shotgun, a nine-millimetre handgun and an eight-millimetre rifle and then I buried them in the ground in case I ever needed to use them.'

Holme Wood is not an area traditionally associated with gun crime. The public perception is that it is mainly inhabited by low-level car thieves as opposed to dangerous armed criminals. How easy was it to get hold of a firearm on the estate?

'Why, are you thinking of buying a strap?' asked Kenny jokingly. 'Nah seriously, you can get a piece within the hour if you need one. I got mine from a fella called Jeff the Gun over in Fagley. That was what people actually called him as well, and I'll tell you what, it fucking suited him. His house was like a military bunker. He took me down into his basement and he had everything you could ever need: grenades, Uzis, MAC-10s, all types of machetes and swords, you name it.'

Fagley is another large council estate to the north of the city. It seemed that while the media were focussing attention on so-called black-on-black gun crime, white criminals there were trading in all manner of different weapons with relative impunity. 'How much did Jeff sell his guns for then?' I asked, curious as to how the prices compared to firearms in other cities. 'I got the .410 for £450,' Kenny told me. 'You could get a secondhand shooter off him for a couple of hundred quid. The grenades were fifty quid a pop and then if you wanted a machine gun or something like that it would probably set you back a couple of grand.'

'Have you ever actually needed to use any of the guns that you bought?' I asked.

'Yeah, they would have been a waste of money otherwise. When he was around sixteen, my younger brother got himself debted up to one of the local coke dealers. The dealer kept hounding him for the cash so I went and had a word with him. I said, "Look mush, you're getting fuck all. If you want your money then you can fight me for it." Five minutes later he'd gone and fetched his dad so that we could straighten things out. His dad was a pussy and he didn't want to face me so I went out and booted his car. The next thing I knew, his big, fat, twenty-stone sister was trying to hit my brother so I smashed her over the head with a barstool. After that, we kept getting phone calls saying rah, rah, rah, I'm going to shoot you and burn your fucking house down. The calls went on for a couple of weeks and then it all died down. I was finally beginning to think that we'd seen the back of it all when the dealer's dad turned up at my mate's house, looking to do me in.'

It was two in the morning and Kenny and his friend were drinking and snorting coke. They had ordered a pizza and they were planning on having a night in, without any trouble for once. There was a knock on the door. It seemed too soon for the pizza delivery and, sensing something was amiss, Kenny's girlfriend peered through the window to see who it was. She could just make out the silhouette of a grizzled-looking man concealing something beneath his jacket. She knew straight away that it was a gun.

'He's got a piece!' she screamed. Kenny ran to the kitchen and grabbed a knife. 'Don't open it,' he shouted but she was already opening the door.

'Where's Kenny?' the angry gunman bellowed in her ear, drunkenly waving a pistol inches from her face. 'I'll count to three and if you don't tell me where he is then I'll shoot you.'

Sensing that the man meant business, Kenny's friend attempted to step in to calm him down. 'Just put the gun down,' he said. 'Kenny isn't here.' It was not a wise move. The next thing he knew, he had been shot in the leg from point blank range and he was hopping around the room in agony.

'He looked like he'd stepped on a land mine. There was bits of his leg everywhere,' said Kenny. 'I ran in and tried to drag him to safety and the mush who shot him did a runner; he must have realised that he'd gone too far. I was wasted at the time, I'd been taking coke and Es all night so I wasn't really thinking straight. I jumped into a car, dug my nine up and went and got the rest of the firm together to go and look for him.

'I went round his house to do him in but his missus was there and she said that he'd took his stuff and fled. A few weeks later I heard that he'd left the country. Good for him, he'd have a bullet in his head by now if he'd have stayed.'

Kenny insisted he would have shot the man had he found him. 'Yeah,' he said. 'I've shot at people before, a few times. A couple of years after I started stealing the sports cars, I developed a serious coke habit and I started selling some bags on to fund it. When you're involved in that type of business, you meet a lot of nasty people and you have to be willing to defend yourself.'

Whereas several of the dealers from Leeds had been able to peddle their wares without the need for violence, the drug game in Bradford seemed a lot more competitive and a gun was an essential tool of the trade. 'The rougher the place you live, the better,' said Kenny. 'If you live in a poofy area, you're going to struggle to find enough people to sell to. Fair enough you'll probably be able to shift a fair bit of coke but when it comes to crack and heroin, Holme Wood is the best round in Bradford. We were selling all three and I was making between two and four grand a day. That's probably more than most judges make.'

Kenny's phone was switched on twenty-four hours a day, seven days a week, and he prided himself upon the fact that his clients could get through to him whenever they needed drugs. 'I was always coked up so I was always awake. Don't get me wrong, coke's probably one of the worst drugs that you can take but it's good for getting things done. People who smoke weed all the time are always half-asleep. If you're on the sniff all day then you're going to be wide awake and looking for things to do.'

In order to supplement their earnings from selling drugs, Kenny and his gang would engage in all manner of other illegal activities. They were particularly adept at ram-raiding and they would steal a jeep, crash it into a cash machine, chain the machine to the back of the vehicle and then drive it back to Holme Wood to count their earnings. 'We had the best driver in Bradford with us,' he boasted. 'We got chased by helicopters a couple of times but we always managed to outrun them. There was usually four of us doing each graft and we ended up with ten grand each.'

Commercial burglaries were another lucrative source of income. The rest of the firm would cut a section out of a shop roof and lower Kenny down through the hole using a wagon strap. 'It was like *Mission Impossible*. We usually made around four grand each, which isn't bad for a couple of hours' work. We didn't like to limit ourselves to one particular crime though, we did everything. Car crime was what we did best but we'd do houses, factories, bikes, trucks – anything.'

So did Kenny spend all of his earnings on cocaine or did he have any left over at the end of each day? 'It didn't necessarily all go on coke,' he said. 'Some of it went on clothes, some of it went on cars and bikes. When you make your money illegally, it's difficult to bank it without the coppers getting onto you so you end up blowing most of it. Saying that though, I've got a fair bit stashed away for when I'm free again. I can't be going out of jail and begging change off people.'

In an attempt to get Kenny to point me in the direction of somebody else from Bradford that I could talk to, I asked him who his main competition was. 'Hmm, that's a hard one,' he mused. 'There's so many lads on the graft nowadays I wouldn't even know where to start. There's a lot of Pakis who are doing well for themselves at the moment. Some of them have managed to put their money into chicken shops and restaurants, which is good for them 'cause it means that it's all washed up [laundered].'

Then he came up with a name from one of the Asian gangs who might tell me more. 'Maybe Imran,' he said. 'He was only a runner but he can tell you what it's like selling drugs for them. Slip him a couple of bags of gear and he'll tell you anything you want to know.'

Imran had been selling narcotics for far too long and the free samples that he'd been given to supplement his payment had left him looking considerably worse for wear. He was skinny and pale, with a mouthful of black, discoloured teeth and a level of personal hygiene that would make a goat hold its nose. His chosen profession had taken away any ounce of dignity that he may have once had and he had reached the stage where he would do anything to get a fix. As well as being addicted to both crack and heroin, he was also a chain smoker and I felt that offering him tobacco would be marginally less immoral than plying him with bags of heroin so that he would tell me about his firm. 'I'll give you a pack of burn [tobacco] if you tell me a bit about the people that you were selling for,' I told him. Whereas certain inmates chose to observe a strict code of silence, others held the view that it was acceptable to talk about their crimes just as long as they didn't incriminate any of the people that they had worked with.

'What do you need to know?' he asked me. 'Throw in an extra half a pack and I'll make sure that I don't leave anything out.'

Although he had been one of the lowest ranking members of his gang, Imran was surprisingly knowledgeable about the inner workings of the firm. 'The people at the top don't want to get their hands dirty,' he said. 'Think of Richard Branson.

When you get a flight with Virgin, he's not there serving you your food on the plane. He's got his workers to do that for him and it's the same with dealers. I was like the flight attendant. I did the things that the main guys didn't want to do themselves.'

'Weren't you bothered that you were getting used to do someone else's dirty work?' I asked him, surprised that he was so accepting of the fact that he was effectively another dealer's lapdog.

'Well when you're on drugs you want them straight away,' he said. 'It's easier working for somebody else rather than having to find your own customers. I got two hundred pounds a week and enough brown and white to keep me going so I was always happy. A lot of Asian dealers will treat you like you're scum if you're a Muslim and you're on gear but my boss was never like that. He was always fair with me and I always got on well with him. He could have paid me a little bit more but I got as much as I needed so I don't think I was getting a particularly raw deal.'

Imran had been fully aware that he was being paid peanuts yet at the same time, he knew deep down that it was the only form of employment that he was ever likely to get. His job was to deliver £10 wraps of crack and heroin to a number of different locations across West Yorkshire. 'My main rounds were in Beeston and Holbeck. All of the runners had their own territory where they would sell their drugs. I'd get driven to Leeds every morning at ten a.m. and then somebody would collect me at eight at night and drop me off in Manningham, where the rest of the firm were waiting for me. I'd give them the money that I'd earned and they would pay me my wage. If I'd sold a lot of gear, they'd throw in some extra bags for me as well.'

Manningham is at the heart of the city's Asian community. It is also a centre of vice, where prostitutes walk the streets and addicts prowl, searching for their next bag of heroin. 'You can criticise us Pakis for selling drugs but ninety-nine percent of our customers were white,' said Imram. 'People are always quick to bring up the fact that the blacks and Asians sell a lot of drugs but it's not us that's taking them. Yeah, fair enough, I take drugs but that's just me. Most Asians wouldn't touch the stuff with a bargepole.'

'How do you square the fact that you're a Muslim with the fact that you're selling drugs?' I asked him. A large proportion of the wing's population were regular attendees at the prison mosque, despite the fact that the vast majority of them were in for selling either crack or heroin.

'Well I'm just a bad Muslim,' he laughed. 'There's plenty of bad Christians about and nobody ever questions them about it. How many Christians do you see who have never had sex before marriage? Not very fucking many.

'The reason that we sell drugs is because we've got morals. We don't believe in stealing from other people or hurting innocent people so we do something that doesn't directly hurt anyone. People choose whether they take coke or crack or Es or whatever, they aren't forced upon them. It's bad but it's not as bad as putting a gun to their head and taking their money from them.'

So would any of the gang ever resort to violence if it came down to it? 'Well some people would, some people wouldn't. I personally wouldn't, there's other people that would sort it out for me. There's a lot of Asians killing Asians nowadays. I don't agree with it but who am I to tell them to stop? If somebody rips you off then you're going to want to get even with them. That's just the way it goes.'

The gangs in Manningham seemed to have a distinct hierarchy to them. Everybody had been on an equal footing in

Kenny's gang, whereas Imran worked for next to nothing whilst his bosses got rich off the proceeds of his crimes.

'Do you think you'll go back to the same people when you get out?' I asked him.

'Where else am I going to go?' he said. 'It's either that or work in a factory and I doubt they'll let me smoke my gear while I'm on the job. I'm not going to lie to you, drugs are my main priority in life and the minute I get through those gates, I'm going to buy myself a couple brown and a couple white. I've thrown away too much of my life to quit now. Crack and heroin are the only thing that keep me going.'

Imran seemed to have abandoned any hope of ever leading a normal, law-abiding existence. He held the view that the only way that he would ever earn enough to support his habit was by selling the very substances that had caused him to turn to crime in the first place. Neither he nor Kenny seemed like the types of people that would ever have a place in mainstream society. They were far too deeply entrenched in the repetitive cycle of addiction and criminality. It is little wonder that Bradford is home to one of the country's highest rates of gun crime. Drugs and violence come hand in hand, with dealers often feeling the need to arm themselves against those who are looking to muscle in on their earnings. Places like Holme Wood and Manningham harbour a hidden world of vice, where the laws of the land can seem to hold little value.

Bristol

IN MARCH 2009, the online magazine AskMen.com published a list of the top ten most dangerous British neighbourhoods. The usual suspects were present: Moss Side in Manchester, Hackney in London, Toxteth in Liverpool – and then a single street in Bristol. All of the other entries were large, spread-out areas but Stapleton Road seemed to be a very precise location for the list to mention. What caused this particular road to be named alongside some of the country's most violent districts?

Stapleton Road is known to the local residents as 'Crackhead Alley', although it goes by many names. Writing for the *Observer* in February 2003, crime reporter Tony Thompson described it as 'Britain's most dangerous hard drugs den', while the *People* newspaper labelled it 'a lawless hellhole infested by ferociously violent criminals and the lowest dregs of society' and 'a moral cesspit where the pavements are heaving with killers, junkies, hookers and their pimps'. Strong words: so how exactly had it gained such a fearsome reputation? Yes it had high levels of prostitution and drug addiction, and reported crimes were running at 130 per month. But perhaps it had more to do with the fact that it was the territory of one of the city's most notorious postcode gangs, the Easton High Street Crew.

Easton has suffered from a wave of gang-related violence in recent years. In April 2010, Avon and Somerset Police were given increased powers to stop and search amid fears of an ongoing battle for supremacy between a local street gang and a rival crime group from the St Paul's district. Tensions were rising between the two communities and the region had already seen an axe attack, a machete attack and a shooting within a few weeks.

Despite extra precautions taken to protect local residents, on Thursday, July 8, eighteen-year-old Abdirisiak 'Mugabi' Mohamoud was stabbed to death on Stapleton Road. According to his cousin, he was killed as part of a vicious turf war between rival gangs from Easton and St Paul's.

Shortly after his death, a shrine was erected in his memory, complete with a large display of the High Street Crew's trademark blue bandanas. The Crew had been at war with the St Paul's-based 573 Blood Gang in the run up to the murder and it was likely that the stabbing had taken place as a result of the escalating feud between the groups.

In the wake of the killing, a number of videos were, almost inevitably, posted on YouTube featuring young teenagers dressed from head to toe in blue, expressing their condolences for a fallen comrade. 'Easton's the jungle so we're down in the safari, R.I.P. Mugabi, you left and it scarred me,' rhymes a small, fresh-faced young rapper in one of the clips. A Somali youth wearing a blue peaked cap brandishes a knife towards the camera and the words 'R.I.P. Mugabi Never Forgotten' flash across the screen during another of the videos. Whether Abdirisiak was an active member of the gang or whether he was a distant associate remains unclear, although it is more likely than not that he was killed because of his friendship with the Crew.

I called a few of my contacts from jail, who managed to get in touch with a young drug dealer affiliated with the 573 Blood

Gang. He agreed to answer my questions on condition that I kept his identity a secret and omitted any details that could possibly incriminate him. I conducted my interview via a pay phone, as he refused to meet me in person and he specifically stated that he didn't want there to be any traceable record of the fact that he had been in contact with a writer.

'I'm not one of these mans that will leave things to chance,' explained my contact, who I shall refer to as Joe.

'It's cool,' I told him. 'I can see why you would be wary.'

I had been given his phone number by one of the black inmates from prison, who had assured me that, although he was not a fully fledged member of the gang, he had grown up amongst a lot of the main players. I asked if he was on good terms with the Bloods.

'Yeah. SP, bang, bang! Everyone on the ends knows about them man. I'm not into dying over postcodes or coloured rags or none of that shit but them man go hard, I ain't gonna lie. Them man have got St Paul's on their back when it comes to the gang t'ing. They ain't gonna let man from Easton take us for no pussy holes.'

'So how did the whole St Paul's/Easton beef start?' I asked.

'Well it ain't no drug t'ing like the papers is trying to say. It's just area beef, innit? Two different zones and both sides want to have the baddest rep. The same thing's happening all over the city only in St Paul's and Easton, the youths have all got guns so it's some next level type of beef.'

He refused, however, to talk about the circumstances surrounding Abdi's murder.

'I ain't telling you fuck all about that,' he bluntly replied. 'You tryna get man on some conspiracy charges or some shit? All I can tell you is that my man shouldn't have been on Stapleton Road if he wasn't on no gang t'ing. He was from some next area, he wasn't even from Easton. He could have stayed well away. Don't get me wrong, he was young and it's always sad when somebody dies before their time but I'm glad it was him and not some youth from St Paul's. Live by the sword and you're gonna die by the sword, that's all I'm going to tell you about that one there.'

I changed the subject and ask him a series of fairly innocuous questions about the levels of violence in the city.

'The media says that Stapleton Road is the most dangerous place in Bristol...' I started.

'Bollocks!' he sneered. 'That's some bullshit right there. Easton is in the shadow of St Paul's. There's a lot of things that never make it to the papers going on round our sides. Easton mans is running up their gums talking their business in public, that's why everybody and their gran knows about what they're doing. Don't get me wrong, Bris' is gully [dangerous] all over but don't believe the hype. Stapes is nothing special. It's just another road.'

The two areas seemed to be in competition to see which part of the city had the highest crime rate. 'Man from Easton think they're bad for shotting a bit of brown,' Joe went on. 'There's fourteen-year-old white boys in Southmead and Knowle West selling drugs. It doesn't make them hard; anyone can hand over a bag of powder to someone and take their money off them. Niggers from St Pauls is eating [robbing] other dealers. I don't just wanna eat my slice of the pie, I want the whole thing for myself. I'm not gonna cut myself off a slice and sit there eating it. I'm gonna be taking yours from you as well.

'When you live in certain parts of the city, you learn to protect yourself by striking before they do,' he continued. 'If people know that you will snap on man for no reason then they ain't gonna fuck about with you. That's how the whole gang thing came about; it's a fear thing, really. The youths don't wanna be seen as an easy target so they start rolling around with a group of niggers that's eating man's food. It's a way of making sure that nobody tries to take them for a joke t'ing.'

What did Joe think could be done to lessen the tension between the gangs? 'To be honest there's not really all that much that can be done. You put them in the same room as each other and they're going to kill each other. There's too much been going on for them to ever make their peace now. You've got to stop these things before they start. Once there's people getting stabbed and shot, people ain't gonna go back to peace times. What's done is done and all you can do now is try and contain the damage and try and stop it from getting worse.'

He had a bleak but possibly realistic outlook. However to get the other side of the story, I had to find somebody from Easton who was willing to answer a couple of questions. Via the wonders of MySpace, I managed to find one of Abdirisiak's friends, by the name of 'Supreme', who was willing to answer a few questions. He turned out to be an intelligent and thoughtful commentator on the Bristol conflict.

'Everyone from Stapleton Road knew Abdi,' he told me. 'Like many of the young people in the area, he was a good person who was a victim of circumstance. He was a real individual, loyal to his religion and his friends and he was somebody you could always catch jokes with. A lot of people were close to him and to say that what happened hasn't caused tension would be a lie.

'Nowadays there is a divide between certain areas in Bristol that never existed before. It seems to be getting wider and wider and postcodes seem to have become a lot more important. My take on them would be just to represent the people from my area and give a voice to where we live, not for some sort of competition as to who's the hardest, which seems to be the way it's used at present. I think it's just a way of dividing people: divide and conquer.

'The media loves a big story to point at and analyse. It gives them something exciting to write about, especially once they've put their customary spin on things. Gangs start out as groups of local friends who look out for each other out of fear of being jumped when they're alone and then the media fuels it by creating a mentality where they don't feel like they're safe any more. When you shine a dark light on an area, less commercial opportunities end up coming to it because of its bad reputation. If Stapleton Road lived up to the media hype, there would be barricades on the streets, no go zones and all sorts. It's like most areas in the UK, it has normal people that work a nine to five coming and going twenty-four hours, seven days a week. There's elderly people there who aren't living in fear and still live a normal life. Obviously there's crime there but most people are just trying to get by and get the most out of life.

'Drugs are the cause of a lot of family problems that can lead to violence. To the younger generation, they represent an easy way of getting rich. They've made the youth a lot lazier, thinking that hard work is no longer necessary when in reality it's the key to real success. Saying that though, opportunities being so few and far between in our areas, they can sometimes be the only available way to go. Drugs aren't the only reason why gangs exist though; there's an array of different reasons from negligent parents to negative influences on TV and the glorification of musicians that have been on the wrong side of the law. Violent films, ignorant school teachers and lack of public funding for positive projects for the youth all contribute.'

Supreme seemed to be very aware of the various factors that had led to violent crime within the city. I wondered whether he had ever been involved in criminality himself or whether he had merely grown up observing the felonies of others. 'Well I've been remanded for twenty-one months for murder before,' he said. 'I was acquitted though because I was innocent.'

Supreme was clearly knowledgeable about the reasons why young people in Bristol were choosing to resort to gangs and drugs. He was able to provide me with a far more detailed insight into the mentality of teenage gang members than Joe had been able to do and he seemed to genuinely care about the youth of the area that he had grown up in. But what could be done to remedy the situation? Was prison a suitable deterrent for those who were caught up in the city's growing gang culture?

'Prison is a deterrent,' he said. 'But as for suitable, I don't know about that one. It's easy for people to get institutionalised and desensitised. Some people are encouraged to do crime rather than being deterred.'

His opinions upon this issue appeared to directly mirror the views that I had formed during my own incarceration. Towards the start of my sentence, I was shocked whenever anybody mentioned that they were in for killing somebody. By the time I was due for release, a 'lifer' was just another type of prisoner and I had heard about all manner of different violent offences, some of them committed for the pettiest of reasons. But then again, how do you prevent young people from joining gangs without the threat of jail to keep them on the straight and narrow? According to Supreme, the answer to this question lies within the communities where these problems arise.

'The police can't solve it. Anything that they handle always seems to crumble because they have a heavy-handed grip on things. It takes a lot of internal pull within the communities themselves to properly combat this type of behaviour. Parents, older family members and respected individuals like musicians need to come together to address the problem and then maybe we'll see a change. I'm trying to do my bit. I'm a hiphop artist and I try to address some of these issues in my music.'

What Supreme had told me was similar to what I had heard from a lot of the other gang members that I had spoken to. The consensus seemed to be that the solution to the problem had to come from the local residents, rather than from any form of government institution. St Paul's and Easton are both fairly insular communities, where the police are often perceived as being the enemy. Anything that the authorities try to implement is likely to be met with suspicion and contempt. Therefore in order to bring an end to the conflict, the only other option is for the residents to come together in order to facilitate a change.

'Not much ever changes on Stapleton Road,' he summed up. 'Even in recent years things have stayed the same in spite of the recession. Things don't change in our types of areas because we don't benefit no matter how much the government wins or loses. Crime will always exist in one form or another, as long as the structure of things remains the same.'

Bolton

I N NOVEMBER 2009, Greater Manchester Police announced plans to set up a special unit to combat drug gangs and armed criminals operating in Bolton. The decision came shortly after the revelation that there were several armed gangs competing for control of the city's drug trade. 'Most of these groups are dealing drugs and causing threats to life and some have access to firearms,' Superintendent John Lyons told the *Bolton Evening News*. 'Hopefully this new unit will help create a safer environment in Bolton because we have obviously got some nasty people who need looking at.'

Superintendent Lyons was speaking as if it was the first time that armed criminals had posed a serious threat to the town. Gangs have existed in Bolton for decades. In the 1970s, the Highfield Boot Boys and the Green Lane Mob fought pitched battles using knives and baseball bats, while the 1980s brought football hooligan gangs with bizarre names such as Mongy's Cuckoo Boys, the Tonge Moor Slashers and the Billy Whizz Fan Club.

The Metropolitan Borough of Bolton contains some of the country's poorest areas. Whilst some of these are within the town itself, parts of the neighbouring towns and villages are also equally disadvantaged. Nearby Farnworth is home to some of the worst housing in the country, with areas within

Newbury, Moses Gate and Central Farnworth all ranking especially low on the scale. It is also the birthplace of the Farnworth Mafia, a loose collective of street fighters and petty crooks who have been fighting with rival gangs since the early 1980s.

In order to get an inside opinion upon how the gangs of Bolton and Farnworth have changed throughout the decades, I arranged a meeting with Mini and Dougie, two former Farnworth Mafia members who had watched the local street gangs become more and more extreme as the years went by. They had been involved in gang violence for thirty years.

Mini and Dougie agreed to pick me up from Bolton train station and take me to Dougie's dad's house in Farnworth. 'We'll do the interview there,' Dougie told me. 'Then you can see a bit of Farnworth on your way.' Sure enough, right on time, a car pulled up at the side of the road and a large, shaven-headed man jumped out and extended his heavily tattooed hand in my direction. 'How's it going?' he asked. 'Jump in the back and I'll tell you a little bit about what goes on in Farnworth.'

Dougie was an imposing figure. Every inch of his body was covered in tattoos and he had the look of somebody who had seen their fair share of trouble over the years. Mini, in contrast, did not look menacing at all. He was still fairly baby-faced and it was difficult to believe that he was the oldest of the pair. 'I was about thirteen when I first got involved with gangs,' he told me, as if to confirm the fact that he was older than his outward appearance would suggest. 'That was probably a couple of decades before you were born.'

As Dougie drove us further and further into Farnworth, our surroundings became less and less salubrious. Groups of Asian teenagers congregated on street corners and hooded white youths traipsed along the litter-strewn streets. The whole town looked like one of the worst areas of Manchester or Liverpool.

'This is my dad's house down here,' Dougie told me. He pulled off down a side street into an area of densely packed terraced housing. 'There used to be a fair few gangs around here back in the day. There was an Asian gang who lived a couple of minutes down the road in Moses Gate. They called themselves The Warriors. They used to drive up here in a white van, jump out on a group of three or four white lads and give them a right good hiding. We soon put a stop to that though. We went down into the Asian part of Moses Gate armed with rounders bats and baseball bats and booted every single door off. I never saw the white van again after that so I think they got the message.'

As I stepped out of the car and walked towards the front door, I noticed an Asian family going into one of the houses on the other side of the road. The area appeared to be fairly well integrated and not the type of place where I would have expected racially determined gangs.

'Do you get a lot of racial tension in Farnworth then?' I asked.

'Yeah, especially in Newbury,' Dougie said. 'That's the most racist estate by far. It's also home to one of the roughest firms as well, the Newbury Cavemen. They used to block the roads off through their estate and only let the white people go past. If an Asian taxi driver turned up, they'd drag them out of their car and beat the fuck out of them.'

Farnworth seemed to be a multicultural place. It was strange to think that a town with such a large Asian population would have tit-for-tat racial attacks taking place. 'It's not so much a racial thing,' Dougie explained to me. 'It's a territorial thing as well. All of the white areas are fighting with each other all the time so the Asians are just another group for them to scrap with, really. That's just how Farnworth is.'

'Right take your shoes off and take a seat,' Dougie told me, as I walked through the doorway and into his dad's front room. 'Ask us anything you want to know. Obviously we can't give you the names of anybody who's done anything that's against the law but whatever else you're after, we can tell you.'

The first thing that I wanted to know was whether the original members had deliberately set out to form their own gang or whether 'Farnworth Mafia' was a label that had been placed upon them by the local population. 'Well there were four main street gangs in Farnworth when I was growing up,' said Dougie. 'There was the Farnworth Arcaders, the Highfield Mob, the Newbury Cavemen and the Moses Gate Mob. As the years went by, we all started drinking in the same pubs and all of the gangs ended up merging together. We had a combined membership of around two hundred lads, which made us Bolton's biggest gang. People started calling us the Farnworth Mafia as a joke at first 'cause if you picked a fight with one of us then you were picking a fight with all of us. In the end it caught on and people started calling us it seriously and it's stuck with us ever since.'

'So apart from fighting with other gangs, what else did the Farnworth Mafia get up to?' I asked him, a deliberately vague question.

'Well some of the firm were into protection rackets,' he replied. 'Some were into robberies and a few have even done time for murder. A couple of the lads were into burglaries. I remember when they robbed the Co-op. They smashed through the ceiling and grabbed a couple of thousand cigarettes.'

'A lot of the firm got into drugs as well,' Mini added. 'It's not surprising really, there were always people taking acid and whiz and stuff like that back when we were younger. There were people that would have cheese and magic mushrooms on toast for their breakfast.'

'There's all sorts going round,' said Dougie. 'There's a lot of smackheads in Bolton and Farnworth. They've got no respect for anybody and I'd say that heroin is the source of a lot of the town's problems. There's a few people who have been killed over drugs over the years. There was a lad called Lee Bonney who's dad used to live on Mini's road, he was involved in all of that. One of his mates Billy Webb ended up with a bullet in him.'

Billy Webb was part of the so-called Great Lever Mafia, a local gang who distributed hard drugs across the north west of England. They were thought to have been responsible for millions of pounds worth of cocaine and heroin hitting the streets and they would dish out brutal punishment beatings to anybody who stood in their way. Those who crossed them would be beaten with hammers and baseball bats and some of them were even forced to watch whilst their girlfriends were raped. Webb's gang were perhaps the most ruthless drug-dealing collective that the town had ever seen and, although they were well aware of their presence, the police had trouble finding anybody that was willing to testify against them.

'[Lee] Bonney was a hard case,' Mini told me. 'The whole family were. Put it this way, you'd know about it if you ever got on the wrong side of the Bonneys. I remember him from when he used to work the doors. He was a nutcase. He definitely wasn't the type of person that you could mess about with. He was Webb's right-hand man and the whole firm were complete lunatics.'

While Webb and his mob became notorious, the police had little firm evidence against them – until they managed to plant a hidden microphone in a café owned by Webb, called Debbie's Diner. They recorded the top players, including Bonney, planning drug deals and organizing their operation, and eventually they were all arrested.

Webb was released on bail. On May 25, 2001, he was lying in bed with his girlfriend at a flat in Ashton-in-Makerfield, near Wigan, when two gunmen let themselves in with a key and shot him at point blank range. His girlfriend also took a gunshot to her left arm. She was unable to identify the assailants. Bolton's Mr Big was dead.

'Billy had a lot of enemies,' said Mini. 'Anybody could have killed him. It was obviously somebody close to him though, seeing as they had the key. A couple of months later, Bonney and the rest of the firm got sent down and then a load of Paki firms started moving in to fill the gap. Nowadays there aren't really any white dealers left at the top. Billy and Bonney were the last of their kind. There are still a lot of white dealers about but the Asians are definitely the top lads.'

Lee Bonney, described as a 'director' of Webb's gang, denied conspiracy to supply drugs but was jailed for fourteen years.

So how common were guns on the streets of Bolton and Farnworth? Were people regularly using firearms to settle their disputes or were shootings still a fairly rare occurrence? 'Well what happened to Billy is happening more and more nowadays,' said Mini. 'Knives used to be the most serious thing that anybody ever used but now there's a lot of guns around and more and more people are using CS gas spray as well. It's not like it used to be when people fought their battles with their fists.'

'Do you think there's another "Mr Big" now Billy's gone then?' I asked him.

'There will be,' he replied. 'I couldn't tell you who it is but there will be. It will undoubtedly be a group of Pakis though. They're the big fish nowadays.'

Billy Webb had ruled with the proverbial iron fist, punishing anybody who refused to buy their drugs from him. He had been instrumental in keeping rival dealers out of Bolton. Now that he was out of the picture, gangs from Manchester and Salford had moved in on the market. 'There's a feud going on at the moment between two rival Asian firms, one from Bolton and one from Manchester,' Mini said. 'Because there are so many smackheads and crackheads in Bolton, people are willing to travel here to make their money. Drugs are attracting people from all over the country and it's causing a lot of trouble for us.'

The feud that Mini was referring to had already led to one fatality. In July 2009, shop worker Nasar Hussain was shot with a MAC-10 submachine gun during a botched 'hit' at Brookhouse Wines in Winton, Salford. Five men were charged in connection with the murder, including Akmal Afzal of Bolton. The police stated that they were investigating whether or not the killing was linked to warring drug gangs in the town.

'There's been a lot of feuding between the Asian gangs in this area too,' Mini went on. 'It used to be white dealers fighting with Asian dealers but now the white dealers just buy their drugs off them. The Asians run Bolton, no doubt about it. There was a firm round here a few years back called the Rawson Street Gang who were always getting into trouble. They all ended up with ASBOs but the rumour was that a lot of the scrapes they got in were over drugs.'

The Rawson Street Gang were responsible for a series of violent clashes across the town in late 2006 and early 2007. On November 5, 2006, a nineteen-year-old was beaten with a baseball bat in Adams Takeaway in Moses Gate before being kicked and punched by up to fifteen gang members. On April 13, 2007, the gang clashed with a rival firm, armed with baseball bats, and a number of men were admitted to hospital with minor injuries. And on April 15 the same year, up to twenty gang members were seen gathering in the street, some holding weapons.

'The new generation of Asian gangs have no qualms about beating somebody around the head with a bat, even when they are unarmed,' Mini told me. 'Things have got a lot worse since I was on the scene. If you drive around the rougher parts of Farnworth, you will always see wreaths of flowers where somebody's been stabbed. There's a new one somewhere every month. It's become the norm.'

So why did he think the situation had got to be so bad? 'It's partly to do with the prison system. Nowadays they've got PlayStations and TVs in all of the cells so people know that if they get sent down it won't be all that bad. They're getting pocket money every week as well. If they knew that they had to work out in the middle of a desert like in American prisons they'd think twice about carrying a knife or a gun but as it is, they really don't give a fuck. Even for carrying a Stanley knife you can get five years nowadays but yet there's still a lot of people going out tooled up with them. There's only one possible explanation for that and that's that prison isn't a deterrent any more.'

'It's to do with the types of families that kids are being born into as well,' Dougie added. 'You've got fifteen-year-olds having kids and they aren't old enough to cope with them so they're bringing them up badly. On top of that, it's all single parent families and the mothers are having trouble disciplining them on their own. Back in the day, we'd always be up for a scrap but we had respect. We didn't pick on innocent people.

The gangs of today don't have any respect whatsoever. They're twice as bad as they were in the past and things are going from bad to worse.'

The fact that Dougie and Mini had managed to keep their ears to the street for the last three decades meant that they were able to provide a relatively objective opinion about how the gangs of yesteryear compared to the gangs of today. They painted a picture of a town where crime had always existed but where the way in which the criminals went about their business had rapidly altered over the course of the last few years. Drug abuse, fatherless families – Bolton has one of the highest rates of teen pregnancy in Europe – and lack of opportunity have all taken their toll and the territorial street gangs are being replaced by armed drug cartels. Those who would have previously used their fists are now carrying knives and those who would have kept a blade on them are gradually converting to firearms as their main source of protection. The gangs are still the same but their attitudes are different; the gloves are off and, in the town's numerous impoverished council estates, random acts of brutality seem to be increasingly commonplace.

Farnworth is a town like many, where drugs are rife and a handful of deeply immoral people are willing to exploit the situation in order to make a profit. So long as desperate people are willing to do whatever it takes to get a fix, the levels of violence will continue to increase. Poverty leads to drug abuse and drug abuse lead to crime. Until the cycle is eventually broken, wars will continue to be fought across the streets of Bolton's poorer suburbs.

The Future

WHAT DOES THE future hold for Britain's street gangs? Is there any way to prevent the country following in America's footsteps, with copycat Bloods and Crips taking hold of our estates? The authorities have been trying novel ways to curb inner-city violence ever since the first Lad's Clubs were set up in Nineteenth Century Manchester, as a diversionary activity for the city's teenage 'scuttler' crews. So does the solution to modern day postcode gangs lie in similar holistic methods, or should law enforcement agencies bear the sole responsibility for keeping these groups at bay?

In June 2010, the Chief Inspector of Prisons, the Chief Inspector of Probation and the Chief Inspector of Constabulary published a high-powered joint report on 'the management of gang issues'. They said:

> Interviews with young people themselves showed that, for young men, gang membership was a source of protection but also a source of fear. Friendship, territoriality and above all 'respect' defined and justified gang activity. Young women's situation was more fluid and less clear-cut: they could be used (particularly sexually), protected or mistrusted, depending on the situation.
>
> Young men generally described their 'gang' associations in terms of friendships or family ties. For some

young people, there was a sense of inevitability in gang membership, linked to living in particular localities. Some saw this as necessary for their protection. There was an acceptance of the risk of having a short lifespan, especially among those who had been on the receiving end of gang violence.

This echoed almost exactly what I had been told in the many interviews I conducted with gang members. As Duzy, a gang-banger from Hounslow in West London, said: 'The gang culture is turning into something bigger now, it's no longer kid's stuff. There are no jobs [for us] and no proper community in London: most of the people these days can't even speak English. There's people trying to take over, lurking in the shadows. You feel unsafe and walk around in a huge group because it's better than getting robbed.'

What I had not been offered were many solutions. The report recommends a rather woolly 'national approach' to tackling serious youth offending, involving 'relevant local community groups and partnerships'. It also advocates a more specific strategy to tackle gang culture among the under-eighteens, to be developed 'by the Youth Justice Board working with local authorities, the Department for Education, the Ministry of Justice, the National Offender Management Service (NOMS) and the Home Office, on behalf of prisons, probation and the police'.

The problem with this list of Government organizations, institutions and other bodies is that most potential gang members have a deep-seated distrust of authority. 'The police don't do shit,' a gang member from Croxteth in Liverpool bluntly told me. 'Things like Operation Matrix [Merseyside Police's anti-gun crime unit] are just fancy names to get the public's eye. All they do is pick up young kids drinking on the streets.' Needless to say, I doubt he would be open to the types of solutions that 'NOMS' and the various other bodies could come up with. He would view them as just another group of 'fancy names'.

'I don't think the authorities even really need to be involved,' said Frank, the former gang member from Gorton in Manchester. 'The problem is that all of these government bodies pump money into trying to make things better but they always assume that they know better than the local people. They say, we're doing this and we're doing that and we're going to spend millions of pounds on doing up the estate, but what's the point of doing that if they don't know what it is that actually needs doing? Some group of so-called experts can't tell you that. You need to ask the people.'

Those within the main gang territories have little faith in the ability of outsiders to deal with their situation. As far as they are concerned, the solution to the violence, crime and anti-social behaviour has to come from within the communities themselves. When asked, as part of the 2010 report, about the attempts of a young offenders' institution to curb his behaviour, one teenage gang member spoke of the authorities' overwhelming ignorance on the subject. 'How can they help?' he said. 'They don't know what they're talking about; all they advise is "just say no" but it's not like that. The only thing that would help is to move away to a totally new area, with my own place and some money, but who's going to do that?'

He made a valid point. In certain areas, gang culture is so deeply rooted that the only way of breaking ties to these groups is to move to a different area – or even to quit that town or city completely. The suggestion that young people should simply refuse to have anything to do with gangs implies that it is a simple 'yes' or 'no' decision and ignores a host of more complex factors. For some, gang membership is their only source of income, or of protection. For others, it is their family, and their crew forms the basis for all of their close friendships. Their gang is their world.

It would be naïve to claim that I had stumbled across a means of eradicating gang-related crime during the course of researching this book. But what did seem blindingly obvious to me is that street gangs will thrive so long as poverty exists. And so Britain's poorer estates will remain fertile breeding grounds for street gangs, from disorganised postcode crews like the Nogga Dogs and the Croccy Crew to serious organised crime groups like the Upperthorpe Crew and the Alien Abduction Gang. Crime is a fact of life, and criminals rarely work alone: gangs have existed since the dawn of civilization. What has changed is their access now to more technologically sophisticated and deadly weaponry that has ever existed before. Gangs may be ancient but the Uzi and MAC-10 are frighteningly modern.

It is only fitting, in this book, that the final words should go to a young gang member. They are not reassuring.

'Gangs will never die,' said Richie, from Croxteth. 'Things will get worse. And if you think that the guns that are being used now are bad then wait and see what it will be like in a few years' time. There's already people with grenades.

'Gangs are caused by rough estates where the kids have nothing else to do. They see gangsters on the telly getting respect and money and they want the women, cars, money and guns that they see them getting. To be honest, the police can't stop gangs. It's impossible. If drugs were stopped in the country then I could possibly see something happening, but until then the gangs will get worse.'

Appendix: Gangs Mentioned

Sheffield

S3 (Burngreave and Pitsmoor)
S4 (Pitsmoor and Burngreave)
S8 Boyz (Batemoor, Greenhill, Lowedges,
  Meadowhead, Jordanthorpe and Woodseats)
S6 Crew (Fox Hill)
Shirecliffe Boys (Shirecliffe)
Birley Boys (Birley)
Parson Cross Crew (Parson Cross)
S5 (Firth Park)
Upperthorpe Crew (Upperthorpe)
S2 Mandem (Park Hill, Arbourthorne, Heeley,
  Manor, Wybourn and Norfolk Park)
S9 Boyz (Darnall and Attercliffe)
S13 Boyz (Handsworth)
Teck 9

Halifax

HX5 (Elland)
Elland Mad Dogs (Elland)
Elland Bongheads (Elland)
HX2 (Pellon)
Mixenden Crew (Mixenden)
Furnace Crew (Illingworth)
Lee Mount Loonies (Lee Mount)
Brighouse Crew (Brighouse)

Glasgow

Real Calton Tongs (Calton)
Brigtonderry (Bridgeton)
Young Shields Mad Squad (Pollokshields)
Shielders (Pollokshields)
Toryglen Nazi Circus (Toryglen)
Young Toryglen Toi (Toryglen)
Bowery Wee Mob (Barrhead)
Sonnyhills Mad Sqwad (Sandyhills)
Gallagate Mad Skwad (Gallowgate)
Castlemilk Young Machrie Fleeto (Castlemilk)
Young Blackhill Toi (Blackhill)

Pollok Bushwackers (Pollok)
Young Tyre Cumbie Troops (Blantyre)
Jungle Derry (Burnbank)
Derry Burdz (Drumchapel)
Gorbalz Burds (Gorbals)
Young X Cross Cumbie (Gorbals)
The Alien Abduction Gang (Possil)

Liverpool
Croccy Crew (Croxteth)
Nogga Dogs Crew (Norris Green)
Moss Edz (Huyton)
Wimborne Gang (Huyton)
Longy Boyz (Huyton)
Hillside Edz (Huyton)
Bakiez (Huyton)
Dovey Edz (Huyton)
Park Road Edz (Dingle)
Somali Warriors (Toxteth)

Lancaster
902 Crew (Ryelands)
808 Crew (Marsh Estate)
Vale Estate Crew (Vale Estate)
602 Ridge Crew (Ridge Estate)
Morecambe Boys (Morecambe)

Edinburgh
Young Pilton Derry (Pilton)
Young Niddrie Terror (Niddrie)
Young Leith Team (Leith)
Young Mental Murrayburn (Wester Hailes)
Young Sighthill (Wester Hailes)
Young Saughton (Saughton)
Broomies (Broomhouse)
Inch Crew (The Inch, Gilmerton, Saughton and
    Broomhouse)
Granton Gang (Granton, Royston and Drylaw)
Young Mental Royston (Royston)
Young Mental Gorgie (Gorgie)

South London
Young Peckham Boys (Peckham)
Stickem Up Klick (Peckham)
Ghetto Boys (Deptford and New Cross)
Brockley Mans (Brockley)
Brixton Boys (Brixton)
Poverty Driven Children (Brixton)
Money Family Gangstaz (Brixton)
Bermondsey Boys (Bermondsey)

C-Block (Camberwell)
Wooly Road Man Dem (Walworth and Elephant and Castle)
ROC (Elephant and Castle)
Latinos Callajeros Cartel (Elephant and Castle)
Original Brooklyn Youts (Old Kent Road)

West London
SMG Mozart Bloods (Queens Park)
Street Diplomats (Queens Park)
Can't Roll in My Ends (Westbourne Green and Maida Vale)
Grimiest Movements (Maida Vale)
Grey Daiz (Westbourne Green)
South Kilburn Firearm Cartel Crips (South Kilburn)
Polish Unit (Hounslow)
Too Many (Hounslow)
Make Paper Regardless (Acton, Hammersmith and Shepherd's Bush)
Grit Set (Southall)

North London
Tottenham Man Dem (Tottenham)
Tottenham Boys (Tottenham)
The Firm (Edmonton)
Shankstarz (Edmonton)
Redbrick Crew (Edmonton)
Edmonton Young Gunnerz (Edmonton)
Dem Africanz (Edmonton)
Young Dem Africanz (Edmonton)
Harlesden Crew (Harlesden)

East London
Latin Kings Royal Chapter Taino Tribe (Hackney)
Hackney Man Dem (Hackney)
P-Block (Lower Clapton)
E5th Ridaz (Lower Clapton)
Mother Square (Lower Clapton)
London Field Boys (London Fields)
B-Block (Homerton)
E9 Kingshold Boys (Homerton)
Beaumont Gang (Leyton)
Oliver Close Gang (Leyton)
M-Block (Leyton)
BDG Bloods (Leyton)
Boundary Boys (Leyton)
Red African Devils (Leyton)

Holly Street (Dalston)
Chingford Hall Boys (Chingford)
Selrack (Chingford)
The Hatch Man Dem (Chingford)
DM Fam (Walthamstow)
Priory Court Grey Gang (Walthamstow)
Can Hall Crew (Can Hall)
Love of Money Crew (Hoxton)

Derby

Browning Circle Terrorist Crip Set (Sinfin)
Young Browning Circle Terrorist Crip Set (Sinfin)
38 Estate (Sinfin)
38 Youngers (Sinfin)
A1 (Normanton and Allenton)
A-Town (Alvaston)

Wolverhampton

Fire Town Crew (Heath Town)
Demolition Crew (Heath Town)
Pendeford Crew (Pendeford)
Flava (Whitmore Reans)

West Bromwich

Raiders

Birmingham

Johnson Crew (Lozells, Aston and Newtown)
Slash Crew (Lozells, Aston and Newtown)
Burger Bar Boys (Handsworth, Winson Green and Small Heath)
Bang Bang (Handsworth, Winson Green and Small Heath)
Blood Brothers (Handsworth, Winson Green and Small Heath)
Birmingham's Most Wanted (Handsworth, Winson Green and Small Heath)
Ghetto Hustla Boys (Handsworth, Winson Green and Small Heath)
Handsworth Town Crooks (Handsworth)
Raleigh Close Crew (Handsworth)
Small Heath Mans (Small Heath)

Manchester

Gooch (Moss Side)
Doddington (Moss Side)
Moss Side Bloods (Moss Side)
Old Trafford Crips (Old Trafford)
Fallowfield Man Dem (Fallowfield)
Rusholme Crips (Rusholme)
Young Cheetham Hill Loccz (Cheetham Hill)

Whizz Crips (Whalley Range)
Longsight Crew (Longsight)
Haydock Close Crew (Stretford)
503 (Stockport)
Gorton The Business (Gorton)
West Gorton Crew (West Gorton)
West Gorton Reds (West Gorton)

Middlesbrough

Pakidom
Donna Network

Preston

Callon Gang (Fishwick)
Farringdon Park Original Gangsters (Farringdon Park)
Deepdale Youth Defenders (Deepdale)
Deep Twisted Youngaz (Deepdale)
Deep Cut Connections (Deepdale)

Leeds

Swarcliffe Warriors (Swarcliffe and Seacroft)
CPT Crew (Chapeltown)
Poole Estate Boys (Crossgates)
Chapel Allerton Crew (Chapel Allerton)
Halton Moorers (Halton Moor)
Beeston Massive Crew (Beeston)
Paki Hater Crew (Beeston)
East Grange Boys (Belle Isle)
West Grange Boys (Belle Isle)
Miggy Boys (Middleton)

Bradford

Kenny's firm (Holme Wood)
Imran's firm (Manningham)

Bristol

Easton High Street Crew (Easton)
573 Blood Gang (St Paul's)

Bolton

Highfield Mob (Farnworth)
Farnworth Arcaders (Farnworth)
Newbury Cavemen (Farnworth)
Moses Gate Mob (Farnworth)
Farnworth Mafia (Farnworth)
The Warriors (Farnworth)
Rawson Street Gang (Farnworth)
Green Lane Mob (Great Lever)
Great Lever Mafia (Great Lever)